Brooding Over Bloody Revenge

From the colonial through the antebellum era, enslaved women in the USA used lethal force as the ultimate form of resistance. By amplifying their voices and experiences, *Brooding Over Bloody Revenge* strongly challenges assumptions that enslaved women only participated in covert, nonviolent forms of resistance, when in fact they consistently seized justice for themselves and organized toward revolt. Nikki M. Taylor expertly reveals how women killed for deeply personal instances of injustice committed by their owners. The stories presented, which span centuries and legal contexts, demonstrate that these acts of lethal force were carefully premeditated. Enslaved women planned how and when their enslavers would die, what weapons and accomplices were necessary, and how to evade capture in the aftermath. Original and compelling, *Brooding Over Bloody Revenge* opens a window into the lives and philosophies of enslaved women who had their own ideas about justice and how to achieve it.

Nikki M. Taylor is Professor and Chair in the Department of History at Howard University. She specializes in nineteenth-century African American history. This is her fourth book.

Nikki M. Taylor

Brooding over Bloody Revenge

Enslaved Women's Lethal Resistance

CAMBRIDGE
UNIVERSITY PRESS

Shaftesbury Road, Cambridge CB2 8EA, United Kingdom

One Liberty Plaza, 20th Floor, New York, NY 10006, USA

477 Williamstown Road, Port Melbourne, VIC 3207, Australia

314–321, 3rd Floor, Plot 3, Splendor Forum, Jasola District Centre,
New Delhi – 110025, India

103 Penang Road, #05–06/07, Visioncrest Commercial, Singapore 238467

Cambridge University Press is part of Cambridge University Press & Assessment,
a department of the University of Cambridge.

We share the University's mission to contribute to society through the pursuit of
education, learning and research at the highest international levels of excellence.

www.cambridge.org
Information on this title: www.cambridge.org/9781009276849
DOI: 10.1017/9781009276818

First published 2023

A catalogue record for this publication is available from the British Library.

A Cataloging-in-Publication data record for this book is available from the
Library of Congress

ISBN 978-1-009-27684-9 Hardback

For Grandmommy,
I still miss you . . .

CONTENTS

FIGURES

INTRODUCTION

That Justice is a blind goddess
Is a thing to which we black are wise:
Her bandage hides two festering sores
That once perhaps were eyes.

~ "Justice" by Langston Hughes

In Clark County, Kentucky, on January 23, 1812, Peggy Daniel, the wife of Captain James Daniel, was viciously attacked in their home by Charlotte, their enslaved woman. Peggy was holding the couple's eight-month-old infant when Charlotte hit her with a block of wood. She then pushed her mistress – or female slave-owner – and her baby headfirst into the fire blazing in the fireplace. According to the press, Peggy used "extraordinary exertions" to lift herself out of the fire, but each time, Charlotte pushed her back into it until she "expired in excruciating tortures." After the murder, Charlotte tried to cover the crime by running to a neighbor's home in a panic, telling them that Peggy was "unwell" and needed their assistance. The neighbor got dressed and followed her back to the Daniel home. Charlotte, running ahead, rushed into the house, and came back out with the Daniels' baby – with its clothing still burning, exclaiming that her mistress had fallen into the fire. The papers reported that although the infant was badly burned, it survived; but Peggy's body was "burnt in the most shocking manner." Because she had gone into the fire headfirst, her head and breast were completely incinerated. One of her arms was nearly burned into two pieces and the other reportedly was "an entire crisp."[1] As shocking as it was, Charlotte's resistance reveals that enslaved women were not always willing to resist slavery covertly or nonviolently. Charlotte is, in fact, part of a large number of enslaved women who exercised lethal slave resistance in the United States.

Charlotte confessed to the murder and was tried, convicted, and sentenced to death in Winchester, Kentucky, in February 1812. When asked by the judge if she had any reason to object to her death sentence, Charlotte, trying to save her own life, claimed to be "quick with child,"– or pregnant, a condition that would have automatically stayed her execution in Kentucky. In response to her claim, the judge impaneled a jury of twelve women to determine whether Charlotte was indeed pregnant. That jury concluded she was not, so she was promptly hanged five days later on February 28, 1812.[2] Many of the enslaved women who, like Charlotte, made the decision to kill their owners suffered the same fate – a death sentence. This book is an effort to tell the stories of these women, particularly why they made the decision to use murder as the ultimate form of resistance to slavery.

Although violent resistance to slavery was not the preferred form among enslaved women, the fact that it happened at all – and despite the constant surveillance and repression women endured – is what makes these actions remarkable. This book is concerned with those moments. Few historians have made this kind of resistance the subject of monographs. Melton A. McLaurin's *Celia, A Slave* and my own book, *Driven Toward Madness: The Fugitive Slave Margaret Garner and Tragedy on the Ohio* and other articles about individual women who used violence to resist slavery are rare exceptions.[3] Without stories like the ones in this book, we are left with an incomplete, softened, or watered-down understanding of Black women's resistance to slavery. We must enrich and deepen the historiography by adding additional layers and complexity to enslaved women's resistance.

It is hard to know with certainty how many enslaved women murdered their enslavers in the United States before 1865. According to David V. Baker, nearly 200 enslaved women were executed in the United States from 1681 to 1865. Most of those were executed for murder, attempted murder, and conspiracy to murder, whites.[4] However, Baker's estimate may be too low. Local authorities suppressed news stories about these incidents because publicizing such crimes could seriously threaten the social, racial, and gender order.[5] Even Charlotte's story was barely mentioned in the newspapers. Another consideration for the low estimate is the fact that in the colonial and early national eras – before the erection of separate judicial processes for enslaved people – owners resorted to their own brand of punishment – or sale. Moreover, because several southern states offered justices the option of transporting convicted enslaved murderers to another region or country as punishment, counting the executions alone misses an entire group of women who were sold and transported for their crimes. In addition to the historical, social, and cultural barriers to obtaining the exact number of enslaved women who murdered their owners or overseers, the archive has been lost, damaged or destroyed. Many trial records about these capital cases have been lost to fire, water, and degradation, especially in the earlier eras. Other records have been simply misplaced or misfiled. Using Baker's baseline number to extrapolate, between 1681 and 1865, hundreds, possibly more than a *thousand,* enslaved women committed, or plotted to commit, deadly violence against their owners. Even with that extrapolated estimate, it must be emphasized that compared to other demographic groups, enslaved Black women were the *least* violent people in American society during the age of slavery.

When enslaved women did sometimes murder their owners, it was not simply murder. It should be understood as slave resistance. When enslaved women did commit murder in the colonial era, 92 percent of their victims were white.[6] In his study on enslaved women and capital crime in antebellum Georgia, Glenn McNair found that enslaved women targeted their enslavers or their agents for murder, including their wives and children, or overseers. They were less likely to seriously injure or harm other African Americans. He found that a higher percentage of enslaved women than enslaved men murdered their owners. According to him, enslaved men who murdered acted out of impulse or momentary anger; women, he insists, used a higher degree of premeditation, which made them more effective resistors ultimately.[7]

Up until now, most historians of women's history have insisted that enslaved women rarely chose armed, lethal, or overt forms of resistance. Stephanie M. H. Camp, for example, emphasized that they rejected explicit or confrontational violence in favor of covert, non-confrontational acts of "everyday resistance," which include insolence, dissembling, disobedience, feigned illness, absenteeism, work slowdowns, temporarily running away, and poisoning food. Women also resisted slavery by pretending to be pregnant or claiming they suffered from debilitating menstrual issues that interfered with their work.[8] Everyday resistance also included appropriating additional food, clothing, hair bows, or other luxury items from their unsuspecting owners.[9] This form of resistance yielded many personal benefits, including reduced workloads, additional time off, or reassignment to different tasks. Despite the varied and creative ways enslaved women practiced everyday resistance, historians have categorized it as nonthreatening and less likely to undermine or challenge the social and racial order the way a slave revolt would. Consequently, women's everyday slave resistance rarely ended in their executions, which meant it was the safer option.

Not only has women's resistance to slavery been exclusively understood as this softer, everyday variety but it also has been mischaracterized as it relates to collective and organized resistance. Historians have categorized slave revolt and uprisings as the preserve of men, leaving the impression that women rarely participated in collective, organized, violent acts of resistance. Women's participation within the histories of the major slave rebellions in the United States is not generally examined; when they *are* mentioned in these texts, they are relegated to the sidelines as mere witnesses or wives of the main organizers of these plots. Historians insist that the exclusion and marginalization of women was a conscious and deliberate decision made by the rebels themselves who did not recruit women to join the frontlines or leadership corps. For example, Douglas R. Egerton insists that Gabriel "chose no women" for the inner circle of his 1800 Richmond plot. Historian James Sidbury, trying to explain why they chose no women in the same plot, suggests that the "conspirators may not have trusted Black women." Yet Gabriel's wife knew about the plot, so they clearly trusted her. Sidbury concludes that women are missing from these plots because they were "planned in the masculine sphere." Historian Edward A. Pearson contends that "Gullah" Jack, one of the organizers of Denmark Vesey's plot in Charleston in 1822, "excluded enslaved women" from the rituals. These historians do acknowledge that enslaved women "knew of the plots," but they portray that knowledge as accidental, or even incidental. For example, the one-time James Sidbury mentions Gabriel's wife Nanny in his book, he states that she "tried" to recruit one man for the insurrection, but adds nothing else, so we are left assuming she failed in that endeavor. Pearson claims that enslaved women in Charleston "inadvertently learned" of Denmark Vesey's plan. Women, he concludes, had a "shadowy presence" in the plot. If we take these scholars at their word, then it would seem that enslaved women hardly ever participated in revolts or, when they did, played marginal, chance, or auxiliary roles. Consequently, slave revolts have been painted as the domain of men, and as uniquely revolutionary and decidedly masculine social movements.[10]

A few recent articles and books are challenging these long-standing beliefs about women's roles in slave revolts. In *Surviving Southampton: African American Women Resistance in Nat Turner's Community,* historian Vanessa M. Holden offers a new way of seeing women's roles within the history of major slave revolts. Revisiting Nat Turner's rebellion, she illuminates sites, sources, and strategies of resistance previously overlooked by historians. By so doing, Holden brings women, children, and free Blacks into sharper focus. She asserts that women's gender roles often enhanced the ways they could assist – and do so undetected. For example, their greater mobility on the specific farms involved in that rebellion led them to play a significant role in "geographies of evasion and resistance." Holden discusses how women contributed to Nat Turner's rebellion by passing information, providing shelter and sustenance, helping rebels evade authorities, hiding weapons, and even physically restraining whites.[11] The merit of Holden's book is that it reveals countless ways women assisted and collaborated in planning and executing rebellions. *Brooding Over Bloody Revenge* also examines collective, violent uprisings, but posits that those led by women functioned differently than the slave revolts with which we are most familiar.

Rebecca Hall's brilliant 2010 article "Not Killing Me Softly: African American Women, Slave Revolts, and Historical Constructions of Racialized Gender," and her recent gripping graphic novel *Wake: The Hidden History of Women-Led Slave Revolts* "engenders" a problematic historiography on slave revolt that assumes women did not lead or substantively participate in them. In order to widen the lens to illuminate women who did, Hall defines revolt as "any violent, coordinated act of resistance that kills or attempts to kill slave owners or their agents." Her definition plus historian Eugene D. Genovese's concept of "simple revolt," which is waged "against unbearable exploitation or ... the overstepping of traditional arrangements" are useful.[12] I use a combination of Hall's and Genovese's definitions to shape the contours of how I use revolt here: organized, coordinated, violent, or lethal acts of resistance that are motivated by unbearable exploitation or injustice. This definition aptly describes the actions of the women in this book.

Like the women in McNair's study, the enslaved women in *Brooding Over Bloody Revenge* carefully premeditated and planned the deaths of their owners. These women decided when and how their owners would die, chose and secured the weapons to be used, recruited accomplices, and plotted how to evade suspicion after the murder. Because of the high degree of planning, they were remarkably efficient at completing the act, even if they eventually ended up being caught. The careful planning debunks any assumptions that these women acted out of impulse or were unjustly enraged.

This book does aim to challenge the field, but that is not the only objective here. I have been led to answer a pressing and recurring question: what factors led some enslaved women to resort to deadly slave resistance? Were they motivated by similar grievances as enslaved men who planned slave revolts or insurrections? Women who murdered their owners did not have a global grievance against slavery itself – at least not one they articulated. They did not strive to end slavery or murder slaveowners en masse unjustly. None of the women discussed in this book killed to secure personal or collective freedom from bondage, not one. Because protection and justice for enslaved women were elusive through traditional moral and legal channels, the only form available to them is what they seized with their own hands – a type of personal justice. Some may question whether revenge *is* justice. According to philosopher Friedrich Nietzsche, "revenge therefore belongs ... within the domain of justice."[13] Personal justice, or revenge – which philosopher Francis Bacon termed "wild justice" – is a means of restoring dignity to the victim of the initial act. Retaliatory justice is pursued outside of legal systems or jurisprudence proved to be the only kind of justice available to enslaved women. Regardless, retaliatory violence is a morally legitimate response to the injustice within slavery.

The historical record includes the names of enslaved women who grabbed their own personal justice in response to wrongs done to them by their owners. Women who exercised this form of justice did so in response to beatings, abusive language, sexual assault, heavy workloads, threats of being sold away from loved ones, and being denied food, time off, and holidays. The primary way in which women's lethal resistance is different from other forms is that personal revenge and judgment were wrapped into it – a bloody indictment of their owners' cruelty and their unwillingness to take the abuse any longer.

It is always nearly impossible to chart the life experiences of individual enslaved women who could not read or write. Usually, historians can only find scraps of evidence about them – numbers, dates, possibly a name, but rarely their voices or opinions, so it can be a challenging task to write about them. The white people who owned them typically are much more discoverable in the historical record. The irony of the research for this book is that these particular enslaved women are more discoverable in the archive than even the white people who owned them – about whom I could barely find their full names, ages, or other pertinent biographical information. Enslaved women who practiced deadly resistance are identified and described in official court proceedings, newspapers, and private papers. Judicial officials, ministers, and reporters made great efforts to document their verbal testimonies, confessions, and modes of execution; they even elicited the reasons these women resorted to lethal force. In other words, it is because of their lethal slave resistance that these particular Black women's voices were recorded and preserved in the archive.

The archival evidence used in this book is hardly new: court records of the women's murder trials have been used previously by other historians, but not in a full-throated examination of Black women's violent resistance to slavery. The confessions of these women and their accomplices are an essential primary source that far too few historians of women's history have examined. Found in newspapers, trial records, and coroner's inquest records, these confessions amplify Black women's voices, illuminate their motivations, and outline their plans. Corroborating evidence in the Journals of the House of Burgesses, compensatory slave petitions, and transcripts from courts of oyer and terminer (meaning to "hear and determine"), state supreme court records, newspapers, and slave execution databases illuminate how pervasive this kind of resistance was among enslaved women throughout the history of slavery.

The women in this book labored in a variety of circumstances from rural to urban, field to house, as chattel and term slaves, and hires. Just as important as their location, era, or type of bondage, are the weapons they used. They used a diversity of "arms" – rat poison, arsenic, fire, water, axes, rusty nails, fence posts, and even a featherbed, reflecting the fact that they weaponized *any* household and farm item they had at their disposal, when needed. Some committed face-to-face murders, while others caught their owners unaware – while they were sleeping or eating. *Brooding Over Bloody Revenge* spans the entire slave era – from the colonial to the early national and antebellum eras; it examines women's overt, lethal slave resistance in the colonies of Massachusetts and North Carolina, the eastern antislavery states of Pennsylvania and New York, the Upper South states of Kentucky and Virginia, and Texas in the southwest.

These women's criminal cases offer a treasure trove of information about them as women and enslaved people, society, the judicial systems, and the very meaning of justice. Enslaved women's sense of injustice (and justice) has rarely been examined.[14] In this book, enslaved women's ideas about justice are juxtaposed against how justice was defined by white local leaders and how it was codified and enforced within the judicial systems. Those clashing and conflicting ideas about justice are revealing. These resisters are presented in their specific, local contexts because they were bound by local slave and criminal codes and judicial systems, which varied across time and space. Some states even erected separate laws, judicial systems, and processes for enslaved people. Hence, this book will examine multiple legal contexts.

My argument is simple: enslaved women did, in fact, resist slavery with deadly violence and when they did, their own ideas about injustice were a central motivation. It is no surprise that injustice would be at the center of my argument because as Eugene

D. Genovese declares in his seminal text, "Violent confrontation with injustice lay at the core of any revolt against slavery."[15] I agree. The enslaved women who committed thoughtful, "coordinated, confrontational, acts of violent resistance" did so within these smaller, local, plots of revenge against their own owners.[16]

I examine enslaved women's lethal resistance within a framework of a Black feminist practice of justice. I term it a Black *feminist* practice of justice (as opposed to simply a Black practice of justice) not because these enslaved women were Black feminists themselves – they were not; but because this theory is rooted in the tenets of Black feminist thought. First and foremost, Black feminist thought prioritizes Black women's voices and lived experiences, which deepens our understanding of, and appreciation for, them as historical agents. Secondly, this theory appreciates that Black women's relationships to their families and communities reign supreme and dictate much of what they feel and do. In other words, Black feminist thought is a community-centered perspective. A significant feature of Black feminist thought is intersectionality, or the idea that the racial, gender, and class/status oppressions that determine Black women's lived experiences and relationship to power are interlinked and intersectional. Black feminist thought seeks collective psychological liberation as a goal. Finally, it insists on respecting Black women's – and Black people's – humanity.

A Black feminist practice of justice emerges from a Black feminist *philosophy* of justice. Enslaved women's philosophy of justice was practical and boiled down to a sense of fairness, decency, justness, and humane treatment. A Black feminist practice of justice has, at its roots, a basic understanding that justice must be centered on the idea of fairness and the humane treatment of all people, regardless of race or status. Any failure to honor that basic premise is itself an act of injustice. Chattel slavery is the biggest example, but other smaller acts of inhumanity also are evidence of injustice, such as sexual assault, denying people adequate food as a form of punishment or disrespectful name-calling of women in front of their children.

Like all Black feminist theoretical approaches, a Black feminist practice of justice is formed from Black women's lived experiences. It prioritizes their perspectives and values, which, in turn, shape the tenets of this theory. Such a theory takes into account how the intersectionality of their oppression – as women, African Americans, and enslaved people – made them *less likely* to obtain legitimate forms of justice in response to abuse, mistreatment, and suffering and, consequently, *more likely* to seize it with their own hands.

This philosophy insists that the American judicial system was constructed within the context of slavery, and never made justice or redress for Black women a goal. It appreciates that they had few legitimate advocates *or* defenders within that system or in society in general. It is in that context that Black women's own brand of retributive justice is born. The irony is that the enslaved women who practiced retributive justice often were condemned and doomed to death sentences, which had retribution as a primary goal.[17]

People would be remiss to conclude that Black women who waged lethal resistance to slavery were irrational, acting purely on emotions. To the contrary, one of the core features of a Black feminist practice of justice is its rationality and forethought. Enslaved women who used lethal violence against their owners were neither impulsive nor irrational; they carefully planned every detail of the murders they committed. Those who marshalled their own justice in the pages that follow had very personal and compelling reasons for murdering their owners, which they usually articulated. They planned these crimes for days, weeks, months, even years in advance. In the course of plotting, they recruited other hands when needed, delegated responsibilities, decided which weapon would be used and who would wield it; they also predetermined the day and time of the fatal attack, and orchestrated fairly sophisticated plans to escape or avoid suspicion afterwards. Some even came up with complex plans to avoid or delay their executions, as Charlotte did. The plots these women masterminded and organized should be considered intellectual acts.

Retaliatory violence must be understood against the backdrop of the injustice the women experienced at the hands of their owners and within social, religious, and legal systems. It must be understood against the backdrop of how their owners treated them. In that vein, these Black women's ideas of justice were local and homegrown. They did not believe it was wrong to do harm to evil people who had hurt them or their families. To the contrary, for them, doing so was a kind of justice. Deadly violence, within a Black feminist practice of justice, is not the first or even second option to deal with unjust peoples or systems; it is often the *last* resort when other options to alleviate injustice, unfairness, abuse, and suffering have been exhausted. Every woman featured in this study tried other forms of resistance before they resorted to lethal violence, including talking back, running away, asking to be sold, or physically assaulting their owners. They used deadly violence only *after* other forms of resistance to obtain relief had been exhausted. For the women featured in this book, lethal violence was their *last* best option.

On first glimpse, it may seem that the enslaved women in this book exercised little restraint in how they murdered their owners. The bludgeonings they delivered often seem out of proportion when compared to the abuse their owners unleashed. These critiques invoke the ancient concept of "just deserts" (pronounced like desserts) – or people getting the punishment they deserve, which is a cornerstone of how judicial systems try to obtain justice. More commonly recognized as "an eye for an eye," the law of "just deserts" can be found in the Hammurabi Code, biblical law, Islamic law, and philosophy.[18] More importantly, the concept of "just deserts" laid the foundation for the construction of the American prison system and sentencing guidelines. A cardinal rule of retributive punishment is the belief that it should be proportionate to the offense. Justice is served and a moral debt is paid when the offender gets his or her (proportionate) "just deserts."[19] Despite its centrality to modern religion and the legal dispensing of justice, the principle was abandoned when it came to punishing the enslaved, who endured punishments that far exceeded their alleged misconduct. In fact, some of the punishments were so disproportionate and incongruous to the misdeed that they fall into the realm of the sadistic. For example, a 1729 Maryland statute outlined that if an enslaved person was convicted of burning homes, the punishment entailed having "the right hand cut off, to be hanged in the usual manner, the head severed from the body, the body divided into four quarters, and the head and quarters set up in the most public places in the county ..." In South Carolina, enslaved people were hanged for petty larceny. In other instances, ears were nailed to posts for perjury and other lesser offenses.[20] So it is in *that* violent context that a critique about the proportionality of Black on white violence seems disingenuous.

A Black feminist practice of justice insists that the proportionality of revenge is best determined by the victims of the unjust acts. They are the only ones who can say when that moral debt has been paid. Many of the women featured in this book offered not even an ounce of mercy to their owners as they murdered them. Within the context of chattel slavery, no level of retribution was too much against slaveowners and others who denied African American women their humanity and rights to freedom and dignity.

A core principle of retributive justice is that it is wrong to punish the innocent. In addition to challenging the dominant standard of proportionality, a Black feminist practice of justice also considers complicity in dispensing "just deserts." All those who advance or benefit from injustice and oppression are complicit agents and parties to it. To the enslaved women in this book, every member of their owner's family was complicit in their abuse and denied humanity; there were no innocents or faultless among them – not even infants, women, or young children. Understanding *this* premise from this perspective helps to better understand the stories in the following pages.

Finally, the women who used lethal violence to resist slavery were always fully aware of the consequences of their actions. Plotting the death of, or killing, a slaveowner would result in certain execution in every corner of the nation, across time. The fact that these women persisted in their plans in spite of that danger demonstrates that they were willing to die pursuing their version of justice. It meant so much to them that they were willing to take the risk of laying down their lives to obtain it. I do not contend that *all* enslaved women who murdered their owners used this Black feminist practice of justice, but that the women in these pages did.

In the end, did these women get the satisfaction they sought through lethal resistance to slavery? Yes. Because, as Frantz Fanon asserted in his seminal text, *The Wretched of the Earth,* violence itself can be cathartic.[21] Violence certainly restored these women's self-respect and insulted dignity and rebalanced the scales of justice. By the dawn of their executions, they had found peace – a peace they likely never had while enslaved. And because spiritual freedom follows peace, perhaps they also found freedom as they stepped onto the gallows.

It is impossible to fully understand a Black feminist practice of justice without understanding it in its proper historical and legal context. In the age of slavery, the formal, legal channel to obtain justice – otherwise known as the judicial system – catered to white Americans exclusively. Neither the Constitution nor legislation, courts, sheriffs, justices, or judges regularly extended justice or protections to Black people – enslaved or free. For Black Americans, "justice" flowed in only one direction – to punish them for various violations of the racial and social order; and it rarely flowed to protect *them* from injustice.

Slaveowners and overseers acted as the embodiments of the judicial system and the front line for meting out punishments on their farms and plantations. They made plantation "laws" or rules that enslaved people had to follow, acted as corrections officers, judge, jury, punisher, and sometimes executioner for every infraction. The exceptions to this internal disciplinary system were in the cases of large conspiracies or rebellions or if the crime involved the death of a white person.[22] Then, enslaved people would be subjected to the formal judicial system. State laws and local statutes governing enslaved people – also called the slave code[23] – exacted rigid control and surveillance over them, and maintained their enslavement, social inferiority, and political impotence. Designed to deter bad behavior and resistance, slave codes tended to be exceedingly punitive for even minor offenses. For example, Virginia made smuggling tobacco, stealing hogs, and receiving a stolen horse crimes punishable by death. By the antebellum era, Virginia, had sixty-eight capital (death-sentence) offenses for enslaved people, including counterfeiting, burglary, arson, administering poison to a horse, and having ten pieces of coin in their possession. Antebellum South Carolina had thirty-six capital offenses for enslaved people, including larceny in the amount of $1.07 or higher. For a conviction on that or other capital offenses, they would be executed and denied the benefit of clergy[24] beforehand. In the nineteenth century, North Carolina had forty capital offenses for enslaved people, including "resisting owner by force," "running away" and "not returning home immediately." Enslaved people could be put to death in Georgia for arson or attempted arson, "grievously wounding, maiming, or bruising" a white person, or circulating "incendiary" documents.[25] The punitive tendencies of the system were not much better for *free* Blacks who, in antebellum Virginia, could be sold into slavery if convicted of minor offenses, including debt. In Virginia, North Carolina, and other southern states, slaveowners would be reimbursed if their enslaved people were executed by the state, illustrating that even as the judicial system failed to offer protections, privileges, or rights to Blacks, it protected – perhaps even *overprotected* – the economic interests of slaveowners.[26]

Although rooted in English common and statutory law, the American judicial system was built on the ideas of justice enshrined in the Magna Carta of 1215. Among the most important rights outlined in that document are the rights to petition, habeas corpus, trial by jury, and "due process." The Magna Carta outlines due process as the guarantee that no person will be deprived of life, liberty, or property without a fair hearing of the matter in court and before a jury of their peers. These essential rights are outlined or enshrined in America's founding documents. For example, the right to a trial by jury is one of the grievances the American colonists articulated in the Declaration of Independence. As it related to Black Americans, the entire judicial system was polluted by systemic unfairness, from the investigation stage of criminal cases to sentencing and execution.

Even before the trial stage, enslaved people accused of capital crimes endured several layers of an unfair judicial system. One glaring example is the investigation stage, or coroner's inquest process. In cases of murder, sudden, or suspicious deaths, the coroner's main job duty was to hold inquests, or investigations, to determine the cause of death. In some colonies/states, county coroners were responsible for doing the detective work in murder cases, which included examining the crime scene to discover the means and circumstances of the murder, as well as the identity of the culpable party. Coroners had the power to impanel a jury composed of white, free, male property holders to help with these death investigations by gathering evidence, identifying and questioning witnesses, and analyzing the crime scene. In slave states, inquest jurors tended to be slaveowners. The stark power imbalance meant that when being interrogated by slaveholding inquest jurors, Black witnesses or suspects may not have been forthcoming or willing to disclose damning details that might get them or their loved ones implicated in the crime. The power imbalance also meant that many enslaved people were often pressured to "confess" or implicate other enslaved people who might or might not have been involved. The irony is that enslaved people were interrogated by these coroners' investigations, but often prohibited from testifying in their own trials later.

Another example of injustice in the legal system happened outside of it – at the hands of white clergy. After their arrests and confinements, enslaved people were visited in their jail cells by local white clergy. These ministers ostensibly were there to share scriptures, pray for the souls of the enslaved people, and prepare them for their execution and afterlife. They pressed convicted slaves to "repent," but also managed to obtain their confessions.[27] The specific tactics white clergy used to elicit confessions are unknown, but more than likely they included manipulation of the Bible, pressure, guilt, berating, and convenient scriptures about hellfire and eternal damnation. Apparently, the ministers' tactics were very effective because they commonly got enslaved people not only to confess to horrific murders but also to provide detailed summaries of how and why they killed. Regardless of the era or geographical location, these confessions follow a similar pattern: a short autobiography, admission of the crime *and* sin, proclamations of regret, and pleas for forgiveness. Because most of the confessants could not read or write, it is not clear how much of these confessions actually were the authentic, verbatim words of the accused, or embellished constructions created by the clergy. After obtaining these confessions, ministers turned them over to officials who used them as evidence in trials. Many of them ended up in local newspapers. By manipulating enslaved detainees, clergy effectively functioned as agents of the judicial system, working against the interests of the enslaved.

A small percentage of other "confessions" were extorted by slaveowners. A teenaged Cloe was threatened with both a beating and hanging to elicit a confession for the death of her owners' children in 1801. In 1842, slaveowners suspected several enslaved people of plotting an insurrection in Purysburgh, South Carolina. In order to obtain their confessions, they stripped their people naked and ordered them to lie face down. The accused were then "cut first lengthwise and then crosswise [lashed across their backs] till [sic] they made confessions of guilt." The beatings were so brutal that it was reported that Billy and Elsy, two of the accused, were so "badly cut" that they "could not bear" to continue receiving the lash. In yet another case, Elizabeth and Ned were beaten with a rope to extort a confession for killing the young son of Elizabeth's owner. According to legal historian Thomas D. Morris, slave confessions actually were quite rare; he found only fifteen in his research on eighteenth-century Virginia. Because of the use of beatings, threats, and torture to extract confessions, Morris cautions against taking them at face value or accepting them as truth.[28] But looking at confessions another way reveals that there was no long-term incentive to confess to a murder because doing so would result in a certain execution. Given that threat, they are more reliable than not.

Enslaved people accused of capital crimes were tried in slave courts, courts of oyer and terminer, or other local criminal courts and defended by court-appointed attorneys. Apparently, the primary reason they received legal counsel was to project a semblance of justice to society, and because enslaved people were considered too valuable to be executed without the appearance of due process to placate their owners.[29] Some slave states did not even pretend to have fair judicial systems: for example, North Carolina did not give accused enslaved people access to legal counsel, juries, or clergy.[30] Without due process, accused enslaved North Carolinians could expect death sentences for all capital charges. Even when defense attorneys were provided in other parts of the South, they rarely made much of an effort to defend their clients. They took a perfunctory approach to their work: many did not bother to build a strong defense – or a defense at all – and offered no alternative theories of the case to counter that of the prosecution. Some defense attorneys did not even bother to cross-examine white witnesses; they accepted their words as truth – even in the face of obvious lies.

The structure of the slave courts or courts of oyer and terminer varied by colony/state. A common formulation is that five justices of the peace presided over the trials – many of whom were slaveowners. Virginia's courts of oyer and terminer were structured in this way. In eighteenth-century North Carolina, a special tribunal comprising three or more justices of the peace plus three other slaveholding freeholders presided over the trials of accused enslaved people. These courts were subjected to the will and financial interests of the slaveholding class, who determined which enslaved people would stand trial for capital cases and whether they would be executed. According to one historian, slaveowners "shape[d] events in the courtroom almost as they pleased and ... acquiesced more readily in the role of the state in the punishment of serious crime."[31] Similar to the coroner's inquest juries, the power and racial imbalance between slave-owning justices and enslaved defendants tipped the scales of justice away from enslaved people. Those brought before these courts faced justices who were often the neighbors or friends of their dead owners. To compound the situation, these "justices" were poorly prepared to execute their duties, "unlearned in the law, susceptible to local pressures and prejudices, and capable of committing grave legal errors." According to prominent jurist and legal scholar A. Leon Higginbotham, Jr., "slaves were doubly damned: not only were they deprived of trial by jury, but, in addition, they were tried by ... inept and unlearned [justices]."[32] In other words, enslaved people faced justices who were incompetent, biased, or ignorant of laws and legal processes. This gross incompetence all but *guaranteed* a miscarriage of justice in these courts.

The procedural rights embedded within the American judicial system are designed to eliminate or minimize injustice. Yet enslaved people accused of crimes were denied many procedural rights granted to white defendants, including arrest warrants, indictments that matched the crime, bail, and writs of habeas corpus. In addition, enslaved people were denied the most basic right of all – a trial by a jury of their peers. Instead, cases were decided by justices in many states. Both slave *and* free states prohibited Blacks from serving on juries through most of the slave era. In fact, it was not until 1860 that the first African Americans were impaneled to serve on juries in the United States.[33] Without a doubt, their exclusion from juries made it difficult for Black defendants to obtain justice. Moreover, laws in most states prohibited Black people – free or enslaved – from testifying against whites in court.[34] There are a few instances in which enslaved people were allowed to testify in their own trials; but that was entirely up to the whims of local justices. Unable to benefit from critical eyewitness testimony, even well-meaning court-appointed defense attorneys could not build a case good enough to exonerate the accused, even the innocent. Consequently, defense attorneys had no choice but to rely on white witnesses who were largely prejudiced against the defendant by the time of the trial. Many of the witnesses in this book were neighboring slaveowners.

In the colonial and most of the antebellum eras, capital trials for enslaved people generally were one-sided affairs with all witnesses testifying for the prosecution. Not surprisingly, enslaved defendants were convicted on the slimmest of "evidence." Much of what was presented by the prosecution at these trials was based on the accused's temperament, hearsay, "suspicious behavior," past acts of resistance, or previously articulated wishes for another owner. Evidence that would have been insufficient to convict a white person in a regular court returned convictions for enslaved defendants. Enslaved people were effectively prohibited from pleading self-defense in capital cases. Because slaveowners had the right to severely discipline and even abuse their enslaved people if they wished, self-defense claims of enslaved people had no merit in the eyes of the court. However, even abuse had its limits; after the American Revolution slave codes often prohibited owners from murdering their enslaved people. Some southern states implicitly granted enslaved people the right to use deadly force to protect their lives from a life-threatening attack, but self-defense arguments usually failed in southern courts – especially because enslaved people were generally prohibited from striking or injuring white people. In other instances, judges and justices failed to admit damning evidence against the white victim, thus eroding all hopes of a successful self-defense argument. For example, during the 1855 trial of Celia, who murdered her owner, Robert Newsom, in Callaway County, Missouri, after years of rape, the judge refused to allow evidence about Newsom's previous threats on Celia's life and ordered the jury to disregard damning testimony about him from a white witness.[35]

Once a case ended in a guilty verdict, enslaved people were not guaranteed the right to an appeal in the full sense, even in the face of gross procedural errors. Appeals are an important element of due process because they open the possibility of a second trial that can lead to an acquittal. Without this avenue, defense attorneys sometimes tried to reduce the worst charges for enslaved people, thereby eliminating the looming threat of a death sentence. Slaveowners reserved the right to pursue an appeal on behalf of their enslaved people who were convicted of capital crimes, but enslaved defendants could not pursue appeals themselves. Newer slave states tended to offer more procedural fairness than the older ones. For example, Texas,

Arkansas, Missouri (Missouri only allowed appeals for enslaved people convicted of murder), Mississippi, Tennessee and Alabama all offered enslaved people the opportunity for appeals, whereas, Virginia, North Carolina, South Carolina, Maryland, and Georgia did not until the nineteenth century. Neither Louisiana nor Virginia had any provisions for appeals in cases involving enslaved people until 1865, the year slavery ended – despite an 1844 Louisiana Supreme Court decision that affirmed that enslaved people had the right of appeal. Similarly, Delaware and Maryland did not allow even one appeal for a capital case before 1865. In Kentucky, enslaved people had the rights to trial by jury and appeal on the books, but the state did not rule on an appeal for one until 1859. South Carolina allowed slave appeals after 1839, but such cases, instead of being sent to the full state supreme court, were heard by just one justice. In terms of sentencing, enslaved people convicted of capital crimes would be executed or sold and transported abroad, which was a type of erasure or disappearing. In Virginia, all five justices had to agree to a death sentence for it to be implemented.[36] Because death cases had to be sent to the governor for examination in Virginia, executive review left open the possibility of clemency. Hence, executive review functioned as a type of appeal that often provided the only hope for a reprieve an enslaved person had in Virginia.

The only component of the judicial system that *did* work for enslaved people was the right to a speedy trial.[37] But even that was handled unjustly. In capital cases, enslaved people charged with murder were convicted and executed within days. Historians Marvin Michael Kay and Lorin Cary found that in eighteenth-century North Carolina, an enslaved person's trial, conviction, and punishment often occurred on the same day.[38] Although this pace was not typical, many were summarily executed within days of the trial and conviction. According to legal scholar Stuart Banner, the speediness of slave murder trials was intended to ensure that the public desire for retribution was quickly satisfied while the memory of the crime was still fresh.[39]

The American judicial system did not work when enslaved people were *defendants;* and justice was even more elusive when they were *victims.* Physical and sexual assault, maiming, and injuring enslaved people were not treated as prosecutable crimes through most of the slave era.[40] No group was more vulnerable to the injustice of the judicial system than Black women. The intersection of patriarchy, white supremacy, and wealth meant that slaveowners wielded all society's power and held the keys to the judicial system – especially because they served as county judges, magistrates, and local and state legislators. Hence, with their intersectional oppression as enslaved persons and women, they were exponentially disempowered and disregarded by the system and, in fact, made vulnerable to the crushing impact of powerlessness and denied personhood and citizenship. For enslaved people, the United States judicial system was a burlesque.

As a disclaimer, this book is concerned with enslaved women who actually plotted and carried out revolts that centered on killing their owners then admitted it. A qualification for inclusion in this book is overwhelming evidence that the women did, in fact, kill or attempt to kill their owners or their owners' families. I also chose women who articulated a reason for using lethal resistance. Another qualification for inclusion is premeditation, organization, and a careful plan to avoid suspicion. This book is organized around several case studies and an interpretative framework for how historians of enslaved women's history might approach the work that lies ahead. Consequently, it is not an exhaustive catalogue of *every* instance when this type of resistance appears in the historical record. It simply provides a blueprint for how we may begin to do this research. Because this is an understudied topic, the secondary sources that would normally contextualize this resistance by women are few and far between. Hence, these stories are contextually situated within local histories and legal contexts as well as the stories of other women who waged lethal resistance using the same means. The following chapters are not the same length and nor should they be: they reflect the fullness or scarcity of the archive across time and space.

As a warning, the pages that follow depict graphic violence that is extraordinarily gruesome. The reader must remember that slavery was a violent institution; slaveowners could be brutal and sadistic. Enslaved women's retaliatory violence is a direct product of, and response to, slavery and the violence required to sustain it. That cannot be stressed enough. Even more troubling than the carnage these women left in their wake is the sadistic, inhumane, and appallingly tortuous state-sponsored execution of these women – who were mothers, daughters, and grandmothers. This final act of state violence committed against Black women underscores the savagery of the violence that defined these women's lives and deaths in the age of slavery.

1

PHILLIS AND PHOEBE
" . . . cut Down the Old Tree, and . . . Hew off the Branches"

I

What sad and awful Scenes are these presented to your View;
Let every one Example take, and Virtue's Ways pursue.

II

For here you see what Vice has done, in all it's [sic] sinful Ways;
By Mark and Phillis who are left, to finish now their Days.

III

The Sight is shocking to behold, and dismal to our Eyes;
And if our Hearts are not o'er hard, will fill us with
Surprize [sic].
  God's Vengeance cries aloud indeed, And now his Voice they
hear, And in an Hour or two they must before his Face appear.

V

To answer for their Master's Blood, which they've unjustly split;
And if not Pardon'd, sure they must, Remain with all their Guilt.

VI

Their Crimes appear as black as Hell and justly so indeed; and
for a greater, I am sure, there's none this can exceed.

VII

Three were concerned in this Crime, but one by Law was
clear'd; The other two must suffer Death, and 'tis but just
*indeed.*¹

On Sunday morning, June 29, 1755, Phillis, an enslaved woman owned by Captain John Codman prepared breakfast as usual. The wealthy captain was a merchant and slaveholder who resided in the town of Charlestown in the colony of Massachusetts. A widower since 1752, Codman lived in the home with his children and enslaved people. Phillis prepared his usual breakfast of a bowl of water gruel – oatmeal – and gave it to his thirty-one-year-old daughter Elizabeth to give to her father. Codman, who had a history of stomach ailments, fell gravely ill shortly after finishing his breakfast. As his condition worsened, his children and enslaved cooks, Phoebe and Phillis, tended to him at his bedside with great tenderness and concern. The captain is said to have "languished for fifteen hours" in his bed, suffering from convulsions. He died two days later on July 1, 1755.

According to the *Boston Evening Post,* upon examining Codman's body, Middlesex County Coroner John Remington noticed that his "lower Parts [had] turned as black as Coal." Perplexed by the unnatural state of his body, Coroner Remington held a coroner's inquest that began on July 2, the day after John Codman's death.[2] After his cause of death came to light, officials uncovered a diabolical conspiracy that dated back at least six years.[3]

. . .

Colonial Charlestown, Massachusetts, was a port city located roughly 2.5 miles north of Boston, and separated from it by the Charles River (Figure 1.1). Both whites and Blacks freely traveled between the neighboring cities of Charlestown and Boston for business and personal reasons. On any given day, enslaved people, merchants, or fishermen took the ferry to and from Boston, underscoring the connection between the two port cities.[4] The economies of Charlestown and Boston both centered on trade, shipbuilding, fishing, and distilleries, but Boston was the more significant of the two. By the 1730s, Boston had the distinction of being the most prosperous port city in the British American colonies. Among the many goods traded on Boston's Long Wharf and destined for other places in Massachusetts, other colonies in mainland North America, Barbados, and even England, were enslaved African men and women.

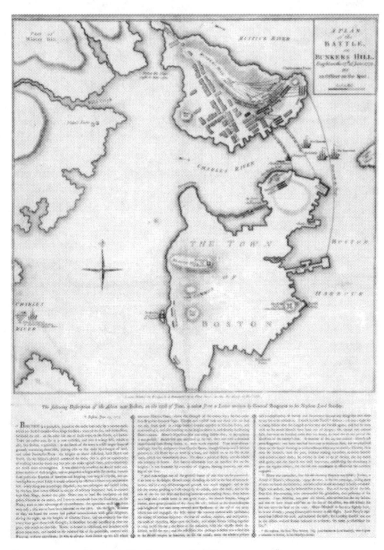

Figure 1.1 1775 Map of Charlestown and Boston
Credit: The Society of the Cincinnati

The earliest evidence of enslaved Africans in the Boston area can be traced to 1638 when a group arrived on the ship *Desire*. Still, slavery never became a dominant feature in Boston's culture or economy. Most Boston slaveowners owned just one or two people as personal servants or artisans. Although it is hard to find accurate census data from colonial Massachusetts, roughly 280,000 people resided in the colony by the mid-eighteenth century. In 1754, when Governor William Shirley ordered a colony-wide census of enslaved people older than sixteen years old, there were 954 of them living in Boston (Suffolk County) – comprising roughly 5.6 percent of the city's estimated total population of 17,000. An incomplete slave census of Middlesex County, where Charlestown was located, recorded just 353 enslaved adults in that county. Yet, together, Suffolk and Middlesex counties were home to the majority of Blacks living in the colony of Massachusetts in the mid-eighteenth century.[5] Even before the American Revolution, slavery was on the decline in the area.

In 1750, 80 percent of Boston's Black community consisted of free Blacks, most of whom resided in the city's North End.[6] Boston's Black community was consequential: several Black Bostonians in the colonial era would later make their mark in history. The future poet Phillis Wheatley; future founder of the first Black Masonic lodge, Prince Hall; and Elizabeth "Mum Bett" Freeman, who successfully sued for freedom after the American Revolution, all lived in Boston in the 1750s.

Great fluidity existed between Boston and Charlestown: some enslaved people living in Charlestown had spouses and other family members living in North Boston, so it was not unusual for them to travel between the towns in both directions to visit their loved ones. John Codman's enslaved people, for example, regularly visited Boston's North End on errands, to visit spouses and friends, and for work and leisure activities. Black Boston, with its healthy and growing population of free Blacks, offered Codman's enslaved people a taste of freedom. Perhaps, it was that *taste* that made them increasingly discontented with their owner.

John Codman was born on September 29, 1696, in Charlestown, Massachusetts, to Stephen and Elizabeth Codman. Both of his parents died by the time he was eight years old, so an older brother cared for him until adulthood. In 1718, John married Parnell Foster, the granddaughter of Mary Chilton, a pilgrim who had arrived from Europe aboard the *Mayflower* and who was, purportedly, the first woman to land at Plymouth. By the time Parnell Codman died on September 15, 1752, the couple had given birth to eleven children. A saddler by trade, Codman also worked as a merchant and sea captain. In those various endeavors, he managed to amass a great deal of wealth: his estate, which was valued at £6,000 in 1749 (equivalent to $1,385,773 today), included a "mansion," a ship, a forge, seven enslaved people, thirty acres of land in Bridgewater and fifty acres of land near Harvard College. Historian Lorenzo Greene's research listed John Codman among the leading slaveholders in the Massachusetts colony. Captain Codman also was an ensign, or junior officer, in the first (and now oldest) chartered military organization in the western hemisphere, the Ancient and Honorable Artillery Company. Posthumously, he was described by elite local whites as a "remarkably upright man both in person and character, and was greatly respected."[7] However, Codman's enslaved people did not think so highly of him as the white elites in Charlestown and Boston.

In 1755, Captain Codman owned seven enslaved people: Pompey, Cuffee, Scipio, Thomas (Tom), Phillis, Phoebe, and Mark, all of whom worked as mechanics, common laborers, or house servants.[8] Phillis had grown up in the Codman household. In her late thirties in 1755, she was described as the "spinster servant of John Codman," which was a seventeenth-century term to describe an unmarried woman. She and Phoebe were the only two enslaved women owned by the captain. According to Mark, Codman "favored" Phoebe and treated her better than the others. Phoebe was "married" to a man named Quacoe. The couple did not legally marry, but were recognized as husband and wife by contemporary Black and white Charlestowners. The archive does not reveal how the two met or where they married. Quacoe lived in Boston with his owner, James Dalton, who owned a restaurant; he sometimes spent the night and weekends with his wife in the Codman garret in Charlestown.[9]

Quacoe had a long and notorious history. Likely born in Africa or to an African mother judging by his Akan name, he may have been transported in the Transatlantic Slave Trade to the Dutch colony of Surinam, where he was enslaved most of his life. Quacoe and a female accomplice had been accused of poisoning in Surinam.

In Surinam, people such as Quacoe, who poisoned and used knowledge of plants and herbs for evil, were called *wisimen* by fellow enslaved people.[10] Quacoe's female accomplice was executed for the crime, but he was sentenced to transportation out of Surinam, which is how he arrived in Boston. The 1755 Codman murder is the second time Quacoe had been implicated in a poisoning; it would not be his last. In 1761, five years after Codman's death, a dying slave named Boston accused Quacoe of poisoning him before he died. That case began with an argument over a woman between Quacoe and Sambo, another enslaved man. Shortly thereafter, Sambo's pigs were found dead – poisoned. Many enslaved people immediately suspected that Quacoe had poisoned the pigs as revenge. Reportedly, he had felt betrayed when his own friend, Boston, took Sambo's side in the dispute. Boston then fell deathly ill, and before dying, he accused Quacoe of poisoning him. Quacoe escaped a conviction and death sentence because the justice overseeing his case did not believe an allegation alone was enough to convict him of the crime.[11] What this history reveals is that Quacoe was a master poisoner who used his craft to exact revenge when wronged. He is, perhaps, the only enslaved person in that era who was implicated in multiple poisoning murders in the Black Atlantic and escaped a death sentence each time.

Mark is the only Codman slave for whom there is more biographical data available – much of it provided in his own dying declaration, *The Last & Dying Words of Mark*. Mark stated that he had been born in Barbados in 1725 and sold as a child to Henry Caswell of Boston. In the colonial era, ships routinely traded between Boston and Barbados so his transportation to the colony was not unusual, but certainly traumatic to the young child who was permanently separated from his family and community. Mark's second owner, John Salter, was a Boston brazier, or brass worker, by trade. Salter had had a transformational impact on young Mark by teaching him to read and write. Mark fondly recalled that Salter "educated me as tenderly as one of his own children. In the colonial era, owners rarely taught enslaved people to read. Owners who recognized their enslaved people's humanity might teach them to read so that they could read the Bible. Mark was a Christian, so being able to read the Bible was important for his spiritual growth. For reasons unknown, Salter sold Mark to

Joseph Thomas of Plympton, Massachusetts, located roughly forty-five miles south of Boston. Thomas subsequently sold Mark to Captain John Codman. Mark had a wife and at least one child in Boston. The record is silent on their identities or whether they were enslaved or free. Mark indicated that Codman "let me live in *Boston* with my Wife, and go out to work." A blacksmith by trade, and literate, Mark had many more freedoms and privileges than typical enslaved people in the colonial era. Codman allowed him to find his own work, earn his own wages, and live with his wife and child in Boston. While hiring out their own time – especially in another city – enslaved people needed to find their own employers and housing. It was not uncommon for hires to reside with their enslaved family members. Living and working separately from Codman and earning his own wages afforded Mark some freedom and independence. For one, he moved freely between Charlestown and North Boston. By his own admission, though, he spent too much of his free time drinking, visiting friends, and "carousing" on Sabbath. His drinking was such a problem that Codman tried to stop it by telling the owner of a pub Mark frequented not to sell any more alcohol to his servants.[12]

In 1752, a warrant was issued for Mark's arrest in Boston after he had ignored its "warning out" notices to leave the city. The warning out process began with legal notices to non-residents ordering them to return to their legal towns of residence. The intention was to ensure that transients and indigents would not apply for poor relief in their adopted towns, but would, instead, put that burden on their legal places of residence. For most white newcomers, warning out was not always enforced, but Blacks could not expect the same privilege of whiteness.[13] The record is silent on whether Boston officials arrested Mark and forced him back to Charlestown in 1752. What is certain is that he continued to spend his free time in Boston.

It is hard to determine, with certainty, the quality of the lives Codman's enslaved people enjoyed. All except Mark lived in the garret of the home. The inventory of Codman's estate after his death provides clues about their material conditions in the garret. There were five straw beds, one feather bed, and ten rugs in that common living space.[14] It was highly unusual for enslaved people in the colonial era to sleep on a feather bed; these typically were found in the homes of the wealthy. Poor whites and enslaved people generally slept on the floor or straw beds. Hence, the presence of the feather bed among five straw beds in the garret where they slept suggests that one of Codman's enslaved people received special treatment. Given what Mark revealed about Phoebe being favored, it is highly likely that the feather bed belonged to her.

None of the people owned by Captain Codman ever explicitly stated that he was an abusive or neglectful owner, but there were clues that he was. Right before his death, he had hit Tom so hard that he injured his eye. Codman's people clearly had their own image of what character traits defined "good masters" because they expressed the desire to have one during the coroner's inquest following his death. Implicit in this expressed desire for "good masters" is the judgment that Codman was *not* a good owner.[15] Codman's people gave the coroner's inquest jury several reasons why they considered him such. According to Phillis, Mark said he was "uneasy and wanted to have another Master, and he was concerned for Phebe and [Phillis] too." Although she was not forthcoming on the specific nature of Mark's concerns, it must be noted that he did not express the same "concern" for Codman's enslaved men; the inference is that the women were enduring a distinctive gendered experience in the Codman household. Perhaps, Mark's "concern" is related to the burden of the women's workload as house servants and cooks or it may be a subtle reference to sexual abuse – a regular feature of Black women's enslavement. The use of veiled terms and euphemisms to discuss sexual abuse is a product of the era; in the interest of decorum and taste, people in colonial American did not discuss sex or rape publicly. It is reasonable to think that as a widower, Codman might have forced his enslaved women to satisfy his sexual needs. Enslaved women were particularly vulnerable in widowers' homes. The fact that Phoebe received special treatment by Codman and a feather bed gives credence to this idea. If these women were being sexually abused by their owner, they did not have the power to stop it or to get anyone to protect them. In colonial Massachusetts, people external to the household would have been disinclined to intervene or challenge the sexual prerogatives of powerful white men – especially as it relates to their enslaved women. In the context of slavery,

Codman's unjust treatment of his enslaved workers was done with impunity. They had no one to appeal to for better treatment. Realizing they were powerless to change their owner's behavior themselves, Codman's slaves hoped that different owners would alleviate their suffering.[16] The dilemma they faced is that they had no power to initiate their own sales to different owners. So they decided to force Codman's hand.

Sometime in early 1749, Phoebe, Phillis, and Mark designed a plan to burn down the blacksmith shop and workhouse. Phillis claimed the arson was Mark's idea, and he claimed Phoebe masterminded this plan. Phillis reported that Mark told the women that he wanted to live in Boston and "if all was burnt down, he did not know what Master could do without selling us." Both he and Phoebe had enslaved spouses in Boston so they may have hoped their next owners would reside in Boston so they could be closer to them. The arsonists calculated that the destruction of the blacksmith shop and all his tools would lead to Codman's financial devastation and force him to sell them to new owners. Although Phillis later admitted that she set the fire, she implicated Phoebe and Mark in the arson, testifying that Phoebe prepared the shavings and coals for the fire and Mark placed them in the shop for her.[17] The fire, set at 1:00 a.m. on June 12, 1749, caused extensive damage. Codman's blacksmith shop and several other nearby buildings burned. A distillery and brigantine docked nearby also caught fire, but escaped serious damage. The captain's damages were estimated at £6,000, a near total loss for him.[18]

But they had grossly underestimated their owner's financial resources: the fire did not force Codman into financial ruin as they had expected. In fact, he did not sell a single slave after that fire. Not one. Codman never figured out that his own enslaved people were responsible for it, although he may have had his suspicions. In the colonial era, fires were remarkably common and most were not the work of arsonists. Phillis, Phoebe, and Mark held the secret between them until 1755 when Phillis admitted to officials that she had committed the arson.[19]

Because the 1749 arson did not result in their sale as they had hoped, Phillis, Phoebe, and Mark decided to *kill* Codman. Consistent with a Black feminist practice of justice, murder was the last option for them to free themselves of Codman for good. Their decision to kill him suggests that they did not think he was redeemable or capable of reform. He had to die.

The conspirators, though, seem to have been spiritually conflicted about whether they could commit murder as Christians. Phillis recounted that Mark read the Bible to make sure that it was not sinful to kill a man. According to her, Mark concluded "that it was no Sin to kill him if they did not lay violent Hands on him So as to shed Blood, by sticking or stabbing or cutting his Throat." Or so he thought. Somehow, Mark missed the dozens of biblical scriptures that forbid the shedding of blood, including the Sixth Commandment (Exodus 20:13) and the one that reads, "Cursed is anyone who kills their neighbor secretly" (Deuteronomy 27:24), which would have covered secretly killing someone with poison.[20] However, most biblical statements on murder condemn the shedding of *innocent* blood or killing *righteous* people. Mark may have concluded that because Codman was neither innocent nor righteous, his murder was justifiable.[21] It was Codman's "just deserts."

The trio decided that poison would be the best way to kill him. Quacoe's history of poisoning is not inconsequential to this case. He may have given his wife the idea and instructed her as to which poisons to use. Phoebe, Phillis, and Mark believed it was possible to get away with killing their owner with poison because it had previously been done with success in their own neighborhood when John Salmon's slaves killed him with poison – and got away with it. Not only were Salmon's enslaved people never suspected of his killing but they also ultimately ended up with what the conspirators concluded were "good masters." This gave Phoebe, Phillis, and Mark a successful poisoning model; and they may have even sought the advice of Salmon's people. Their comment about Salmon's people getting "good masters" after his death, suggests that freedom from slavery was not their ultimate goal, just obtaining "good masters."[22] This logic is consistent with that of other enslaved women who killed their owners. Their actions were more a moral condemnation of Codman than slavery itself.

Phoebe (possibly along with her husband, Quacoe) masterminded the poison plot. Although Mark insisted that he was nothing more than Phoebe's and Phillis' pawn, the evidence implicates him for being actively involved in obtaining the poison. As a male who hired his time, traveled to, and worked and lived in Boston, Mark had greater mobility and access to a wide network of enslaved people who worked for apothecaries or doctors and could readily access poison. Robbin, enslaved by Dr. William Clarke in North Boston, procured poison from his owner's business and became a frequent supplier of arsenic to disgruntled enslaved people. Mark later admitted that he initially told Robbin "horrid lies" to get the poison, including telling him he needed it to kill three pigs. After that initial lie, Robbin did not appear to question Mark about why he needed so much arsenic. Sometimes Robbin took the ferry to Charlestown and delivered the poison to Mark and other times Mark ferried to Boston to pick it up from him. In the last month of Codman's life, Phillis said that Robbin had come to the house in a black wig to disguise himself – obviously nervous about being identified by anyone in Charlestown. Another enslaved poison supplier was Kerr, who was enslaved to Dr. John Gibbons in Boston. Kerr typically sent the poison to the women through Phoebe's husband, Quacoe. Phoebe had also made the trip to Boston to collect the poison directly from Kerr at least once. Even Mark had received poison from Kerr at least twice. But in June 1755, Kerr was no longer willing to provide any more arsenic because Phoebe told him that she was poisoning someone in the Codman home and that revelation made him nervous. When the arsenic proved too weak to finish Codman off, Mark obtained some lead used in pottery glazing from Essex, who was enslaved to Thomas Powers.[23] What is interesting is that all of these enslaved people knew Codman was being poisoned, and most of them participated in the plot or facilitated it, passively or actively; not one of them betrayed the plot before his demise. On some level, they surely believed he deserved what was coming to him.

Although Mark procured the poison, Phoebe and Phillis administered it to Codman in his food and drink. For two years, the women fed the captain an array of poisons, including arsenic, ratsbane (rat poison), potter's lead, and possibly raw cashews, which contain urushiol, which can be fatal if ingested before boiling. These women were quite knowledgeable about the poisons' efficacy and potency and even how to administer each kind without detection. For example, the people who interviewed Phillis determined that she "seems to have thought [lead] was the efficient poison compared to arsenic." She also knew a good deal about rat poison.

Phillis confessed that when Mark gave her ratsbane, she discerned that it was just "only burnt allom [*sic*]," and not real ratsbane. She doubted its authenticity because she knew that when people took ratsbane, "they would directly swell, and Master did not swell." Phoebe agreed with Phillis' suspicion about the counterfeit ratsbane. The fact that both women knew the effects of rat poison suggests a high degree of familiarity with its effects in humans. The men were just as knowledgeable about poisons: Robbin had told them that arsenic should be dispensed in cold water because it would have no taste. He also instructed them that if used with "swill or Indian meal (cornmeal) . . . it would make 'em swell up." Moreover, he had also advised Mark to give the vial of arsenic in two doses – directions the trio apparently failed to follow. Quacoe's own history proved that he also knew about using poisons to harm or kill.

The women's strategy was to kill Codman slowly, over time. Phillis claimed that when Robbin learned they had not followed his instructions, he said they were "damn'd Fools [because] we had not given Master that first Powder at two Doses, for it wou'd have killed him, and no Body would have known who hurt him, for it was enough to kill the strongest man living . . ."[24]

The larger enslaved community possessed extensive knowledge of palliative and medicinal herbs, plants, *and* deadly poisons. Women, in particular, learned different uses for any given plant. Collard greens, for example, could be eaten or used to cure headaches by tying the leaf to the sufferer's head. Particular plants could have a dual function – to alleviate illness or to murder. Jimsonweed, for example, could be used to treat headaches, asthma, or dropsy, or to kill someone. In 1841, in St. Augustine, Florida, an unnamed enslaved woman along with Jake, an enslaved man, poisoned the entire Hyde family by putting the seeds of the Jimsonweed (a corruption of "Jamestown weed") into their coffee. Every part of the Jimsonweed is extremely toxic if ingested, but especially the seeds: ingesting as little as 15–25 grams of the seeds can be fatal. The Hydes were immediately sickened after drinking their coffee, so it was obvious that their enslaved cook had poisoned them. The pair were promptly arrested. They confessed the following day and were executed shortly thereafter.[25]

As that case demonstrates, there was a thin line between using plants to heal and using them to kill. Practitioners could do both. Chelsea Berry found that in the West African language Igbo, the phrases for preparing medicine, practicing sorcery, and neutralizing poison are very similar – "-gwọ ọgwù (to prepare medicine), -kọ ọgwù (to practice sorcery against), and -rụ ọgwù (to neutralize effect of poison)." Among the Akan speakers, the word *aduru* means medicine and poison. In spite of this striking similarity of the root words and verbs in traditional West African languages, enslaved people in colonial American understood the difference. Slaveowners were equally fearful of the medicinal knowledge and practices of enslaved people. As Berry asserts, "unsanctioned medical practice" by enslaved people was extremely threatening to slaveowners, especially when used as a form of resistance. Because poisoning was done in secret, slaveholders had to live with the fear that every bite of food they took – every sip of drink – could lead to their death. That persistent, gnawing anxiety prompted some colonial authorities to legislate against enslaved people's medicinal practices. Colonial Virginia, for one, made the "practice of medicine" by enslaved people a capital offense, punishable by death.[26]

The cultural knowledge African and African American medicinal practitioners held about plants, roots, herbs, and fruits must be distinguished from knowledge about deadly poisons and chemicals. Plants mostly nourish, heal or cure – although some can also kill, as demonstrated above; manufactured poisons and chemicals, by contrast, are always harmful when ingested or when in contact with the skin. Enslaved people possessed sophisticated knowledge about both categories and where they overlapped. At times, the weapons enslaved people used to poison their owners were common household cleaners and products. For example, in nineteenth-century Louisville, an enslaved girl asked a vendor for something to kill flies. The vendor was clearly accustomed to enslaved household workers procuring insecticides so her inquiry did not raise his suspicion. Unfortunately, the "flies" this girl sought to kill were her owner's children. She mixed the insecticide with molasses and gave it to the children to drink; all three children immediately fell ill, but did not die.[27]

In 1859, in Richmond Virginia, an enslaved girl obtained oxalic acid from her mother who was enslaved sixty-three miles away in Fredericksburg, Virginia. Oxalic acid, then (and now) commonly used to removed laundry stains, was widely recognized as toxic and required handwashing after contact. As a product used in laundering, her possession of oxalic acid would not have raised any alarms. The young girl mixed the poison in her owner's water and gave it to him to drink. Although when mixed with water, oxalic acid is colorless, the slaveowner noticed that it tasted acidic so he did not finish the drink, but rather, set it aside to be analyzed by a chemist. Had he finished it, he would have suffered severe gastroenteritis, vomiting, convulsions, metabolic acidosis, and kidney failure. Ingesting as little as 15–30 grams of oxalic acid can be fatal.[28]

Enslaved people's access to, and shared communal knowledge of, herbs *and* poisons allowed them to wield a social capital and power that could be used to resist oppression, and decide whether their oppressors were maimed or died. They even chose how much or how long their owners suffered before dying. The fact that the "weapons" were often common plants grown in nature, household cleaning agents, insecticides, or raticides made it difficult to prevent these types of crimes.

In June 1755, Phoebe and Phillis increased the poison dosing. On June 13, 1755, Phillis received a tiny package that consisted of a white piece of paper that had been folded into a square and tied with twine. Inside the carefully wrapped package was nearly an ounce of white powder. She transferred the powder into a tiny vial, added water, and stored the concoction in Codman's kitchen cupboard. For the next two weeks, she and two other people in the Codman home, Phoebe and Mark, seasoned his food and drinks with the arsenic mixture. When arsenic failed to do the job, the duo added potter's lead to Codman's poisonous meal seasonings.[29] As the only people responsible for the family's meals, Phoebe and Phillis possessed unlimited power to determine when and how the poison would be administered. Although Codman's daughters lived in the home, they were not responsible for preparing the meals for their widowed father. Phoebe and Phillis poisoned Codman's meals, snacks, drinks, and even the tea infusions he took for his lung issues. They mixed it into his barley drink, breakfast water gruel, tea, and even in his favorite luxuries, such as a chocolate drink and sago – a type of pudding made from the pith (starchy center) of the sago palm grown in Barbados. It also seems that the Codmans were not as so vigilant as they could have been: they never discovered the mysterious vial of arsenic in the kitchen cupboard, nor did they notice how the meals had changed in taste, although there was one complaint that the water gruel tasted "gritty." On occasion, though, the Codman daughters expressed curiosity about the food, asking the cooks what the black substance was in the porringer or why the water gruel had turned yellow. The fact that none of the Codmans ever suspected that poisoning was the root of the patriarch's health issues underscores how deeply the family trusted Phillis and Phoebe.[30]

Poisoning is categorized by historians as secret, or *covert,* slave resistance. Because it was done secretly and did not directly confront the slaveowner's power or result in freedom, people assume this form of covert resistance also was nonviolent. It is anything *but* nonviolent. The poisons Phoebe and Phillis used guaranteed a violent reaction in John Codman's body. The symptoms of arsenic poisoning include blood in the urine, stomach cramps, seizures, vomiting, diarrhea, and organ failure. The symptoms of high levels of lead toxicity include stomach pains and cramps, vomiting, muscle weakness, and seizures.[31] Mark reported that his owner suffered from "a wracking Pain in his Belly." According to reports in the local papers, Codman "was seized with an exquisite Pain in the Bowels." In addition, he seemed to have also suffered convulsions in the last few days of his life.[32] Poisoning should be recategorized as a form of armed resistance due to the extensive damage it does to the human body.

The genius of using poison to murder someone is that it can be masked as a chronic illness, as was the case with Codman. Shortly after his death, Abigail Greenleaf wrote a letter to her brother, Robert Treat Paine, who was Codman's friend, "Capt. Codman departed this life yesterday having been ill with a cholick [sic] ever since you drank tea with him." In the eighteenth century, colic – with stomach pain as its primary symptom – would have been the presumptive diagnosis because it was very common among adults then. It was not until five years later, in the 1760s, that physician-researcher Sir George Baker discovered that lead poisoning caused adult colic. Of course, by then John Codman was already dead.[33] The fact that his symptoms could easily be mistaken for chronic illness illustrates how remarkably disciplined Phillis and Phoebe had been in the dosing amounts.

Phoebe and Phillis did not kill their owner suddenly and elicit immediate suspicion. Instead, they murdered him piecemeal over several years. If they were to get away with his murder, people needed to believe Codman had died of a chronic illness. This is the likely reason the women were so disciplined and resisted the impulse to administer the poison in larger doses. Phillis revealed that Phoebe sometimes had "put in more [poison] than she should" and that "her hand was heavy" when she added it to their owner's food and drink. Phillis argued against using too much poison at once – likely concerned that a quick death would make people suspicious. Phoebe subsequently scaled back the poison.[34] Regardless of whether Codman suffered a while or died instantly, as a white, wealthy man, his untimely death would raise questions. Unfortunately, Black women cooks were the objects of suspicion even when such people died of natural causes. In this case, however, the evidence is conclusive that Phoebe and Phillis murdered John Codman and were assisted by Mark and various other enslaved men.

When Middlesex County Coroner John Remington began his autopsy on Codman's body the day of his death, the captain's black lower extremities gave him pause. Remington suspected poisoning because hyperpigmentation is a sign of chronic arsenic toxicity. Upon cutting Codman's body open, Remington reported that "some of the deadly Drug was found undissolved in his Body, which, 'tis said, was calcined Lead, such as Potters used in glazing their Ware ..."[35]

Massachusetts coroners could hold an inquest and impanel a jury comprised of white, free, male property holders to assist in the questioning and cross-examining of witnesses. Remington formally began a coroner's inquest on July 2, 1755. At least four members of this jury belonged to the same family: Samuel Larkin, Samuel Larkin, Jr., Thomas Larkin, and John Larkin, underscoring how much the cards were stacked against Codman's enslaved people from the beginning. Quacoe, Phillis, Robbin, and Mark were arrested and held in the local jail. Suspicions about Mark's culpability were confirmed when the coroner's justices searched the property and found the potter's lead that Mark had hidden in a wall plate, or candle sconce, in the blacksmith shop. It looked similar to the lead found in Codman's stomach. The arsenic was never found but once the lead poison was discovered inside the blacksmith shop where Mark worked, no lie would help him escape a certain execution. The inquest jury concluded that Mark poisoned Codman; the jury assumed the women were innocent.

A grand jury was convened shortly thereafter in Cambridge, Massachusetts, Middlesex County.[36]

Quacoe was questioned by the county justice of the peace on July 12. He stated that he had only recently found out about Mark's efforts to acquire poison. Quacoe claimed that when he did learn of it, he told his wife not to become involved. Since his wife was the ringleader, it is unlikely that Quacoe had only recently heard about the plot – as he claimed. Given her husband's history as a poisoner, Phoebe certainly had consulted him. But Quacoe had learned a lot from his poisoning conviction in Surinam, including how to avoid the same mistakes that had led to his discovery, conviction, and transportation. This time, he simply claimed he knew nothing about it. That strategy worked for him.[37]

Phillis and Mark – in that order – were then questioned by prosecutor Thaddeus Mason and Attorney General Edmund Trowbridge. Had the women feigned ignorance of the plot, they might have gotten away with murder; after all, neither had the reputation Mark had for "roguery" and defiance. But the trio's bond had been broken the day the poison was found in Mark's possession. Phillis, whose testimony began on July 26, fingered Mark as the mastermind and Phoebe as the primary poisoner. Phillis admitted to participating in the conspiracy, but minimized her own role, testifying that she only mixed the poison into the food a few times. She blamed Phoebe, and to a lesser extent, Mark, for the actual poisoning. Phillis told the inquest jury that she often felt "ugly" – a reference to her conscience – about what they were doing, which led her to throw away the tainted food several times instead of serving it to her owner. Phillis provided all the details about how they procured the poison, how the poison was served, and their motive. The transcript of this interrogation is the only surviving record of the women's perspective of the crime.[38]

By the time he was questioned, Mark had already been named as the mastermind by Phillis and possibly Phoebe as well. Regarding Phoebe, Mark testified that she had visited him in jail "to desire me not to confess any Thing for they could not hurt me." She might have been trying to plead with Mark to keep quiet so that they could all escape convictions and death sentences. Perhaps she calculated that without the testimony of the three of them, the authorities did not have enough evidence to convict. Regardless, Phoebe left the jail uncertain about where Mark stood and doubtful about whether he would confess. In that moment, she might have believed that she could no longer trust him because his bitterness towards her was becoming nearly palpable. She might have decided to betray Phillis and Mark to save herself from a certain execution. According to Mark, Phoebe "was an Evidence in Behalf of the king," which means she testified against him for the prosecution. This claim was later corroborated by founding father Dr. Josiah Bartlett in his book, *An Historical Sketch of Charlestown, in the County of Middlesex and Commonwealth of Massachusetts*, "Phoebe, who was said to have been the most culpable, became evidence against the others."[39] She was never interrogated, arrested, indicted, tried, or convicted of the murder she masterminded.

Mark tried his best to convince officials that the women had killed their owner and that he had no foreknowledge of their plot, despite admitting that he had given them poison several times. When asked by the prosecutor why he had potter's lead in his possession, Mark lied and said that he was testing it to "see if it would melt in our Fire."[40] When asked if he had reason to suspect that the poison he was supplying to the women was being used to poison his owner, his reply was "No other Reason than hearing Phoebe the Saturday night before master died ask Phillis, if she had given him enough, to which she replyd [sic]. Yes. I have given him enough and will stick as close to him as his shirt to his back; but who she meant I did not then know, nor untill [sic] after master died." Mark claimed multiple times that he only learned of the plot after Codman's death when he had confronted Phillis and she had admitted it to him. At the end of his testimony, Mark signed his deposition, an act of agency that underscored his literacy and ability to construct his own historical record.[41]

Using those interviews as evidence, a grand jury indicted Phillis, Mark, and Robbin on August 5, 1755. Instead of murder, Phillis was indicted for *petit treason*, an English common law statute 25 *Edw. III c2* that dated back to 1352, that made the murder of a social superior a capital offense. The legislation was designed to protect the social hierarchies in England (and New England) by severely punishing three distinct groups – servants or slaves who killed an owner; wives who killed husbands; or a member of the clergy who killed a superior. Convictions under *petit treason* in colonial New England dictated that women be burned to death and men be drawn to the place of execution and there, hanged. Phillis' indictment stated that she had acted "of Malice forethought willfully feloniously and traiterously [sic] poison kill & murder the said John Codman ... against the Peace of the said Lord the king [and] his Crown & Dignity." Robbin and Mark were named as accessories. The indictment stated the men "did traiterously [sic] advise & incite [and] procure & abet the said Phillis to do and commit the said Treason & Murder." Mark was charged only as an accessory to Phillis' *petit treason*. Despite her prominent role, Phoebe was not indicted, a fact that gives credence to the idea that she may have betrayed her co-conspirators. Despite their prior confessions during the coroner's inquest, both Phillis and Mark pleaded not guilty at their arraignments. For his part, Robbin's charges seem to have been dropped by the time Phillis and Mark were arraigned.[42]

The judicial system that enslaved people faced in colonial Massachusetts, a society with slaves, was different from what they might have experienced in slave societies. For one, they were not subject to separate, slave courts. Enslaved people had their cases heard in the Superior Court of Judicature. Based on the principles in the Magna Carta, colonial Massachusetts prohibited death sentences without due process for anyone, including enslaved people. Enslaved people also enjoyed the right to a grand jury, legal counsel, legal challenges, and juries. They had the right have their indictments read to them and to testify in court, except against whites.

The pair's trial commenced on August 6, 1755, in the Superior Court of Judicature, Court of Assize, in Cambridge, Massachusetts. Chief Justice Stephen Sewall and Associate Justices Benjamin Lynde, Jr., John Cushing, and Chambers Russell presided over the trial.[43] The historical record is silent on whether these justices owned enslaved people. Neither defendant was provided with a member of clergy to counsel them, owing to an English law that dictated that those charged with intentional and premeditated murder would be denied that right. More than twenty witnesses were subpoenaed to testify for the prosecution against Phillis and Mark, including six Codman children. The rest of the Codman slaves, including Pompey, Thomas, Cuffee, and Scipio also received subpoenas. Multiple other enslaved people also testified, including Essex, the servant of Thomas Powers, a person enslaved to Dr. Rand, Dinah (who belonged to Richard Foster), the servants of John Gibbins and John White. There is no extant record of their testimonies. Interestingly, Phoebe received no subpoena despite her extensive and intimate knowledge of the plot. White people sometimes served as proxy witnesses for enslaved witnesses, and testified in court about what enslaved people told them directly. The long list of prosecution witnesses was insurmountable for Phillis and Mark's defense.[44]

Phillis and Mark were convicted of their charges of *petit treason* and sentenced to death. Their death warrants, signed by Richard Foster, the Middlesex sheriff, scheduled their executions for September 18, 1755, between 1:00 and 5:00 p.m. The death warrant for Phillis indicated that she was "to be drawn from our goal [*sic*] ... to the place of Execution & there be burnt to Death." Phillis' sentence was exceedingly harsh, but it was the prescribed sentence for *petit treason*. Mark's death warrant stated that he was "to be drawn from our goal [*sic*] ... to the place of Execution & hanged up by the Neck until he be dead." "To be drawn" meant to be dragged by a horse across the ground. Although it was typical for men to be drawn to a place of execution in the colonial era, the practice was rarely used on *women*. In that way, as a woman, Phillis was defeminized and subjected to a level of public humiliation typically reserved for men. While being dragged, there would be no way to stop her dress from going up (women, without exception wore dresses in colonial America), exposing her private areas. Massachusetts changed the mode of women's punishment for *petit treason* from burning to hanging in 1777 and ended charges under the *petit treason* statute altogether in 1790 – too late to benefit Phillis.[45] Phoebe was condemned to be transported to the West Indies for her role in the murder.

On the eve of his execution, Mark wrote a dying declaration (Figure 1.2). His is one of just a few surviving dying declarations written by enslaved people in the colonial era. By the time he wrote his declaration, he was consumed with resentment that Phoebe had not received her "just deserts," so he exposed her true character to white Charlestowners. He expressed contrition and regret and admitted his role in the poisoning death, but insisted that the women had "enticed" him to get the poison. Referring to the 1749 arson, Mark claimed that he had nothing to do with it, claiming to have been sick in bed when the shop was set afire. He accused Phoebe

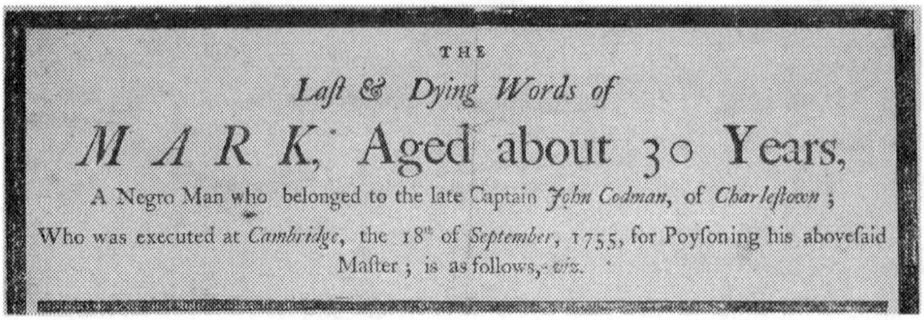

THE
Laſt & Dying Words of

M A R K, Aged about 30 Years,

A Negro Man who belonged to the late Captain *John Codman,* of *Charleſtown* ;
Who was executed at *Cambridge,* the 18ᵗʰ of *September,* 1755, for Poyſoning his abovefaid
Maſter ; is as follows, *&c.*

Figure 1.2 *The Last and Dying Words of Mark (1755)*
Credit: Massachusetts Historical Society

of thievery while the shop burned: she "wickedly stole some of the cloaths [sic], thrown of the Window to be sav'd [sic] ... and to my certain Knowledge, she was a great Thief ..." Mark continued, "She stole Money from my Master ... *One Hundred Pounds* in Money, Part of which, I believe to be in Phoebe's Sisters Hands ..." There is no way to determine if his accusation is true or merely a final ploy to get Phoebe in trouble. In this version – his last – Mark provided details different from those he had previously shared with the coroner's inquest jury about the days preceding Codman's death. In his dying declaration, he claimed that when one of the other enslaved people in the home had asked Phoebe how their owner was faring on his deathbed, she referred to him as "the old dog" and promised that she would "stick as close to him as his Shirt to his Back and not only so, but she would cut down the *Old Tree*, and then would hew off the Branches" – a chilling reference to killing Codman and then his children. Mark had previously testified that *Phillis* was the one who made the reference to sticking as close to Codman as his shirt on his back, but later attributed those words to Phoebe. He also recounted that although Phoebe had sat at Codman's bedside with his children as he lay dying, behind his back she celebrated his impending death and mocked his suffering. Mark claimed that as their owner lay dying, Thomas and Phoebe gleefully rejoiced at his impending death, "when [he was] in the bitter Pangs of Death." Mark alleged that after having witnessed Codman's convulsions Phoebe "got to dancing and mocking master & shaking herself & acting as master did in the Bed." He claimed that Thomas reportedly told the others that he did not care what happened to their owner and "hop'd he wou'd never get up again." Mark painted Phoebe as a conniving, heartless thief and monster. He also implicated Quacoe, insisting he was "as knowing in this Affair as I was."[46] Mark's dying accusations had no effect: Phoebe was never indicted for Codman's death and there is no record of her having been transported from colonial Massachusetts, much less out of British North America. She got away with murder. Testifying against one's fellow conspirators is the *only* way Black women could proactively escape executions in colonial America.

As Mark's dying declaration reveals, he still felt deep regret and harbored resentment towards Phoebe on the eve of his death. For Phoebe's part, by turning state's evidence on her co-conspirators, she had escaped the death penalty and, instead, was condemned to transportation. By contrast, Phillis accepted her fate, admitted her role in the crime, repented for it before man and God, and apparently felt peace within herself before her execution. Unlike Mark, she made no bitter pronouncements, failed to implicate anyone else, and refrained from accusing Phoebe of additional crimes. The difference between how Mark and Phillis responded is that Phillis admitted her guilt and was resigned to accepting the consequences of her actions. On September 18, 1755, Phillis and Mark were drawn and executed at the gallows in Cambridge, not far from Harvard College (now University). According to the *Boston Gazette,* their executions were "attended by the greatest Number of Spectators ever known on such an Occasion."[47]

Britain's 1752 "Murder Act" denied convicted murderers the right to a church burial unless they had received a post-mortem punishment. The irony of a "post-mortem" punishment is that the offender was not alive to experience it; instead, the person's family and community witnessed the horrors of the desecration of their body. Hanging a corpse "in chains," whereby a corpse was placed in a gibbet, or cagelike structure, and displayed in public as a deterrent to others, had been popular in England, but its usage peaked in the 1740s. After the passage of the Murder Act, anatomical dissection was the most common post-mortem punishment in England until 1832; by contrast, gibbeting was less common. Britain's North American colonies only rarely followed the mandate for post-mortem punishment. When they did, they preferred gibbeting to dissection. However, in the English Caribbean, gibbeting was used as a form of torment/execution, with the convicted person being placed in chains while still alive.[48] After Mark was hanged to death, his body was prepared for an impromptu gibbeting. Although he had not been officially condemned to a post-mortem punishment, local officials made the decision to hang Mark's body in chains, possibly to satisfy local demands. Gibbeting was a gendered practice limited to men; consequently, Phillis escaped this gruesome post-mortem punishment. After his hanging death, Mark's body was measured and fitted for a gibbet. The gibbet was then quickly constructed. Once the body was placed in the irons, the gibbet would then be raised thirty feet or more above ground – too high for anyone to remove the corpse. Customarily, bodies were hung in chains as close as possible to the actual crime scene. Popular attractions or spectacles for locals and travelers alike, gibbets were placed at crossroads or popular landmarks to maximize the number of people who saw them. Mark's body was hung in chains at the Charlestown Common (about ten yards from the gallows) or town square.[49]

Locals intended to keep Mark's body hanging in gibbets until "the elements or the ravages of birds of prey" would pick all the flesh from his bones. For those who lived near the gibbeted body, the stench of a decaying corpse could be unbearable, as were the rodents, scavenging birds, and bugs it attracted. There was no specified time frame that bodies would hang in gibbets. Many, like Mark, remained for decades and became local landmarks.[50] The remains of Mark's body hung in that gibbet for *at least* twenty years as a chilling local landmark. Dr. Caleb Rea, a traveler who lodged near Mark's gibbet in 1758, remarked that the "skin was but very little broken" even after a few years. Paul Revere, recounting the events of his famous ride on April 18, 1775, to alert the American colonists that the Redcoats were approaching, referenced that he was nearly overtaken by them "where Mark was hung in chains."[51] It is not clear *when* Mark's corpse was ultimately removed. By the mid-eighteenth century, British society – which had invented the grisly practice – found the prolonged public display of decaying and dismembered bodies for decades distasteful, if not also incomprehensible. Gibbeting also became increasingly less popular in the mainland

North American colonies, eventually fading as a practice after the American Revolution.

On the same day Mark was hanged, Phillis was burned at the stake. The difference between hers and Mark's modes of execution is a reminder that Phillis was considered one of the masterminds and far more dangerous than him. Being burned at the stake, or burned alive, was typically reserved for the most vicious and unrepentant murderers in colonial America and beyond. Rarely was it ever done to women. Even the women convicted in the Salem Witch Trials were not burned at the stake like Phillis. In spite of the prolonged gibbeting of his body, Mark at least died instantly; Phillis, on the other hand, was tortured slowly. Burning someone at the stake was particularly sadistic and designed to inflict intense suffering. Historian Quito Swan, who wrote about Sally Bassett's burning in Bermuda in 1730, reminds us of the visceral nature of such a scene of horror. It would have affected the senses of those who witnessed it. Phillis' unnatural wails and screams of anguish would have pierced the air – echoing from the Common through Charlestown's streets, alleys, and homes. They would have been impossible to miss – or ignore – in a town that size, even for those who did not attend the event. Those present would have witnessed Phillis' physical response to the pain of fire destroying her flesh: her body must have twisted and convulsed in agony. Spectators would have seen her flesh melt from her bones as the flames consumed her. The combination of smoke and burning flesh, hair, and bones would have been noxious to smell. We will never know whether the spectators were aghast or covered their eyes and noses. Did they wince in horror or revel at watching her slowly burn to death? Did they cheer or pray for her as her soul departed?[52] We will never know. What we do know is that Phillis' mode of execution says more about the inhumanity of the society in which she lived as an enslaved woman than it does about her humanity or final act of resistance.

Despite the fact that Phoebe and Phillis conceived, planned, and led this act of resistance, prominent historians have reduced them to background players in *Mark's* plot.[53] The reality is that Mark was charged and convicted of being only an *accessory* in Phillis' plan. Mark was given the mantle of leadership by historians because he was male and some are incapable of imagining enslaved women as leaders of slave revolts. In the historians' defense, Mark's gender and literacy did make him loom larger in the historical record. But the inability to see the outsized role the women played corrupts the history. The Codman case illustrates Black women's capacity to organize and execute a lethal collective action against an abusive slaveowner – and in Phoebe's case, escape the consequences.

Every aspect of this case reflects the Black feminist practice of justice. Codman's enslaved people initially wanted more humane and just owners. Their arson conspiracy did not result in their sale, as they had wished. When that plan failed, Phoebe and Phillis handed Codman a death sentence if for nothing else than enslaving, abusing, and denying his enslaved people their humanity. Murder was their last best option to remove themselves from his authority. The conspirators were remarkably patient, killing him slowly over six years. They delighted in his suffering and privately mocked him at his weakest moments. To these women, prolonged physical suffering was an essential part of Codman's "just deserts." This is what they felt he deserved.

. . .

Phillis was only the second enslaved woman executed this way in the colony of Massachusetts. (Maria, who was burned at the stake in Boston in 1681 for arson, was the first.) According to the ESPY database of executions in the United States, only twelve Black women were burned at the stake during the entire slave era. The other enslaved women sentenced to be burned alive were either convicted of arson or poisoning murders. Enslaved men were, by contrast, far more likely to be burned to death during the age of slavery. In the colonial era alone, thirty-two Black men met that fate.[54]

Phoebe and Phillis are not the only enslaved women convicted of using poison to kill or attempt to kill their owners in the long history of American slavery. In January 1751, and across the Charles River, Phillis Hammond was accused of a poisoning death. *That* Phillis was a sixteen-year-old girl owned by a prominent apothecary, Dr. John Greenleaf, and his wife, Priscilla. Priscilla had given birth to three children, all of whom died as toddlers, within a short span of time. The death of the last Greenleaf child – their only son, John Jr. – caused them to believe that it was not fate playing a cruel joke, but a human culprit who had prematurely ended their children's lives. Within days, Phillis was arrested for the death of the eleven-month-old John. The *Boston Evening Post* reported that he had been killed by "arsenic or ratsbane." The paper noted that Phillis also confessed to having previously poisoned the Greenleafs' fifteen-month-old daughter. Young Phillis was hanged in May 1751 for those crimes.[55] Certainly, Phoebe, Phillis, and Mark heard about that story and may even have personally known young Phillis, given how much time they spent in Boston. They also would have known that she was hanged for the alleged crime. The fact that they knew the harsh consequences of poisoning in colonial Boston and still persisted with their plan underscores how much they were willing to risk to ensure Codman's death.

The Boston area poisoners were not alone. In the colonial era, hundreds of enslaved Black women were convicted of and executed for poisoning their owners. For example, on January 10, 1738, Bess, an enslaved woman owned by John Beall of Prince George's County, Maryland, was accused of his attempted murder. Poison was her weapon of choice. Bess was tried, convicted, and sentenced to death in March and hanged for that crime on June 7, 1738.[56] On March 20, 1738, Judy of Queen Anne's County, Maryland, was executed for the poisoning death of her overseer. In 1747, in Prince George County, Virginia, Abbe was accused of poisoning her owner, Dr. James Tyrie. She escaped a certain execution by hanging herself in her jail cell. In Charles County, Maryland, in July 1755 – the same year as Codman's death – Jeremiah Chase's enslaved worker, Jenny, was tried, convicted, and executed for conspiracy to murder him by poison. In Anne Arundel County, Maryland, Tida was accused of attempting to poison her owner, Ephraim Glover, on February 1, 1757. She was executed for the alleged attempt on April 7 that year. An unnamed, enslaved South Carolina woman owned by a Mr. Fickling was hanged on January 14, 1761, for poisoning him. In Calvert County, Maryland, two enslaved people – Rachel, owned by John Hamilton, and Samuel, owned by William Hickman, were accused of the attempted poisoning of Mrs. Smith "some years ago." They were both hanged for the basis of that suspicion on October 15,

1761. Curiously, in that same county, three years later, three additional enslaved people were convicted of the same crime of attempted poisoning against what may have been the same victim, a Mrs. Smith and her husband, William Smith. This time, Betty, Sambo, and Joe were executed on June 20, 1764, for the alleged attempted poisoning. In 1772, an enslaved woman named Judith Harrison was hanged for poisoning in Brunswick County, Virginia.[57]

In the early national era in Nash County, North Carolina, an enslaved woman named Beck was tried and convicted of poisoning the men in the Taylor family in 1793, including Henry Taylor and his two sons, Henry Jr. and Samuel. In North Carolina in 1800, Sue (owned by John Cates) was convicted of poisoning William Cooke and his family.

On January 28, 1803, Chastity Lawson was hanged for poisoning her owners in Virginia Beach. On February 28, 1806, Fanny Goode was hanged for poisoning in Charlotte, Virginia. In the antebellum era in South Carolina, Eve was convicted of administering poison to her owners in 1829. Three years later, Renah and Fanny Dawson were executed for the crime in Prince Edward County, Virginia, on January 5. Later that same year, 1832, Lucy, an enslaved woman of the Bouligny family in Jefferson County, Louisiana, was hanged for poisoning. Aurelia Chase was hanged on December 20, 1833, in Baltimore for the same crime. On January 12, 1849, two enslaved women in Brunswick, Virginia, Eliza Griffin and Roberta Ezell, were hanged for poisoning. In 1851, Mily Fox was executed in Louisiana. In September 1854 in Thibodaux, Louisiana, an enslaved woman was accused of putting arsenic in her owner's food. Mr. Rawlings, her owner, suspected it had been poisoned so he allegedly gave the food to a dog, which killed the animal within minutes. Rawlings then allegedly consulted a chemist who confirmed that arsenic was in the food. In 1857, an enslaved girl tried to poison the entire slave patrol of New Kent County, Virginia, by pouring muriatic acid in a liquor decanter kept for their entertainment. She confessed and was convicted of the crime.[58]

In 1859, Lucy, an enslaved woman belonging to Araminta Moxley in Prince William County, Virginia, who reputedly was also the daughter of Moxley's late husband, Gilbert (1778–1811), poisoned the entire family with arsenic. Araminta died immediately and Lucy was convicted and executed for her murder on April 22, 1859. Lucy cited poor treatment as her motive. On September 7, 1860, in Franklin County, Kentucky, Frances Berry was hanged for the crime of poisoning. Later that year, in Louisville, Kentucky, Watt Clements reported that five of his enslaved people, including two women, had put poison in his family's milk.[59]

One of the most interesting instances of enslaved people's use of poison as a weapon against their oppressors in American history was when it was used in revolt plots. In May 1805, whites in Wayne County, North Carolina, uncovered a widespread plan to revolt. Having been inspired by the Haitian Revolution, the conspirators planned to use poison to kill all the powerful white men in the region. After those men were dead, the plan was to subdue and enslave the remaining whites. Dozens of enslaved people were implicated in this plot; however, the very first person to be convicted of it was an enslaved woman who was accused of poisoning her owners and two others. Like Phillis, she was burned alive. One observer noted that several enslaved men were hanged, and one was "pilloried, whipped, nailed, and his ears cut off, on the same day," for their roles in the plot.[60]

It is nearly impossible to know with certainty if these other enslaved women actually poisoned their owners or were just *suspected* of it. For enslaved people, the result was the same – execution. Often the only information historians have about these poisoning cases is the nature of the conviction, name, and dates of execution. Unlike the Phoebe and Phillis case, only a few of these other incidents have surviving records of their trials, court testimonies, or "confessions."

Surely, all manner of unexplained or sudden sicknesses before the nineteenth century were attributed to "poisoning" and blamed on the enslaved people who prepared the food. In fact, even food poisoning, which is very common now and even more so in an era before refrigeration (1851) and pasteurization (1862), likely would have been blamed on enslaved people. David V. Baker estimated that as many as one-third of the enslaved women executed for poisoning had not actually poisoned *anyone*, but the cases stemmed from foodborne illnesses, instead. For example, in Orange County, Virginia, in January 1746, an enslaved woman named Eve was convicted of the murder of her owner, Peter Montague, who became gravely ill in August 1745 and finally died on December 27 that year. Before dying, Montague indicated that he had fallen ill in August after he drank some milk. He came to suspect that the milk had been poisoned by Eve. With milk at the center of the case, many doubts are raised about whether Montague had, in fact, been poisoned at all. Before the pasteurization process was developed in 1862, consumption of raw or unpasteurized milk was extremely dangerous because it contains a harmful bacteria cocktail, including *Brucella, Campylobacter, E. Coli, Listeria, Salmonella,* and *Cryptosporidium.* There is a possibility that one or several of these bacteria caused Montague's extended illness, suffering, and death. Regardless, like Phillis, Eve was drawn to the site of her execution and burned at the stake for a murder, real or imagined.[61]

The vast majority of those charged with poisoning before 1865 were enslaved people. On a micro level, 100 percent of those convicted of poisoning in antebellum Virginia were Black. Consequently, poisoning accusations became associated with African Americans. Besides being raced, poisoning accusations were also gendered: Black *men* were more likely than women to be convicted of using poison to murder during the slave era. In fact, 71 percent of Blacks convicted and executed for this crime were male, contrary to the popular belief that women were the ones who poisoned the food.[62] In colonial Maryland between 1726 and 1775, 67 percent of the enslaved people convicted of poisoning were males and just 33 percent were women. Similarly, in antebellum Virginia, Black men comprised 60 percent of those executed for poisoning; and 40 percent were Black women. In South Carolina, between 1824 and 1864, nine enslaved men and two women were arrested for poisoning.[63] Hence, although poisoning is one of the most prevalent methods enslaved women used to murder their owners and oppressors, men used it as a deadly weapon more often. Women only account for one-third of all executions of enslaved people for poisoning before the Civil War. Although the death penalty was not applied evenly for men and women in every state, the data does suggest men were more likely to get caught at the very least.

Regardless, along with arson, poison was the most common weapon enslaved women used to commit murder and the top crime for which they were convicted and sentenced to death.[64]

In the end, the secret, powerful, and deadly weapon of poison is the one thing that terrified slaveowners daily. The more cruel, violent, and abusive ones had good reason to fear that every bite of food or sip of drink could lead to their untimely demise through an intentional act of revenge. And sometimes revenge was served cold by enslaved women.

2 ANNIS, PHILLIS, AND LUCY
"[Your] begging is in Vain"

*Revenge is barren of itself: it is the dreadful food it feeds on; its
delight is murder, and its end is despair*
~ Johann Christoph Friedrich von Schiller

In 1770, in the small town of Bath, North Carolina, Henry
Ormond, a twenty-eight-year-old bachelor from a wealthy and
powerful family, was found dead on his horse late one July evening.
His body, found some distance from his home, was lying across the
horse with one foot in the stirrups. It was clear that he had not ridden
to the location on his own. And unusually, too, Ormond was still
wearing his bedclothes. The investigation of Ormond's death would
reveal that he had been killed with the most unusual weapon. The
subsequent arrest and trial of his killers offers significant insight into
the character of Henry Ormond.

. . .

Bath, North Carolina, located in Beaufort County, near the mouth of
the Pamlico River, became the colony's first incorporated town in
1705. Once the colony of Carolina split into two in 1712, Bath Town
(as it was called then) became a significant town in North Carolina.
The governor of colonial North Carolina, Charles Eden, and other
officials initially settled in Bath, making it the unofficial center of the
colony's government between 1714 and 1719. In order to facilitate
trade and travel, in 1715, Bath settlers established the Port of Bath –
North Carolina's first port of entry, to take advantage of the town's

location. The little port town earned its claim to fame in 1718 when Captain Edward Teach, otherwise known as Blackbeard the pirate, arrived there – seeking a pardon from Governor Eden.[1] Bath Town was one of the most significant towns in North Carolina in the first two decades of the eighteenth century.

The Ormonds were one of the "oldest and most renowned families" in colonial Beaufort County. The family's bloodline had been in Beaufort County, North Carolina, since its founding in the early eighteenth century. In fact, Blackbeard's thirteenth and last wife, Mary Ormond, was the sixteen-year-old daughter of William Ormond, an earlier ancestor of this same family. In the mid-1730s, brothers William and Wyriot Ormond migrated to the region from England, following other relatives into the colony. In 1738, William I. Ormond (1696–1739) purchased his first 205 acres of land in Beaufort County, near Mallard Creek. That same year, he became county land commissioner and sheriff. William later served as the Beaufort County clerk of the courts from 1749 to 1752. His brother, Wyriot (1707–1758), an attorney by profession, became deeply involved in colonial politics, holding multiple positions in local and county leadership. Wyriot served in the lower and upper houses of the colonial assembly in 1746, 1749, and 1753. He also served as the colony attorney general, tax receiver for five counties, and receiver of tonnage duties in the Port of Bath.[2]

The Ormond brothers gained their wealth through land grants given to settlers in the North Carolina colony. On March 16, 1742, the colonial government recorded a land grant of 410 acres in Beaufort County to Wyriot Ormond.[3] This appears to have been a headrights grant, a parcel of land granted to settlers in which the total acreage was determined by the number of people the settler brought to the colony. That same day, he received a deed for 640 acres of land in Beaufort County. By 1754, Wyriot owned 972 acres of land north of the Pamlico River in Beaufort County.[4] Like so many of their neighbors, the Ormonds also owned enslaved workers. According to the 1755 county tax records, Wyriot owned at least twelve enslaved people.[5]

In 1735, Wyriot Ormond married Anne Darden (1701–1750), a two-time widow who previously had been married to Abraham Adams and Wyriot's older brother, William. The Ormonds had three sons, Wyriot (1738–1773), Roger (1740–1775) and Henry (1742–1770). Roger served as the county sheriff in 1766 and representative in 1773 until his death in 1775. Wyriot followed his father into politics, serving in a variety of political positions including county clerk, customs clerk for liquor, Bath Town representative, receiver of tonnage duties, port commissioner, and county representative. He also served in the North Carolina militia.[6]

The Ormond children lost their parents within eight years of one another. Anne died when Henry was eight years old; Wyriot passed away in 1858, when their youngest child was sixteen. Henry's oldest brother, Wyriot, who was just twenty years old himself, became his guardian and the family's patriarch. Wyriot would have been legally and emotionally responsible for managing the Ormond property and Henry's affairs into adulthood. The land and enslaved people Henry inherited from his father's estate would have been held in trust for him until he reached adulthood. When he matured, Henry received a portion of his father's land and five enslaved people to start him towards manly independence – possibly the same five he owned six years later – Annis, Phillis, Cuffy, Lucy, and one unnamed person.[7] According to the records, Henry's brother Roger also received five enslaved people from their father's estate by 1764.[8]

Henry Ormond never married or had any children. His neighbors labeled him a "bachelor." Today, the term is associated with masculine autonomy and virility, and is not necessarily tied to financial stability or independence. In other words, today the term bachelor is a synonym for any unmarried man. In his study on bachelorhood in America, John Gilbert McCurdy demonstrates that in colonial America, the term bachelor had a more nuanced definition. Before the mid-eighteenth century, "bachelor" was a negative term applied to adult males who had not yet obtained a level of independence. Bachelors remained at home and unmarried until they could achieve the autonomy and financial stability expected of men and husbands. Not until a young man had his own property, a profession, or an independent household was he considered worthy of all the privileges and respect of manhood, particularly as a husband, father, and citizen. By the time Henry Ormond came of age in the 1760s, however, bachelorhood was beginning to be perceived more positively. Instead of being considered a stage of *dependence*, it had come to be associated with freedom, especially from the burdens and responsibilities of being a husband or father. Some men consciously chose to delay marriage – or chose not to marry at all, and reveled in that freedom. However, people still expected them to be independent.[9] Based on the fact that he still lived in his brother's household, Henry did not achieve manly independence at least until he reached twenty-two years of age. He moved into his own household on adjoining land, taking his five enslaved people with him.[10]

Bachelorhood also had other implications. As conservative and sexually restrictive as the mid-eighteenth century was for unmarried people, bachelors were not necessarily virgins or celibate. Although fornication and adultery were illegal in many colonies, bachelors, nonetheless, indulged in premarital sex with women in spite of the laws and religious mandates; but it may have been difficult to convince white women of a certain class to indulge in premarital sex. The fine for fornication in colonial North Carolina was twenty-five shillings and there were even more punitive social costs, such as fines, imprisonment, and public shaming, if a woman became pregnant outside the bounds of marriage. Consequently, slaveholding heterosexual bachelors likely fulfilled their sexual needs with their enslaved women, who were an easy target because there were neither societal nor legal jeopardies for using them to fulfill one's sexual needs.[11]

It is notable that Annis was labeled a "house wench" in local papers. The phrase "house wench" was originally used as a synonym for girl; by the Middle Ages it was used to designate a woman of lower social standing or a female servant. Even when used of white women, the term implied a lower-class woman with loose sexual morals. For example, English poet Geoffrey Chaucer used the term to refer to a wanton woman or mistress. As a socioeconomic pejorative, wench distinguished between the higher morality and decency of "good" middle-class women and the lower morals of poor white women in England. By the eighteenth century in the British North American colonies, it was mostly used to refer to poor Black and white women, but also implied that the woman in question was a whore.[12] Colonial Americans typically referred to an enslaved woman as a "Negro woman" or "house servant," so the use of "house wench" is loaded in this context. When an enslaved woman owned by a slaveholding bachelor was labeled with this pejorative, one possible implication is that he used her for sexual purposes.

Again, these are white perceptions; from the perspectives of the enslaved women, sex between them and their owners was not consensual and therefore was rape. Certainly, like so many other slaveholding bachelors and widowers, Ormond posed a menacing problem to the enslaved women he owned. These unmarried slaveholders were more likely than married slaveholding men not only to be physically and sexually abusive but also to die at the hands of enslaved women.

The archive does not reveal whether the Ormond enslaved people were related to one another, nor does it provide any other biographical details about them. However, Phillis was significantly older than the rest of the group, based on her value. Phillis and Lucy had anglicized names, suggesting they were second- or third-generation Black Americans. The name Annis likely was the Ebonics version of Agnes, also an English name. On the other hand, Cuffy – or Cuff, as he was called – seems to have been a version of Kofi, an Akan name for male infants born on Friday.[13] The spelling Cuffy would have been how whites understood the spelling of this Akan name and likely not how he would have spelled it himself. Cuffy might have been either African by birth or a first- or second-generation creole.

The world in which Ormond's enslaved people lived is not easy to recreate because the records of the Black experience in colonial North Carolina are scarce. There were 6,000 enslaved people in the colony in 1730; in 1765, the governor estimated that between 30,000 and 37,000 Blacks resided there. In 1770, the year of Ormond's murder, there were 69,000 Blacks out of a total North Carolina population of 266,000, which means they formed 26 percent of the colony's population.[14] Beaufort County, where Henry Ormond resided, had a small population: in 1764, just 731 people lived in the county, but 377 – or 52 percent – of them were Black. The higher percentage of Blacks in Beaufort meant they enjoyed a bigger community in which to find mates and friends. Certainly, this may have emboldened them toward resistance. After all, there is strength in numbers. In terms of their quality of life, historian Alan D. Watson found that both the diet and clothing for enslaved people in colonial North Carolina was insufficient regardless of the wealth of their owners. In fact, Watson asserts that many of them starved and went naked in this era.[15]

Enslaved people living in Beaufort County and other parts of
the North Carolina colony were governed by the 1715 and 1741
slave codes which, among other things, made it very difficult to
manumit them unless the owner could prove they had performed
"meritorious service." Freed Blacks were required to leave the colony
within six months of manumission. Enslaved North Carolinians had
to carry a pass to leave their farms and were prohibited from gathering in groups for any reason. The slave code offered no legal protections for enslaved people. For example, North Carolina slaveowners
could not be indicted for assaulting, maiming, raping, or injuring
their enslaved workers, and until 1774, killing a slave was not even
considered homicide.[16] With no protections under the law, the only
protection or justice enslaved Black people could obtain in colonial
North Carolina is what they seized with their own hands or feet.

. . .

One July evening in Bath, North Carolina, Henry Ormond was on
horseback searching for one of his enslaved people who had escaped.
The record fails to identify which of them escaped or why, but all
indicators point to it having been Annis. The colony had instituted
a slave patrol system in 1753, but it may not have been effective in
every corner of the colony by 1770. Perhaps this is why Ormond
went looking for the unnamed fugitive himself. He captured her, tied
her up, and brought her back home, where she would have suffered
a whipping before Ormond retired to bed. Likely deeply frustrated
about the failed escape, Annis decided that Ormond would die that
night. It was her decision. She enlisted Phillis, Lucy, Cuffy, and
another unnamed enslaved man to assist her. As enslaved people
who had lived together for years, they naturally bore witness to each
other's abuse. Their conspiracy may have been forged in that common grievance. The decision the others made to assist Annis suggests
that they also believed Henry Ormond deserved to die. The fact that
they did not decide to kill his brother Wyriot, too, suggests that he
was not quite as objectionable as an owner as young Henry.

Annis and the others waited until Ormond had fallen sleep
and then went up to his room and strangled him with a handkerchief.
The fact that they chose a handkerchief as a murder weapon may
reveal that they did not have access to traditional weapons or that

they did not want to leave any evidence that Ormond had been murdered. Strangulation is also a relatively quiet murder that muffles the screaming. Then, in a time before autopsies, a strangling murder could easily be mistaken for a natural death. Ormond eventually stopped struggling and Annis and the others believed him to be deceased, so they left his bedroom and went downstairs. In actuality, Ormond just may have been rendered unconscious or pretended to be dead, because shortly after they left him for dead, he began to recover. They heard him moving about and returned to his room. Their return reflects a commitment to ensuring his death. Theirs was a twice-premeditated act. Ormond reportedly "begged very earnestly for his life," to no avail. Annis, whom the press and court officials identified as Henry Ormond's "house wench," told him that he "must die" and that "his begging was in vain."[17]

As a house servant, Annis, at the very least, would have had a somewhat intimate relationship with the slaveholding bachelor just in performing her usual duties. She would have been responsible for all the duties of a colonial era wife, including cleaning the home, cooking, and keeping his clothes clean and pressed. She might have drawn water for his bath, turned down his bedding, cut his hair and nails, and helped him shave. The personal intimacy required for enslaved women to care for a bachelor was more intense than what was required for married men. And clearly, Ormond abused her in some capacity – sexually, verbally, or physically. So it is rather ironic that the woman closest to Ormond had planned his murder, recruited accomplices, and acted as judge, jury, and executioner. When he begged for his life, his so-called "house wench" Annis declared that "as he had no mercy on them, he could expect none himself."[18] Her comments underscore the Black feminist practice of justice: they delivered personal justice in return for Ormond's past merciless abuse and mistreatment. And because Ormond had not afforded his enslaved people any mercy, in their opinion, Annis did not intend to give him any in return. Instead, she watched a man with whom she essentially had a degree of personal intimacy – even if nothing more than as his personal servant – suffer and beg for his life and extended him not an ounce of mercy. In essence, she insisted on reciprocating *mercilessness*. There is no better indictment of Ormond's character, abuse, and mistreatment or example of a Black feminist practice of justice.

After denying Ormond the mercy he sought, his own enslaved people threw him "between two feather beds, and all got on him [and jumped] till he was stifled to death."[19] Featherbeds could weigh as much as eighty or ninety pounds depending on the size, so, the weight of one of the beds, plus five people meant he not only suffocated to death, but may have been crushed by the sheer force of more than eight hundred pounds on top of him. His was a dishonorable death, despite his being a young man of means from a highly respected family of politicians. Neither his wealth nor his family's local respect could protect him from the judgment of Annis and company.

It must be noted that there is a difference between the acts of strangling and smothering someone to death. Strangling or choking murders require sustained pressure around the victim's neck and a great deal of strength. Enslaved men tended to use strangling over smothering when killing their owners and overseers – although there are notable exceptions. For example, in 1859, an enslaved woman nearly choked a white woman to death during an argument in West Virginia.[20] Smothering or suffocating deaths, involve cutting off the nose and mouth airways. Smothering can be done with hands, but can also involve the use of an object – such as a pillow – to stifle the breathing. Enslaved women were more likely than enslaved men to use smothering as a means to murder – especially infants. The Ormond case, then, fits into the pattern that enslaved women preferred smothering as a means of murder.

To deflect suspicion away from them, the five conspirators carried Ormond's body downstairs and out of his home and laid it across his horse. To ensure that his body would not fall off the horse, they placed one of his legs in the stirrups. They then led the horse to the main road and set it running. Ormond's body was found the following day at a distance from his home.[21] His death led to a coroner's inquest, which uncovered that his own enslaved people had killed him. They were arrested and taken to the jail at the end of Craven Street between Water and Bath Creek streets.[22]

What kind of justice could Ormond's enslaved people expect in colonial North Carolina? They were charged under An Act Concerning Servants and Slaves (1741), which made consulting, advising, or conspiring to rebel or murder, of three or more enslaved people, a capital offense punishable by death. Four of Ormond's enslaved people, plus Cuffy, were charged with this crime. The trial for Annis, Phillis, and Lucy was set for July 21, 1770. In colonial North Carolina, enslaved people were tried in the special court, otherwise known as the slave court. They would not have the benefit of a trial by jury; enslaved people would not get that right in North Carolina until 1793 – too late for Annis and company – but even then their juries were comprised of slave owners. So their case would be decided by a tribunal made up of justices of the peace and slave-owning freeholders. Until 1741, the law in colonial North Carolina dictated that three justices of the peace and three slave-owning freeholders who lived in the precinct of the accused should preside over these cases. In the aftermath of the 1739 Stono Revolt in South Carolina, the North Carolina General Assembly aimed to tighten slaveholders' grip on the special court by passing An Act Concerning Servants and Slaves (1741), which mandated that the composition of the tribunal include two justices and four freeholding slaveowners. Slaveholders were essentially given more power over the slave court. More often than not, the justices of the peace were also slaveholders. These courts were subjected to the will and financial interests of the slaveholding class, who determined which enslaved people would stand trial for capital cases and whether they would be executed. According to one historian, slaveholders "shape[d] events in the courtroom almost as they pleased and ... acquiesced more readily in the role of the state in the punishment of serious crime."[23]

An Act Concerning Servants and Slaves (1741) also directed this court to "take for evidence [against the enslaved person] the confession of the offender, the oath of one or more credible witnesses, or such testimony of Negroes, Mulattoes, or Indians, bond or free." In other words, the testimony of enslaved people could be used in the case for the Crown (prosecution) after 1741. The caveat is that they faced extreme penalties for false testimony, which included having both ears nailed to the pillory and then cut off, followed by thirty-nine lashes on the person's bare back. Nailing slaves' ears to the pillory and then cutting them off as the punishment for perjury was copied from the colony of Virginia. In colonial Maryland, enslaved people would be subjected to having their ears nailed and cut off only if they could not pay a fine. Although enslaved people could testify against Blacks accused of crimes as in so many other colonies, North Carolina did not allow enslaved people to testify against whites in court after 1719. Per the General Assembly of 1746, "all negroes, mulattoes, bond and free, to the third generation, and Indian servants and slaves, shall be deemed to be taken as persons incapable in law to be witnesses in any case whatsoever, except against each other." Given the countless cards stacked against them in the colonial North Carolina judicial system, enslaved people accused of crimes had only a small chance to beat the conviction – their owners. After 1741, North Carolina allowed owners or overseers to testify on their behalf.[24] For Ormond's slaves that meant they had no one.

Annis, Phillis, and Lucy are among the small percentage of enslaved women who stood trial in the North Carolina slave court for any crime between 1715 and 1785. According to Alan D. Watson, only 10 percent of defendants were women. In colonial North Carolina, enslaved women committed fewer crimes and offenses or were less likely to stand trial for them because of gendered assumptions about women and crime. The trial transcripts no longer exist, but the court documents indicate that Annis confessed to the crime before the trial. That confession, plus witness "evidence produced against her" resulted in her being found guilty of murder, as charged. All decisions in the colonial North Carolina slave courts required mandatory unanimity among members of the tribunal overseeing the case. The record does not explicitly state that Phillis and Lucy were found guilty, but one can infer that they were because as required by North Carolina law for enslaved people convicted of capital crimes, the court affixed values for all three women.[25]

Annis, Phillis, and Lucy are more visible in the albeit faint historical record of this act of resistance; the men who participated have been rendered anonymous by records that fail to record one of them by name. The fifth conspirator – whose identity is unknowable to historians – confessed to the crime and became a witness for the Crown against the other four. In exchange for his testimony against his fellow conspirators – who may have been his friends, co-workers, or even family members – this man's life was spared.

Cuffy's trial was held in the same venue four days later. Although all three women had been charged with murder, Cuffy only faced charges of "aiding and assisting in the murder." The difference in the charges suggests that colonial Beaufort officials believed that the three women led the efforts to kill Ormond, while

Cuffy played only a minor role. Like the women, he also faced an unjust judicial system in the slave court. His trial was presided over by seven white men, including four freeholding slaveowners and three justices for a total of seven, which is one more justice than outlined in the code. Two of the justices and one of the freeholders who heard Cuffy's trial had also presided over the trial of Annis, Phillis, and Lucy. One can only imagine the built-in biases they brought to Cuffy's trial. The weight of the evidence led Cuffy to confess. His confession, plus the witness evidence led to his conviction. Hence, Annis, Phillis, Lucy, and Cuffy were all condemned to die for Henry Ormond's murder.[26] To put their executions in context, between 1755 and 1770, almost 25 percent of enslaved people sentenced to execution were convicted of murder.[27]

Annis and her crew could not expect humane treatment from the tribunal that sentenced them because the punishments of enslaved people convicted of capital and felony crimes in North Carolina were excessive and sadistic, at best. Convictions for killing, stealing, "misbranding" or "mismarking" a horse, cattle or hog would result in a sentence of having both ears cut off, followed by a public whipping. Between 1758 and 1764 in an effort to save the colony the expense of reimbursing slaveowners for executed slaves, the General Assembly restricted the death sentence to only enslaved men convicted of rape or murder. That was the simpler sentence; felony convictions of enslaved men for crimes other than rape or murder resulted in castration during this period. Thankfully, that legislation was repealed in 1764, but not before several barbaric castrations had taken place in the colony. Enslaved women were spared the death penalty in the six-year period from 1758 to 1764, but executions resumed for them and men in 1764 for all felony convictions. Hanging was the most common mode of execution of slaves for capital crimes in colonial North Carolina, but even that sentence could be delivered in sadistic ways. In 1763, after his hanging death for murdering his owner, the head of an enslaved man was cut off and stuck on a pole as a deterrent. Brutalizing enslaved people convicted of murder was as much an effort to deter crimes of murder or insurrection as it was about punishment.[28]

Consistent with that culture, on December 11, 1770, Annis was burned at the stake. At that time, condemning someone to be burned alive was rare in colonial North Carolina. Perhaps this punishment was considered more barbaric than other death sentences and was, therefore, reserved only for the most heinous cases. In the few decades before this case, it had only been carried out twice and both times to men. So this mode of execution conveys the message that Annis' crime and her role as its mastermind was considered by contemporary colonists to be exceptionally wicked. Lucy and Phillis were executed by hanging. The difference in their means of execution underscores the fact that local whites understood that Annis had masterminded Ormond's murder. Annis reputedly went to her death vowing to follow Ormond into the afterlife and kill him again.[29] Her comment speaks volumes about how she still felt about Ormond's abuse even after she had killed him; at the very least it indicates that Annis was not satisfied that he had suffered enough, given what he had done to her. Cuffy managed to escape from custody and fled the area before his scheduled execution. His whereabouts were unknown as long as a month later; but he was eventually captured and executed by hanging.[30]

Pursuant to North Carolina colonial law that mandated that slaveholders be reimbursed for the value of their bondspeople if executed, and jailers for their expenses, both Anderson Elleson, the county sheriff, and Wyriot Ormond applied to the colonial General Assembly for reimbursements. The sheriff was awarded £8 "for his trouble and expense" in executing them and Wyriot was compensated £70 for Annis, £20 for Phillis, £80 for Cuffy and £65 for Lucy.[31]

Based on these values, with the exception of Phillis these enslaved people were in the primes of their lives. Annis and Lucy, by comparison, must have been of childbearing age, which is why their estimated value as women is slightly lower than Cuffy's, a man in his prime. Phillis was likely near the end of her childbearing or working years, and therefore less valuable in the slave market. The General Assembly set the valuation of her dead body, or what historian Daina Ramey Berry terms a "ghost value," at the low value of £20. This value has no relation to what she was worth to her community.[32] As an elder, the others would have valued Phillis for her wisdom and experience. She might have been the mother of some of the others; nonetheless, the values affixed to Annis, Phillis, Lucy, and Cuffy in death is a reminder that in a society in which Black bodies were commodified and executed with alacrity, enslaved people's opinions about mercy or justice simply did not matter.

Interestingly enough, in 1786 the North Carolina General Assembly passed a law acknowledging that some owners drove their enslaved people to murder because of "cruel treatment."[33] Despite seeming progressive on the surface, this legislation was passed not out of empathy for enslaved people but to reduce the state's burden of reimbursing slaveowners' estates for their executed enslaved people.

The Ormond case reflects a Black feminist practice of justice on the part of the women involved who planned, directed, and executed this slave revolt. Annis, Phillis, and Lucy did not rise up and kill their owner to gain freedom from, or to end, slavery; instead, they simply wanted freedom from Henry Ormond. This case reveals that some enslaved people harbored deep convictions about their rights to justice and mercy. When denied those rights, Annis meted out justice to her owner with the same disregard for his pleas for mercy as he had provided to her. In that act, she obtained justice and Ormond his "just deserts." Although they tried to conceal his murder, all of the conspirators were resigned to accept their fates. For her part, Annis confessed to the crime and the others testified against her in her case. Annis' confession and her accomplice's testimony is forever lost to history, but the weight of their resistance as women will live on into perpetuity.

. . .

Although the era, place, circumstances, and reasons for murder are different, another case that bears some similarity to Ormond's is an 1852 Virginia murder in which the bedroom was the site of deadly contestation, bedding used as a lethal weapon, and smothering the means of murder. In Powhatan County, Virginia, in August 1852, Jane, an enslaved woman, was charged with "assaulting and beating, choking, strangling, smothering and suffocating" to death Tamezen Beazley – a sixty- or seventy-year-old woman suffering from arthritis. Gus Depp was Jane's actual owner, but he hired her out to Tamezen Beazley, who treated her poorly. Jane told one witness that Beazley denied her food to punish her. That, coupled with beatings and incessant work, made Jane conscious of the injustice and inhumanity she endured. According to Jane, the battle began on July 7. Beazley was vomiting and asked Jane to get her a pan. Apparently, Jane did not respond quickly enough, so Beazley struck her with an iron poker. Jane grabbed the poker and used it to beat Beazley before she began choking, strangling, and finally smothering the woman to death with a pillow that was "tolerably full of feathers." These two cases also illustrate how any household object – even soft things – could be weaponized by those resisting slavery, from featherbeds to pillows. When they found her body, two of Beazley's teeth had been knocked out of her mouth; her other injuries included scratch marks on her face, fingernail marks around her throat, blood that had run from her mouth and eyes, a bruise on her right shoulder, swollen lips, one side of her mouth "mashed," and eyes that were "very much blood shot" (petechial hemorrhage is a sign of strangulation). As these cases demonstrate, kitchens were not the only workspaces that became, in Vanessa Holden's words, "sites of resistance and survival, murder and attempted murder." Bedrooms functioned the same way, although as intimate and personal spaces, the violence and resistance within them seems more ruthlessly personal as well.[34]

3 CLOE
"To Bring all the Misery I Possibly Could . . ."

Out of the night that covers me,
Black as the pit from pole to pole,
I thank whatever gods may be
For my unconquerable soul.

In the fell clutch of circumstance
I have not winced nor cried aloud.
Under the bludgeonings of chance
My head is bloody, but unbowed.

Beyond this place of wrath and tears
Looms but the Horror of the shade,
And yet the menace of the years
Finds and shall find me unafraid.

It matters not how strait the gate,
How charged with punishments the scroll,
I am the master of my fate,
I am the captain of my soul.

~ "Invictus" by William Ernest Henley

On Saturday morning, January 24, 1801, in Carlisle, Pennsylvania, Mary Carothers sent her three daughters, Sally, Polly, and Lucetta to do washing with Cloe, the family's teenaged enslaved servant.[1] Cloe and the Carothers girls washed clothes at a creek near the Carothers' home. According to Mary, they returned around 3:00 p.m. that afternoon. That is the last time she saw her four-year-old daughter, Lucetta, alive. Around sundown, Mary's husband, Andrew Carothers, noticed Lucetta was not in the home and began asking his family members and Cloe if they had seen her. The family began to search for the child on the family's property – in the kitchen and the family's barn. Andrew Carothers called out to Cloe, asking her if Lucetta was with her, to which she responded with a simple "No." Andrew then went to the creek to see if she was there. He found his baby daughter's body lying in the shallow water.[2] By all appearances, Lucetta had fallen into the creek and drowned.

Carothers carried his daughter's body up the hill to his family's home. His wife recounted that she rushed to her husband and put her finger down Lucetta's throat, possibly in an effort to get her to cough up water. She stated that she could barely open her daughter's mouth – indicating the body was in rigor mortis, a stiffening of joints and muscles that begins on average two hours after death but sooner for bodies in cool water. Once the Carothers got Lucetta back to their barn, they removed her wet clothing and "tried all means to bring it [her] back to life," but her body was cold and stiff. They sent their other children to get their neighbors. They then placed Lucetta's body in a barrel – which served as a makeshift coffin – and proceeded to hold her wake service immediately. Four-year-old Lucetta was buried the following day.[3]

The Carothers family suffered an incalculable loss with the death of their youngest child. Even Cloe had been distraught to learn of little Lucetta's death. It seemed to be nothing more than an accidental drowning. Then, the following week, on Saturday, Cloe found Polly Carothers' dead body in the same creek.[4]

. . .

Cloe had been born into "term slavery" on December 15, 1782, in Carlisle, Pennsylvania. The historical record is silent on the identity of her parents, but whoever they were, the birth of their daughter that year was an augur of freedom. Fortunately, Cloe had been born two years after the passage of Pennsylvania's Gradual Abolition Act of 1780, the nation's first abolitionist legislation. The legislation had been born of the spirit of the American Revolution among Pennsylvania legislators. Uncomfortable with immediate and total freedom, those abolitionist legislators compromised on the first attempt to end slavery in the young nation. The Pennsylvania Gradual Abolition Act stipulated that those, like Cloe, born after March 1, 1780, to enslaved mothers living in the Commonwealth of Pennsylvania would be freed at the age of twenty-eight. Until then, they would be subjected to "term slavery," which was envisioned to be similar to an extended indentureship. Like people enslaved for life, *post-nati* slaves could be subjected to "correction and punishment" by their masters; but, unlike them, term slaves were entitled to relief if "evilly treated by his or her master or mistress." In other words, the law provided recourse if they were unduly abused. Upon their release from service at age twenty-eight, term slaves would receive "freedom dues and other privileges" from their owners, which might include tools or a new set of clothing. Section 10 of the legislation prohibited the retention of enslaved people brought into the Commonwealth for terms longer than six months.[5] In fact, it was this aspect of the law that forced President George Washington to remove his enslaved people back to Virginia every six months during his Presidency.

On the surface, this legislation seemed to be a radical step that signaled a death blow to slavery in Pennsylvania. But according to historian Gary Nash, the Pennsylvania 1780 Gradual Abolition Act was "a cautious document that protected the property rights of slaveholders and freed no slaves."[6] Although abolition was in its title, the Act actually would not free its first person for twenty-eight years, in 1808. The legislation guaranteed that slaveholders would have the financial benefit of enslaved people's labor and wombs during their most productive and *reproductive* years (Figure 3.1).

Other northern states followed Pennsylvania's lead and passed their own Gradual Abolition Acts between 1784 and 1804. Connecticut's Gradual Abolition Act was nearly identical to Pennsylvania's, except the length of the term slavery was shorter – ages twenty-one and twenty-five, for women and men respectively. Rhode Island's 1784 Gradual Abolition Act was stronger than other states; it held that children of enslaved mothers born after March 1, 1784, should not be "servants for life or slaves." It also provided

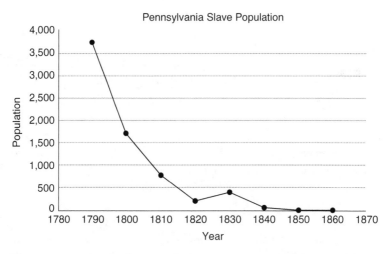

Figure 3.1 Pennsylvania slave population
Credit: Kaia M. Amoah

that those children would remain with their mothers for a year, and after that year the town would provide the cost of their care. To recover those expenses, the town had the authority to apprentice women until age eighteen and men until twenty-one. Hence, not only did Rhode Island exchange slavery for an apprenticeship system, but also the length of that service was significantly shorter than the term slavery in Pennsylvania. Rhode Island also mandated that these children be educated. New York's Gradual Abolition law, finally passed in 1799 after two failed attempts – one in 1785. It also freed no enslaved people immediately, but, instead, obligated the service of those born after the legislation for more than two decades: women would be freed at age twenty-five and men at twenty-eight. New York also mandated that they be educated. New Jersey passed its Gradual Abolition legislation in 1804.[7]

Despite such seemingly abolitionist legislation, it would be several decades before slavery was fully eradicated in Connecticut, Pennsylvania, New Jersey, New York, and Rhode Island. For example, New Jersey abolished slavery in 1846, but instituted "perpetual apprenticeship" in its place. Connecticut did not end slavery until 1848. The Gradual Abolition Acts in the north proved to be weak as abolitionist legislation. By contrast, Massachusetts, Vermont, and New Hampshire ended slavery more decisively in their first state constitutions or by judicial interpretation after the American Revolution.[8]

For those fortunate to have been born in Pennsylvania *post-nati*, term slavery was not freedom, but it was much better than slavery for life. At least it gave such people hope for a better future. However, those born even one day prior to the passage of the Gradual Abolition Act would still be enslaved for life. Consequently, this legislation could result in vastly different experiences for siblings or spouses. For example, it was possible to have one sibling born into life slavery, and others into term slavery. The law did provide some relief to enslaved people by prohibiting owners from importing or selling them out of state. It also left loopholes for freedom if their owners failed to register them with the county clerk of the court by November 1, 1780. Any person not on that registry by that date would be considered free.[9]

Cloe was a beneficiary of the first "abolitionist" act in her state, and the nation. Through the good fortune of the date and location of her birth, she could expect to be fully freed in her twenty-eighth year of life. Admittedly though, the Gradual Abolition Act did little to alleviate the dehumanization or brutality of slavery, despite the clause providing for relief if she was "evilly treated." Nor did the clause that prohibited the sale of enslaved people out of state do anything to prevent her multiple sales *within* the state. Cloe endured all of these conditions as a term slave in the Commonwealth of Pennsylvania.

Cumberland County, halfway between Philadelphia to the east and Pittsburgh to the west, was in the heart of rural Pennsylvania. Slaveholders in Cumberland owned an average of 2.4 enslaved people each. In many ways, the county differs from typical towns in Pennsylvania: neither Quakerism nor abolitionism was a dominant philosophy in this part of the state. Unlike other regions of Pennsylvania, there was no pressure to manumit enslaved people in Cumberland County in the late eighteenth century.[10] In 1790, the total enslaved population in the Commonwealth of Pennsylvania was 3,000 – 7.43 percent of whom lived in Cumberland County. In 1800, 14 percent of the state's enslaved population resided in that county; by 1810, the county was home to nearly 40 percent of all enslaved Pennsylvanians. This data demonstrates that even as the rest of the state moved away from its dependence on slave labor, Cumberland County residents clung more tightly to it. In other words, the county was increasingly angular to the manumission spirit in the rest of the state. According to Michael B. McCoy, Cumberland farmers were reluctant to dispense with their enslaved laborers because they depended heavily on them for agricultural work. He also points to their racial anxieties over what Black freedom might mean for them economically and socially. If nothing else, for poor, rural farmers, slaveownership increased their sense of personal power and racial superiority. Despite Cumberland County's comparative crawl towards abolition, its enslaved population did decrease each decade. For example, there were 773 enslaved people in the county in 1780; two decades later, that population was down to 228.[11]

In 1780, 322 Cumberland County slaveholders complied with the Gradual Abolition Act and registered 773 enslaved people. Because Cloe – as a term slave – did not fall into that category, Kelso did not initially register her. The Act was amended in 1788 to close loopholes and to offer more protections to enslaved people. The amended law required that those born after March 1, 1780 – term slaves – be registered by the county clerk by April 1, 1789. Any owner who failed to do this would forfeit all claims to said persons.[12]

Although historians make distinctions between "slave for life" and "term slaves," Cloe did not indicate that she was aware of any such legal distinction herself. According to her, she had been "born a slave," a declaration that is rather revealing about how she perceived her own status. She never used the phrase "term slave" and did not reveal any consciousness about her twenty-eight-year limited term. Her owner, Mary Carothers, only used Cloe's name or "the girl" when referring to her in historical records. Contemporary journalists referred to her as "Chloe, a negro woman [and] servant" or simply, "Negro Chloe," which reflects a collective consciousness that she would not be subjected to slavery for life.[13] Regardless, it is not clear whether the legal distinction made any difference in the quality of Cloe's day-to-day life.

Cloe provided the details of her biography that were recorded in her confession. In her version of her life history she stated, "I was born a slave to William Kelso, who died when I was young, and willed me to his daughter Rebecca, in whose service I lived four years and an half, at the expiration of which time, I was sold to Mr. Pollock ..."

Cloe's first owner was William Kelso, a Pennsylvania farmer who owned land in Paxton and East Pennsboro townships in Dauphin and Cumberland counties, respectively. In addition to farming, Kelso also operated a ferry on the Susquehanna River that ran from Lemoyne to Turkey Island. His 1770 Cumberland County tax records list his taxable property as one ferry, one slave, livestock, and 240 acres of land. In 1773, Kelso secured an operator's license to open a tavern at his ferry house. Kelso was also a slaveowner in Dauphin County. In compliance with the 1780 Gradual Abolition Act, he registered four enslaved people who could have possibly been Cloe's parents and siblings: Will, eighteen years old; Dina, twenty-three years old; Peter, four years old; and Sib, aged one year. Kelso did not register anyone in Cumberland County in 1780, but with just four days to spare before the deadline, Kelso registered Cloe with John Agnew, the clerk of the Court of Session for Cumberland County, on March 27, 1789. The registration read, "William Kelso … returns Cloe a negro child Born in December 1782 to be registered according to law." When Kelso registered Cloe, 148 other term slaves had been registered in that county that year.[14]

Kelso passed away shortly afterwards, in his early fifties. By then, his wife was also deceased, so Rebeckah, his minor daughter, inherited Cloe from her father's estate. Michael Simpson, her uncle by marriage, was appointed guardian to care for her affairs. For reasons unknown, when Cloe was just eleven years old, Simpson sold the balance of her service (sixteen years plus five months) to John Harland, a Philadelphia merchant on July 17, 1794.[15] This sale may mark the first time Cloe had been separated from her community in East Pennsboro Township in Cumberland County. At the very least, it is the first county record to specify her exact date of birth on December 15, 1782.

Cloe did not remain with John Harland, a Philadelphia clothing and carpet merchant, for even one full month. On August 11, 1794, Harland hastily sold her to Peter Gerandan for 118 Spanish milled dollars. Then, just a little more than two months later, on October 25, 1794, Gerandan sold the eleven-year-old Cloe to another Philadelphia merchant, Louis Crousillat, for the same exact price – 118 Spanish milled dollars. Crousillat only had the girl until March 6, 1795, when he sold her to Oliver Pollack for 118 Spanish milled dollars.[16] Not one of her three Philadelphia owners made a profit from Cloe's sale, so there is no clear financial incentive to explain why she had been sold repeatedly, and at such a dizzying pace among Philadelphia merchants. As a preteen who had been ripped away from her family and community, Cloe simply may have been too rebellious and unmanageable. She later admitted that she had "high passions" and was prone to swear.[17] Cloe may have been subjected to sexual abuse in one or all of these homes. If so, her behavior may have been a result of that trauma. What is certain is that Cloe endured much disruption and instability in her first twelve years of life. Enslaved people, on average, were sold three times at most in their lifetimes; by contrast, she had six owners in twelve years.

Cloe's sixth owner, Oliver Pollack, originally from Cumberland County, had a very colorful career. He had been a merchant, financier, and United States Commerce Agent from 1777 to 1783, and a farmer who had financed the American Revolution. He had lived in Havana, Cuba, for a number of years while serving as United States Commerce Agent. After having had his Havana property seized by Spain, Pollock returned stateside to Philadelphia in 1784 and deeply in debt. The United States government finally paid him $90,000 as partial payment of the debt it owed him in 1791, which he used to purchase Cloe and a tract of land in Cumberland County called Silver's Spring. He had ongoing financial problems that eventually forced him into debtors' prison in Philadelphia in May 1800.[18]

Of all Cloe's owners, she had positive feelings only about her time with the Pollock family. She stated, "I never received an education; no pains were taken by any of my owners, to instruct me in any duty I owed God; save while I lived with Mr. Pollock, I was taught my prayers, and other duties, by his youngest daughter." Here, Cloe's reference is to Oliver and Margaret Pollock's seventh child, Lucetta, who was born in 1783. Her comment is at once a condemnation of all her other owners who never tried to improve her mind or soul through instruction, and a compliment to the Pollocks for doing what no one else had done. Pollock's daughter, Lucetta, likely developed a friendly affection for Cloe since they were peers, and possibly playmates; she may have shared her faith with her in that capacity.[19] After nearly two years, Pollock sold Cloe to her seventh and final owner, Andrew Carothers on November 21, 1796, for £60.[20]

. . .

The beginning of the end of Cloe's story began with her sale to the Carothers family. Andrew Carothers and his wife, Mary, were farmers in East Pennsboro Township, in Cumberland County, Pennsylvania. The couple had eleven children: Andrew, William, Samuel, John, James, Sarah, Levitate, Mary, Mayann, Polly, and Lucetta. In 1790, the Carothers owned 150 acres adjoining the Susquehanna River, but by 1798 their acreage had nearly doubled, to 298. They had two structures on their land: one included the family's kitchen, which measured fourteen by twenty-two feet, plus another separate room that measured twenty-two feet square. The Carothers' main dwelling was a two-story, two-room log cabin with four windows and two large rooms that measured twenty-three by sixteen and twenty-three by twenty feet. In basic log cabins of that era, the second floor typically was a loft used as sleeping quarters. Based on its description, the Carothers' home was very modest. By contrast, wealthier farmers and planters lived in brick or stone homes that boasted a parlor and at least four rooms. Additional evidence of the relative modesty of the Carothers family home is found in the local home values: the Carothers' two dwellings were collectively valued at $265 in 1798. In the immediate vicinity, the home values ranged from $110–800, with the higher end being stone structures.[21] So theirs was at the lower end. Insight into the material quality of life of the Carotherses can be found through the survey of the furniture listed in Andrew Carothers' will, filed in 1817. He listed two bedsteads, two bureaus, six chairs, a walnut cupboard, kitchen furniture, and a large mirror.[22]

Cloe was the first enslaved person the Carothers family purchased. They were a working-class family of thirteen, and the likelihood that Cloe would be the first and last slave they purchased was high. Their ownership of one slave did not catapult the Carothers to the upper echelons of Pennsylvania society, but she was young and could have children. Any hopes they may have had that they could double their investment when Cloe gave birth, were dimmed by the stark reality that slavery was dying in Pennsylvania.

In nineteenth-century rural Pennsylvania, other enslaved people were scattered throughout the county, separated from each other by quite a distance.[23] There is no evidence that Cloe saw her family often, had any Black friends, or attended church. In other words, she was without a support system or anyone to relate to or listen to her grievances. The absence of a Black community, coupled with the fact that she was the Carothers' only enslaved worker, meant that Cloe was perpetually surrounded by whites and may have only rarely left their farm. The degree of social isolation must have been debilitating. Equally sad is the fact that it is unlikely that Cloe had any space or time to herself. Working for a family that size with little to no personal privacy must have been frustrating at best. Her duties included working alongside the women in the family on household chores, but as the only enslaved worker they had, those chores would have been endless.

Most of what people understand about slavery has focused on the enslaved people who lived and worked on southern plantations or large farms.[24] Cloe's enslavement to a family with modest means in the north is different from that typical pattern of enslavement. In many ways, though, her experience is representative of rural northern slavery: enslaved people lived isolated in households where their work duties were not sharply demarcated.[25] Cloe was not a house or a field slave; she was both. She did farm work like planting and harvesting crops and household duties like cooking and cleaning. Cloe's workload had no bounds, temporally or corporeally.

In terms of the power structure of the household, Mrs. Carothers assigned and supervised her daughters and Cloe in their daily chores and her husband supervised their sons. Cloe likely did more than a fair share of the women's work duties, especially because several of the Carothers' daughters were too young for real chores. Mrs. Carothers acted as the primary disciplinarian for Cloe, and she trained her daughters to assist in her management and discipline. Even the youngest Carothers girls had specific roles: they were assigned to keeping an eye on Cloe and reporting any bad behavior to their mother. In that way, they were proxies for their parents. Such management responsibilities taught young white female children lasting lessons about the power and authority they held over enslaved people.[26] Even threatening to tell their parents about the behavior of enslaved people was a powerful instrument of tyranny – akin to the threat of the whip. Despite being closer to Cloe's age, the fact that the Carothers' daughters assisted their mother in her management, surveillance, and discipline precluded any genuine friendships between them. For Cloe, the girls were an extension of their mother.

Apparently, the Carothers girls took their management responsibilities seriously, surveilling and tattling on Cloe's behavior daily, ever eager to report back every breath she took to their parents. Their surveillance led to severe beatings that Cloe believed were too excessive given the wrong. According to Cloe, she would be "severely corrected, far beyond the demerit of the fault." Hence, the disproportionality of her discipline was unjust. Naturally, Cloe began to resent the entire family, and plotted to end the endless surveillance, tattling, and beatings.[27]

In order to end it, she would invoke a Black feminist practice of justice. She planned and attempted several forms of slave resistance to push back against the workload, constant surveillance, and beatings. Cloe stated, "To effect this [revenge], one day my master and mistress being from home, I felt a strong propensity to burn the barn; and so far yielded to the temptation, that I carried fire twice to the hog house which was near to the barn, and did my utmost to burn it, but could not effect my purpose." Certainly, burning the barn of a farming family would have bankrupted the Carothers, who lived a very modest existence by slaveowners' standards. Cloe may have calculated that a devastating financial loss would have forced the family to sell the balance of her indenture. After the arson failed, she admitted that a "second temptation came with force, that I should destroy my master's youngest son, but fail[ed] in this also ..." Consistent with the Black feminist practice of justice, plotting murder was Cloe's last resort after prior resistance had failed to remove her owners from her life. She provided no details about the concrete actions she took to kill the boy or why her plan failed. Her third and final plan was to kill the Carothers' youngest daughter, Lucetta.[28]

Cloe may have targeted those children in particular because they were younger and smaller than her and, subsequently, easier to kill than their parents and older siblings. But she specifically chose to go after her owners' youngest son and daughter, whom the family may have spoiled, doted on, and put on a pedestal. Her careful selection of her victims required a great deal of reasoning and critical thinking. Cloe framed her thoughts about taking revenge as "temptations."[29] Her use of this term is consistent with how Christians conceptualize sin, with Satan tempting people to do evil things. In other words, she did not consider herself innately evil; she believed sin was external to her. In her mind, Satan had led – tempted – her to such thoughts and deeds. Cloe may have invoked this language of Christianity because it was more palatable to nineteenth-century society than admitting it was a deliberate decision she made herself.

. . .

On January 24, 1801, the day Lucetta would die, Cloe, then eighteen years old, took the child with her to the creek to draw water. According to her later confession, while standing there on the edge of the creek, she made the decision to hurt Lucetta. However, that is a dubious claim given the fact that she later confessed that she had premeditated the murder. Cloe confessed, "I immediately laid hold of her mouth and held it as long as I could [no longer] perceive any breath; then [I] threw her into the run; took the water, and entirely forgot what I had done, until about an hour after." She claimed that she forgot about the murder until Andrew Carothers asked if Lucetta was with her.[30]

    Even after the search party recovered Lucetta's body, no one immediately suspected that a murder had been committed and believed Lucetta had drowned in the shallow creek. Cloe admitted to being somewhat relieved by the thought that her beatings would diminish now that her mistress was busy grieving, "but I found it otherwise." She recalled that Lucetta's funeral on Sunday the 25th was "scarcely over" when Mary Carothers "made me strip off my short-gown and gave me a severe whipping, with a cowskin . . ." By her own admission, Mary Carothers did not suspect Cloe at that time, so this beating may have been the usual routine for her – beating Cloe naked for any trivial offense. By beating Cloe naked, Mary Carothers aimed to maximize the pain she inflicted on the girl's body with the strap. Undoubtedly, such a beating in the nude would have left Cloe scarred and bruised. Yet a semi-public beating while nude in front of the large Carothers family, which had boys her age, would have been deeply humiliating to a girl in her teens. On Tuesday, Carothers whipped her again, and "on the following Saturday she gave me a third [beating]." It was after her third beating in one week that Cloe "determined on further revenge."[31]

Cloe set her designs for revenge on six-year-old Polly. She went to the creek, taking the girl with her. Cloe recalled that after they got to the creek she asked Polly "why she told every thing upon me." Polly responded that her mother wanted her to do so. Cloe's retort to Polly was, "you shall never tell any more on me." Cloe then killed Polly the same way she had done to Lucetta, later admitting that "I laid my hand upon her mouth and held it near the space of half an hour, then I threw her into the run." After the murder, Cloe coolly returned to the home, and by her own words, "without any fear or distress." When the family realized Polly was missing, a search commenced and Cloe went to the creek to look for the girl where she "found" her body.

According to Mary Carothers' account of the events, which was carefully documented in her deposition published in the *Carlisle Gazette* on June 24, 1801, there were several things that made her suspicious about Cloe's role in Polly's death, but it wasn't until after the funeral that she became more certain. She recounted that when Cloe "discovered" the girl's body, "she came running up and wringing her hands and pretending to be crying." Mary Carothers testified that after Polly's funeral she suspected Cloe for several reasons. First, Mary believed Cloe had fake tears; she also stated that when she told Cloe to fetch liquor to try to wake Polly up – a common practice for unconscious people then – she brought wine instead, which does not have the same effect. Reflecting on the events, Mary Carothers found that mistake odd, as if Cloe did not *want* to awaken the child. Mary stated that after her Polly's burial, "I thought and it run in my mind that she (Chloe) had drowned them – I think I began on Monday to accuse her. She said she did not do it, had no hand in it, and still denied it till Monday was a week." Living under suspicion of double murder in a routinely abusive household must have exponentially increased Cloe's terror and abuse. The matriarch admitted, "I could not bear the sight of her about the house; I was sure she had done it."[32]

Mary Carothers repeatedly confronted Cloe with her suspicions. According to Mary, Cloe told her she "did not do it, had no hand in it" and continued to deny her involvement. Mary used several strategies to get Cloe to confess. First, she offered to have Cloe confess to two white female neighbors. Cloe initially refused, but Mary claimed that Cloe later told one of her daughters that she would rather confess to Mrs. Huston than to Mrs. Carothers. On getting that report from her children, Mary immediately summoned Cloe and urged her to confess to her directly. Cloe refused and continued to deny culpability. Mary told Cloe that she knew that her children would have "crawled on their hands and feet out of the [creek] if somebody had not held them in." The second strategy Mary used to elicit a confession was to threaten Cloe, admitting that she told her "She would be hanged for it, [it would be] better to confess it ..." Mary failed to specify whether Cloe would be hanged extralegally or as part of a legal death sentence, but either way her comment was a clear death threat. When that threat failed to elicit a confession, Mary then threatened Cloe again – this time with being sold away. She testified that she told Cloe "maybe her master would send her away to Philadelphia and sell her."[33] Mary's threat about selling Cloe to someone in Philadelphia is a very specific threat that is undoubtedly related to what must have been Cloe's traumatic experience in that city – a past that Mary used to strike fear into her heart. It was a low blow. Still, threats – including death threats or promises to return someone to past traumatic sites – would have grossly undermined the reliability of any confession Carothers managed to elicit.

Mary Carothers also tried using a third party to obtain Cloe's confession. She understood that Cloe was too afraid of her to confess directly, so she sent for a neighbor, Elizabeth Clendinen, who took Cloe into the kitchen away from her mistress to speak with her about the girls' deaths. Allegedly, Cloe confessed to Lucetta's death, but not to Polly's. Mary then grilled Cloe on the specifics of how she had killed Lucetta. There, in the Carothers' home and in the presence of the woman she hated most in the world, Cloe claimed she had thrown a bucket into the creek and told Lucetta to go after it. When Lucetta turned to go after the bucket, she allegedly said she kicked her into the water. Cloe kept insisting she had not killed Polly, though. Mary then offered to leave the room so that she would feel comfortable enough to confess to Mrs. Clendinen about her hand in Polly's death, too. When Cloe did not respond to that offer, Mary admitted that she snapped, "I said she would be hanged any way; she had confessed to one, and she might as well tell me [about Polly]." So once again, Mary invoked the likelihood of her being hanged to get the answers she wanted. Eventually, Cloe confessed to Polly's murder, too, saying she pushed her into the creek. After that second confession, Mary Carothers asked Cloe if she "had any spite at her master, or me, or the children." Cloe claimed that she did not have any spite. Mary then recalled, "I said you drowned these children, you have done this wonderful action, don't you deserve to be hanged?" According to her, Cloe responded with a simple, "yes."[34] With that "yes," Cloe seemingly accepted that she deserved to pay for her actions with her life.

Cloe's account of her time in the household after Polly's death is much different from her mistress' account. She reported that the Carothers had not extorted a confession with words, but with the lash, "I was much whipped by my master, to extort a confession ..." Despite the violence, Cloe emphasized that it was not the whippings but her own conscience that led her to admit to the murders. This is a last subtle act of defiance. With that comment, she stripped the Carothers of their mastery, power, and dominance over her. Her own agency and personal power trumped theirs. After Cloe's confession, she was arrested and taken to jail.[35]

Murder was just one of many capital offenses for enslaved people. Other actions that carried the death penalty for enslaved Pennsylvanians included "buggery" – which covered oral or anal sex and bestiality – rape or attempted rape of a white woman, murder, robbery, and theft of more than £5. Slaveowners had little interest in allowing their enslaved people to be executed because of the economic ramifications until 1726 when the law was changed to guarantee compensation for those executed by the Crown.[36]

Cloe was indicted in Cumberland County for the first-degree murders of Polly and Lucetta Carothers. She pleaded "non-culpabilis," or not guilty, to both charges. She may have pleaded not guilty despite her confession on the advice of her court-appointed attorney. Cloe was tried separately for both cases on the same day, March 4, 1801, at the court of oyer and terminer in Cumberland County, Pennsylvania before the Honorable John Joseph Henry. In Pennsylvania, all criminal proceedings were held in the oyer and terminer courts. The justices in those cases were appointed by the state supreme court justices. The witnesses against Cloe were all white and free and consisted of Andrew and Mary Carothers, neighbors John and Elizabeth Clendinen, and Izabel Humes. Charles Smith, a court-appointed attorney, led her defense. He focused on attacking the legality of her indictments, and moved that her charges be vacated because of "irregularities in the indictment." Specifically, Smith took issue with the wording in the indictment for Polly's case, which read that the court would be held "*at* Carlisle, *for* the County of Cumberland" instead of stating that Carlisle, Pennsylvania is *in* Cumberland County. In the case of Lucetta, Smith raised the fact that the term "feloniously" had been written into the indictment. According to him, throwing someone into water does not qualify as a felony. He also raised the issue that no time or date of the crime is listed in the indictment for Lucetta's murder.[37]

Technical errors in the indictments – even minor ones like this – were sufficient grounds for the dismissal of charges in Pennsylvania. However, Cloe was not so lucky: Judge Henry upheld the legality of the indictments, despite the errors. According to journalists who witnessed the trial, the main argument for her defense was that the creek water was too shallow for the children to have been held underneath the surface. The all-white, all-male jury deliberated just a half an hour before returning with a verdict of guilty for both murders. Cloe was returned to her cell to await her sentence. Three days later, she was sentenced to be "hanged by the neck until she be dead." The court added, "And may God have mercy on her Soul."[38]

After conviction and sentencing, local newspapers reported that Cloe had previously threatened another Carothers girl, eleven-year-old Sally. According to the story printed in the paper, Cloe asked the child to "do something for her." When the child refused, Cloe allegedly "shook her fist and told her she would be the next." This exchange cannot be corroborated by any other source. Regardless, printing it in the press helped to paint Cloe as a threat to society, possible serial killer of children, and deserving of a death sentence in spite of her age.[39]

Cloe was executed by hanging in Carlisle on Saturday July 18, 1801. It was reported that "she appeared very penitent," before her execution, and made a full confession of the crime, the manner of its commission, and her motives in doing it. In her confession, which was printed in local and national newspapers in early September, Cloe finally identified her motive in her own words:

> My motive in the first place, was this; I knew that the children were compelled by my mistress to give

> information respecting some parts of my conduct; for
> which I was severely corrected, far beyond the demerit
> of the fault. To cut off this means of communication, was
> the first end I promised myself, but my second and great-
> est motive was, to bring all the misery I possibly could
> upon the family, and particularly upon my mistress.[40]

Another paper reported that Cloe declared that her mistress "had
been very cruel to her." In no uncertain terms, she admitted that her
motive for killing both girls was to maximize misery for this family,
and especially her mistress.[41] In other words, Cloe believed that the
misery brought by losing her daughters was her mistress' "just
deserts."

What was it about Cloe's relationship with her mistress
that led her to exact revenge on her children? Historian Thavolia
Glymph ably demonstrates that plantation mistresses were active
perpetrators of the violence committed against enslaved people. She
asserts that "mistresses became expert[s] in the use of psychological
and physical violence, and from their perch in the household,
influenced" how enslaved people experienced slavery. Although
Glymph's thesis is about plantation mistresses, the same holds
true for mistresses of small farms like Mary Carothers. Whether
on plantations or small family-owned farms, mistresses like Mary
Carothers were unnecessarily cruel and punitive to their enslaved
people – especially the women. Glymph affirms Cloe's claim about
her mistress when she indicated that "sometimes the punishments
of hell required no transgressions at all." At times, the punishment
was disproportionate to, or absent of, the wrongdoing.[42] As Cloe
reveals in her confession, her mistress often beat her for no apparent
offense and even out of her own frustration and suspicions. Her
observation about the disproportionality of the discipline strikes at
the heart of why she felt her treatment had been unjust and why
retaliatory justice was the remedy she sought.[43] The constant surveillance by the Carothers females was an added degree of terror. So
many eyes watched Cloe, even in her private moments, that the
Carothers family effectively became omnipresent in her life. The
fact that the Carothers girls' surveillance always led to beatings
made Cloe resent them and feel contempt for them. From her
perspective, the entire Carothers family was complicit in her

abuse – even the young girls who eagerly reported her behavior. Cloe's story demonstrates that even very young enslaved women had a strong sense of justness and injustice.

It must be underscored here that Cloe did try other options before resorting to murder, including everyday slave resistance, rebelliousness, and arson. None of that resistance stopped the daily and unrelenting pattern of surveillance, tattling, and abuse. The provisions of the Gradual Abolition Act should have given Cloe legal recourse for such abuse, but she could not reasonably expect it to be enforced in Cumberland County. The reality is that she was without advocates or avenues of redress; for example, even Elizabeth Clendinen – with whom Cloe felt comfortable enough to share her confession – did not come to Cloe's defense, but instead helped Mary Carothers extract a confession from her and then testified against her in court.

By the time she gave her widely published confession, Cloe projected remorse. In it, she admitted that a "desire of revenge" led her to murder two children she now believed were "innocent." She also admitted that she had no "spite or malice against them." To the contrary, she said, "I loved them both."[44] In a complicated way, perhaps she did. Her confession revealed that Cloe was then aware of the magnitude of what she had done and feared death, damnation, and judgment from God:

> Oh! Where shall I find a balm to heal its wounds? Oh! What have I done? In avenging the injuries I suffered, I have drawn the fierce indignation of heaven on myself. The voice of the blood of two innocent children, crieth against me from the ground. Is my sin too great for the mercy of God to parden [sic]! ... I trust that his unbounded goodness will not suffer me to perish.[45]

In other words, she may have regretted her actions and found no peace. Unlike others in this book, Cloe did not go to the gallows defiant or resigned to dying. She is the only one who expressed love for her victims and proclaimed they were innocent as children. If genuine, her practice of personal justice had failed because she seems to have humanized her victims enough to regret her actions.

. . .

Cloe is not the only teenaged girl to kill her slaveowners' children. In Boston in January 1751, Phillis, a sixteen-year-old girl owned by prominent apothecary Dr. John Greenleaf and his wife Priscilla, was accused of killing their children. Priscilla had given birth to three children, all of whom died as toddlers, within a short span of time. The death of the last Greenleaf child – their only son, John Jr. – caused them to suspect that it was not fate playing a cruel joke, but a human culprit who had prematurely ended their children's lives. Within days, Phillis was arrested for the killing of the eleven-month-old infant, John Jr. The *Boston Evening Post* reported that he had been killed by "arsenic or ratsbane." The paper reported that Phillis also confessed then to having previously killed the Greenleafs' fifteen-month-old daughter by poisoning. Young Phillis was convicted and hanged in May 1751 for those crimes.[46]

A much younger enslaved girl – ten-year-old Julie Ann – was accused of poisoning an infant in her care in New Castle, Delaware, in 1826. Her owner concluded that the girl had a "character and disposition of the most dangerous kind." Impugning Julie Ann's character is easier than acknowledging the real reason for her animosity. Her owner successfully petitioned the court to sell her out of state.[47]

In Crawford County, Missouri, in 1837, a thirteen- or fourteen-year-old enslaved girl named Mary was accused of the drowning death of her owners' two-year-old daughter, Vienna Jane Brinker, in a case with remarkable similarity to Cloe's. On May 14, 1837, Mary's owners and Vienna's parents, John and Sarah Brinker, sent her to collect firewood. Mary took the toddler with her, but returned home alone. After a brief search, a neighbor found Vienna's body, with bruises on her left temple, in the stream on the Brinker property. The Brinkers' neighbor, William Blackwell, admitted that he tied Mary to a log and "pulled up her coat [clothing] as if I was going to whip her." Fearing the whipping, Mary agreed to tell the truth, confessing under duress that she "threw it [the child] in the branch with the intention to drowned [sic]." When asked about the bruises found on Vienna's right temple, Mary admitted that when little

Vienna's body floated back to the surface, she had used a stick to push it below the water. During the same confession, Mary also said she had murdered a neighbor's child the previous fall. Mary was subsequently indicted and arrested for Vienna's murder, but the coroner could not determine whether the child had met her demise by the blow to her temple or drowning, so Mary was charged with both causes of death. When questioned about her motive, Mary stated that she "did not like Mr. Brinker." There may have been unspoken reasons she did not like him. Hence, like Cloe, Mary resented her poor treatment and took revenge on her owner's child. Mary's indictment declared that she "did not have the fear of God," which is another way of saying remorse. Up to that moment, she had expressed none. On August 18, 1837, Mary was convicted of two causes of Vienna's death: beating the girl with a stick and the drowning. Her attorneys appealed to the Missouri Supreme Court on the basis of procedural errors. Surprisingly, the higher court reversed Mary's conviction on account of the two errors, determining that "the child could not come to its death by both of these modes" and that the prosecution had examined witnesses after the discovery period. Mary was granted a new trial, but was convicted and sentenced to death a second time by an all-white jury of twelve men. She was hanged in Steelville, Missouri, on August 11, 1838.[48] Just thirteen or fourteen years of age at the time of her death, Mary is in fact the youngest person ever executed in the state of Missouri.

Cases involving enslaved children or very young adults who killed their owners' children are difficult to imagine. Because white children are perceived as innocent in society, their murders seem particularly unwarranted and loathsome. But what if we were to look at these white children through the eyes of an enslaved child who worked for them and their families? Slavery ensured that they were not, and never would be, equals to white children, either as playmates, or as friends. Their childhoods were marred by a loss of innocence, abuse, and trauma. Girls, in particular, endured a loss of sexual modesty and innocence. Cloe was routinely whipped naked in front of the boys in the family. In Missouri, a neighbor tried to strip Mary's clothes off to whip her when the Brinker child was found dead. Black and white childhoods were not the same. White children were imbued with all the power, privilege, and authority of slaveholders – and adorned with all the power and authority of whiteness. Even at the tender ages of two, four, and six years old, Vienna, Lucetta, and Polly already were the heiresses of a system predicated on white superiority. And to these enslaved children waiting on their every need, this seemed wholly unjust.

4 ROSE BUTLER
"... more malignant than murder"

Repenting at Christ's feet I stand,
A criminal condemn'd to die!
O! reach me out thy healing hand,
That to Thy Bosom I may fly.
It's just the sinner should be hung,
Before the world for my black crime;
For with the serpent I was stung;
But save me by Thy Glorious Arm.
Almighty God, I dread thy wrath,
While standing by Thy sacred cross;
As I have stray'd from virtue's path,
And now they say my "Soul is lost." [1]

In the early morning hours of March 4, 1818, the Morris home at 28 Chrystie Street in New York City began burning while the entire family and their term slave slept in second-floor bedrooms. The smoke and crackling of the fire awakened the Morris' youngest son, who shared a room with the family's eighteen-year-old term slave, Rose Butler. Concerned about the noise, the boy twice asked Rose if he should go wake his father. She told him to lie down and the noise was "only the cat jumping about." Apparently sensing danger, the boy eventually went to awaken his father who alerted everyone else in the house about the fire. [2]

Mr. Morris broke open the front door of the home, which had been bound from the outside, so his family could exit the second floor by the front stairs. Everyone in the household got out safely and Mr. Morris extinguished the fire, which consumed three kitchen stairs, but nothing else. Morris and a neighbor discovered "combustible materials" in a pail that seemed to have been deliberately placed on the stairs.[3] A second pail, a broom, and a washing machine (likely a wooden machine that rotated clothing in the water, with an attached wringer) had been stacked on the stair next to the first pail.[4] The pail full of flammable items was a dead giveaway that this fire had been the work of an arsonist. The very next day a suspect was arrested. A month later, while that same suspect was still in custody, the Morris' home was set on fire again. And then, a third time. It was clear that the Morris family had been the target of a group of arsonists working together.

The Morris' servant, Rose Butler, was the first person to shed light on the identity of the arsonists. She repeatedly insisted that the culprits were two shadowy white men with a vendetta against her mistress. In the ensuing months, Rose unraveled a complex plot that included a fortune teller, mysterious men in large brimmed hats, unpaid debts, death threats, and a letter hidden inside a loaf of bread.

. . .

There are four first-hand accounts of the Rose Butler case: Dorothy Ripley's *An Account of Rose Butler: Aged Nineteen Years,* John Stanford's *An Authentic Statement of the Case and Conduct of Rose Butler,* Eliza Duell's statement; and Rose Butler's own autobiographical statements.[5] According to Rose, she was born to an enslaved mother in Mount Pleasant in Westchester County, New York, in November 1799. At the time, Westchester was a rural county of 1,037 inhabitants, and made up of several villages. Mount Pleasant was one of those villages. In 1790, census takers counted just fifty enslaved people in the village. Ten years later, the number of enslaved people in the village had increased by only six.[6] Both Rose's hometown community and its African American population were very small.

Rose and her mother were owned by American Revolution veteran Lieutenant Colonel Gilbert Strang.[7] The 1790 census reported that he owned one person at that time, and he never owned more than two enslaved people; Strang freed two enslaved people, Robert and Phebe, in his will in 1825.[8] There is a possibility that one or both were Rose's parents. His posthumous act of manumission did not necessarily mean that he was an abolitionist, though: he had freed his enslaved people upon his death – after he no longer needed them, and only two years before slavery was legally abolished in the state.

By extremely good fortune, Rose had been born just a few months after New York's Act for the Gradual Abolition of Slavery, which went into effect on July 4, 1799, so she was destined for freedom. New York's white legislators believed that slavery contradicted the ethos and ideals of the American Revolution and they hoped to put an end to it gradually. The legislature also received pressure from the state's free African Americans, members of the New York Manumission Society, and other white allies. As early as 1785, the New York legislature tried to pass gradual abolition legislation but failed.[9] After two failed attempts, the legislation finally passed in 1799, after Pennsylvania (1780) and Rhode Island (1784). By the terms of the New York legislation, females born after that date would owe service until the age of twenty-five and males until twenty-eight. After that they would be freed.[10] This meant that Rose Butler was bound to service to an owner until 1824. In 1810, the legislation was amended – An Addition to the Act Concerning Slaves and Servants – to require owners to provide enslaved and term slaves four quarters of schooling before they turned eighteen, or sufficient education to be able to read the Bible. The penalty for owners who failed to honor the letter of that law is that their enslaved people would be freed. In accordance with that legislation, Rose Butler did receive some education and learned to read and sign her name. New York's Gradual Abolition Act was amended one final time in 1817 to end slavery ten years from that date – on July 4, 1827 – for all those born into lifetime slavery (or, before July 4, 1799).[11] Those born after the 1799 legislation went into effect and before July 4, 1817, when it was amended, still owed their full terms. This uneven approach to abolition meant that it would be another two decades before every New Yorker was finally freed from all forms of servitude (Figure 4.1).

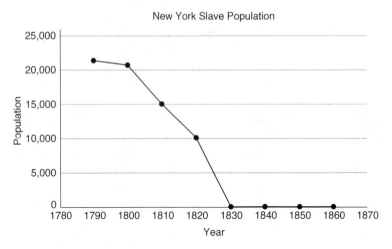

Figure 4.1 New York slave population
Credit: Kaia M. Amoah

Not all enslaved New Yorkers knew about the gradual abolition legislation or believed it to be true, especially those living in rural areas; others knew about the legislation and used it to assert their freedom at every opportunity. They invoked it to make claims that their owners had failed to register or educate them or had kept them in service longer than the law allowed. *Post-nati* African Americans such as Rose benefited from liberal laws that guaranteed their future freedom and identified them on paper as indentured servants, but their lived realities did not reflect much distinction in their status or treatment: in fact, they lived their daily lives like enslaved people. New York's gradual abolition also produced varying freedom dates within the same African American families. Sojourner Truth, for example, received her freedom in 1827, but her children born after 1799 and before 1817 still owed service and would not be freed until their terms ended.[12] As historian Sarah L. H. Gronningsater stated in her article on enslaved children in New York, "being a black servant was little different than being a slave."[13] *Post-nati* African Americans enjoyed some freedoms and legal protections, including an 1801 law that forbade people from importing or exporting enslaved people into or from New York, an 1808 law that prohibited kidnapping of free Blacks, and the 1813 legislation that legitimized slave marriages and extended the right to trial by jury.[14] They also enjoyed the right to an education, but not necessarily to attend public schools. However, the most important freedoms, such as determining their own destinies and living independently, remained elusive. Term slaves like Rose could still be sold and physically, emotionally, and sexually abused. They could not move freely or create their own households; and their work was still compulsory and unpaid. Among other things, servants such as Rose continued to be subjected to the rules and cruelty of owners bent on dominance and mastery. Finally, some still considered people with Rose's status to be slaves. The language of slavery was used when referring to them and those who owned their indentures (i.e., owner, master, mistress). How Rose perceived her own status is unknown.

When she was nine years old, Rose's indenture was sold to Abraham Child of Manhattan, New York, and she was taken roughly thirty miles from her hometown. New York City was a far different world than what she was used to experiencing in Mount Pleasant. It had a sizeable Black population – the largest one in the state; 32 percent of the state's entire Black population resided in New York City. The city also boasted a high population of free Blacks who had already built independent churches, and benevolent and mutual aid societies. By 1810, the 8,137 free Blacks living in New York City far outnumbered the 1,686 who remained enslaved. And the number of enslaved people living in the city kept shrinking. By 1820, only 518 African Americans remained in slavery there.[15] The presence of so many free Blacks provided Rose with an idea of what Black freedom looked like. It would have been impossible to remain content with her status in that environment. Moreover, being a part of a shrinking minority of African Americans who did not own their own labor or lives must have been demoralizing to a young Rose. She may have taken some comfort in the fact that she was not alone in the city: her aunt, Sally, lived nearby on William Street, enslaved to a Mr. Graves. When Rose was sixteen years old, Child sold the balance of her indenture to William L. Morris, a New York attorney with offices at 2 Park Place. The Morris household in the tenth ward on Chrystie Street consisted of Morris, his wife, their children Alisce and Catherine plus three other children whose names are unknown.[16]

By all accounts, Rose hated her new mistress, Mary Morris, and was intent on challenging her authority. She reported that the two had "frequent disputes." In addition to arguing and talking back, she defied her mistress' authority by stealing time for herself, especially in the evenings. Rose frequently lied and told the Morrises she was going to church in the evenings, but instead she chose to party, or "frolic," at the "Hook." The Hook, or Corlears Hook, refers to an eastern Manhattan neighborhood near the shipyards, which was then at the center of New York City's subeconomy. The Hook was known for bars, drinking holes, gambling, brothels, and dance halls. Here, people indulged in selling, trading, and fencing ill-gotten goods, the sex trade, and petty larceny. Rose loved dancing and drinking at her favorite den, an establishment named Mrs. Bundy's. Slaveowners did not generally approve of nighttime outings for their enslaved workers because it led to reduced work productivity the following day. These outings were also threatening because they offered enslaved people a taste of bodily freedom. Once they had experienced it, it became nearly impossible to extinguish those desires. Historian Stephanie M. H. Camp, writing about women's resistance to slavery, contends that antebellum South Carolina plantation owners worried about, and tried to discourage, their enslaved people's nighttime parties, drinking, and trading, but found it difficult to eradicate them completely.[17] These activities persisted on South Carolina plantations and in New York City dens despite slaveowners' best efforts.

Rose also appropriated silver coins and valuables from her owners, which she then pilfered, traded, and fenced in the city's subeconomy. She admitted to stealing "dozens of pounds" of thread and silk and even cash from her previous owner on many occasions. Rose would take the items to an African American woman who would sell them for her. The money she obtained from these transactions was used to fund her "frolicking" at Mrs. Bundy's. She continued stealing at the Morris' home. Rose admitted to two separate people that she stole $300 ($5,435 today)[18] in silver coins from Mary Morris. Had she been caught, prosecuted, and convicted of this theft, her jail sentence would have been up to four years. To erase any evidence of her guilt, Rose took the stolen coins to a local grocer to change them to paper bills. She then used the paper bills to shower gifts and good times on her friends and loved ones. She gifted her aunt Sally a silk dress and took her and friends on a carriage ride through the city, paying for all of their fares. On the Fourth of July, Rose paid her friends' fares on a party steamboat ride on the Hudson River. These entertainments were beyond the reach of most free African Americans, much less enslaved people. Rose also noted that she spent a fraction of the stolen money at the Hook, "I squandered away [all] the money I had stolen – in frolicking and rioting in the dance-houses and other places at the Hook."[19] Stealing and appropriating goods should be understood as resistance, and using her ill-gotten funding for excursions can be seen as an act to seize a measure of bodily freedom and pleasure.

Rejecting the idea that their bodies were primarily instruments of labor for white families, women such as Rose used them as vehicles of pleasure, amusement, and self-expression. Rose's explicit, public enjoyment of her bodily freedom through partying, dancing, and carriage and steamboat rides made these "politically loaded acts," as Camp asserts.[20] Certainly, these activities were done in defiance of the norms and behaviors New York society set for African American women. The audacity of paying for carriage and steamboat rides for other African American women in the last days of slavery in New York City cannot be overstated. Even gifting her aunt Sally a silk dress defied racist ideas that dictated that such a dress was exclusively reserved for wealthy white women. It must also be emphasized that it was unusual for anyone except elite white women to don silk dresses in 1818 New York City. In a world in which African American women dressed in drab work clothes most of the time, a new silk dress offered an ounce of softness and femininity to their bodies. By wearing a silk dress, an African American woman could feel rich, beautiful, and free, thereby transcending her material, social, and economic reality. Yes, even wearing a silk dress in that context was a political act of resistance. Such an expensive gift also declared that Rose believed her aunt to be worthy of nice things despite her race, gender, and status.

These accounts of Rose Butler's life reveal that she was part of a wide network of African American women – including her aunt, the woman who fenced her goods, and the women who accompanied her on carriage and steamboat rides. It is not unusual that African

American women spent a great deal of their non-working time with each other, carousing, trading, singing, and enjoying life.[21] They found support, affirmation, advice, comfort, and laughter in each other's company. Certainly, Rose Butler lived a full life and had a great deal of bodily freedom while living with the promise of full freedom when she turned twenty-five years old.

Rose's history of resistance sets the tone for the March 4, 1818 fire. Rose admitted that she and Mary Morris "had some high words together" that night. According to Rose, her mistress "asked me why I did not clean up the kitchen and the wooden things," to which she retorted that it was impossible to do that and get dinner ready on time. Rose's complaint is that Mary Morris had unrealistic expectations about what was reasonable for her to accomplish in one day given her heavy workload. After staying up late washing the dishes and cleaning the kitchen and furniture as directed, Rose went to bed around 10:30 p.m. She stated that Mr. Morris went to the kitchen at 1:00 a.m. and retired again an hour later. The fire began shortly thereafter.[22]

A day later, on March 5, Rose Butler was arrested for burning the Morris home. It is not clear why people suspected Rose of setting the fire, but she seemed to blame her mistress for raising the suspicion against her, recalling that after the fire Mary Morris consulted with a fortune teller on Division Street to figure out who was responsible. According to Rose, this fortune teller told her mistress that "it was I that did it, and none but me." Rose also added that Mary Morris paid the fortune teller before the woman accused her.[23] Here, she aimed to discredit both her mistress and the fortune teller by implying that the latter had been paid to name her as the culprit – essentially painting the visit as part of a larger plot to falsely accuse her. According to Rose, after her mistress returned home from the fortune teller, she sent her to stay with her aunt because she no longer trusted Rose in the home – with good reason. Police officers Bernard O'Blenis and Josiah Hedden arrested Rose from her aunt's home "on well-grounded suspicion," and placed her in Bridewell, the city jail (Figure 4.2), which stood on what is now City Hall Park.[24]

Although no one in the home was killed or injured in the fire, in New York, arson of "an inhabited dwelling house" was a felony by law. Before 1808, arson of all stripes was punishable by prison

Figure 4.2 Bridewell (circa 1828)
Credit: The Miriam and Ira D. Wallach Division of Art, Prints and
Photographs: Print Collection, The New York Public Library. "Old
Bridewell" New York Public Library Digital Collections:
https://digitalcollections.nypl.org/items/510d47da-27ba-a3d9-e040-
e00a18064a99

sentence; but in 1808, the New York legislature made a distinction
for arson of "an inhabited dwelling house." The emphasis was on the
fact that people were inside the home at the time of the arson. This
kind of arson was particularly heinous because of its capacity to kill
others, and therefore was punishable by death.[25]

During her initial police interview, Rose relayed a twisted
plot to burn the Morris home and kill the family, insisting that two
white men had conceived of the plan and set the fire. According to
her, three weeks before the fire, two mysterious white men, in "snuff
coloured clothes" and "large brimmed hats," followed her to the
water pump, asking her questions about her mistress, which she
chose not to answer. She stated that they asked her name and she
told them it was Jane. She then asked the strangers their names and

they introduced themselves as David Redman and Robert Johnston. No David Redman is listed in the 1818 *New York City Directory* – which lists the names, occupations, and addresses of every head of household. However, there is a *John* Redman who lived on Chrystie, down the street from the Morris family.

It is possible that that man had a young son named David. The directory lists two Robert Johnstons – both living on Division Street – one a physician and pharmacist and the other a "tallow chandler," or soap and candlemaker. It is difficult to imagine a physician trying to hatch a plot to kill a white family with an enslaved servant woman so, it is doubtful he is Rose's co-conspirator. Nonetheless, Rose claimed that these two characters, Redman and Johnston, begged her not to tell her mistress about their conversation.[26]

When asked for more information about Redman and Johnston, Rose claimed they were "constables" (possibly security guards), in an office or store near the Battery (a reference to the Battery Park area in the southern tip of Manhattan). She gave remarkably detailed descriptions of the men: one was "thick and short but one was a little taller than the other. One was a Dark complexion, with black hair. The other had sandy hair." According to Rose, these men wanted to burn Mary Morris' home because her first husband owed them money and would not pay them. After his death, they had visited her several times but she refused to pay the debt. These two men resented the fact that although Morris was "flourishing with the money," she refused to pay them "what they ought to have."[27] If we believe Rose's claim, the arsons were a vengeful response to Mary Morris' willful refusal to pay the debt.

Rose stated that she had run into these same men two weeks later; then, they asked her if she was married. Rose lied and told them she was, possibly to ward off any unwanted sexual advances or propositions. She claimed that the men asked her to meet them later that night, but she refused. According to her, Redman and Johnston tried to convince her to "run away and go to the Hook" and promised they would pay for a hotel.[28] Apparently, this is a veiled suggestion that they propositioned her to prostitution. Certainly, such propositions by white men were not uncommon for African American women in New York City at the time. The Hook also was the usual venue for such illicit activities.

Rose's narrative of the crime continued: she stated the men came by the Morris' home several times as she did her chores, trying to convince her to burn the house. She claimed she refused each time. According to her, Redman and Johnston even invited themselves into the family's kitchen to light their cigars one day. She added that the shorter of the two men promised he would "burn her out," in reference to Mary Morris. Rose claimed that the men said, "if I told of their conversation they would take away my life."[29]

The police asked her some direct questions about the fire, "Did you put the pails and other things on the stairs when they set them on fire?" She responded, "I did not, the men did it." Her interrogator then asked her, "How did they get in?" to which she replied, "by a false key." Rose also claimed that these same two men who had repeatedly tried to recruit her to help with the arson arrived at the Morris home the morning of the fire, pretending to be concerned neighbors. According to Rose, they asked Mr. Morris whether "he knew the girl that lived with him and he said yes, she has lived with me a great while."[30] So this first version of Rose's story blames these two mysterious men for planning and executing the arson. They not only disclosed their motive to Rose, but pressured her to help them burn down the Morris home. In this version, these men let themselves in with a duplicate key and started the fire themselves. They then left and came back to the scene that morning asking Mr. Morris questions that could be interpreted as an attempt to point suspicion toward Rose.

About twenty days into her confinement, the Morris home was torched again, but this time the family barely escaped with their lives. The house and all their belongings burned to the ground. The family relocated to another home and that house was also set on fire soon thereafter, but did not completely burn.[31] Because the Morris family's homes had been twice targeted by arsonists while Rose was in Bridewell, it is certain that she had accomplices. When asked how she came to find out about the subsequent fires, Rose explained that she learned the news from a letter that had been placed inside a loaf of bread and given to her inside her jail cell. She believed the letter had been sent by the two men, but the name was "so queer and bad we could not make it out." Supposedly, the letter read, "Jane, We are going away and shall come back again. You are in no danger, you will be cleared. We have consumed the house pretty near down.

Don't tell what we said to you." Rose claimed she burned the letter after reading it.[32] This incredible tale of a letter hidden in a loaf of bread and passed to her in her cell reveals either the creative minds of her accomplices or the complexity of Rose's plan. The second and third arsons while she was incarcerated plus the letter in the loaf of bread were designed to affirm Rose's innocence altogether. Had she not confessed multiple times and relayed key details, one might doubt whether she had anything to do with any of the arsons.

During Rose's year-long incarceration in Bridewell, she told many people what she knew about the crime, and some of them recorded these statements. In one version of her story, told to Baptist minister and Chaplain to the Public Institutions Reverend John Stanford on June 2, 1819, Rose insisted, "The statement I made in the Police – office was true – I DID set the fire MYSELF, but was advised to do it by two men." She continued, "they gave me the matches, and advised me when and how to set the house on fire." In this version, she admitted she started the fire, but insisted that the men provided the matches. Rose positioned herself as just a minor contributor in a plan devised by the white men; the thirst for revenge was theirs – not hers; the plan was theirs; and she merely set the fire at their urging. In this version, she also provided other details that revealed her own intellectual work in planning the fire. She stated, "I affixed a string on the outside of the front kitchen door, to prevent the family escaping the flames in that way, and also cut the door a little, with an old knife, that the family might think some person had broken in, and not suspect any one in the house."[33] It is no minor matter that she bound the front door from the outside so the family could not escape the fire. This statement reveals the true nature of what Rose Butler intended for the Morris family: death. What is not clear, though, is the path Rose herself planned to take out of the burning home: the part of her plot where she planned to save herself is forever lost to history. Still, it is certain that Rose Butler did intend to escape the fire she set. Her being upstairs with the Morrises would make her look like a victim and less like a suspect.

While in Bridewell, Rose Butler confided in Eliza Duell, a white woman responsible for cleaning her cell, who later betrayed her trust by providing a statement to authorities. Perhaps Rose expected this level of surveillance and reporting by whites, but because Duell was not an authority, she likely may have developed a modicum of trust in this woman. There are key differences between Duell's account and Rose's versions of her story. In the version relayed to Duell, Rose incriminated a different man as the arson plot mastermind – someone named John Williams or James Edwards. Are these the real names of her accomplices, told to a trusted confidant? Multiple men named John Williams are listed in the city directory, but there is no one named James Edwards. Perhaps Rose could no longer remember the names of the men she originally provided to police in March 1818?

Interestingly, neither Redman nor Johnston are mentioned in this version of her story. According to Rose, Williams/Edwards had been a clerk in a store owned by Mary Morris' first husband. That husband died owing the clerk. The clerk had frequently applied to his widow to repay that debt, but she refused. According to Rose, this clerk was "determined to have satisfaction" by getting revenge. In this version of her story, Rose "assisted" him in placing the flammable items in the pail. After doing so, she went to her room and remained in bed until after Mr. Morris retired for the evening. She then snuck downstairs, unlocked the front door, and let the arsonist into the home. After setting the fire, he advised Rose to return to bed since the fire would take some time.[34] In this version, she incriminated herself, but only as an accomplice. According to her, the motive, initiative, ingenuity, planning, and execution were all his.

In another version of the story later printed in Reverend Stanford's publication, Rose claimed that the evening before the fire when her mistress was scolding her for not doing her work, a man overheard their cross words. Outraged, this man remarked to Rose, "The d – d old bitch why don't you burn her out?" to which she allegedly replied, "I don't care how quick it is done." She claimed the man told her it would be done that same evening. Rose promised him she would come down and open the door for him to set the fire, which happened later than she anticipated because Mr. Morris had gone to bed so late. Rose continued, "When I went down, and found the man cutting the door, which I opened and let him in. He took from his pockets some newspapers and matches, and put them on the pail, together with my wet frock: they were set on fire by a rush-light which he brought in with him." According to her, this man then advised her to return to bed because the fire would not burn much before daylight; after he left, Rose locked the door and fastened it with string so that the family could not escape. She stated that she knew her co-conspirator from the Hook and had once given him $19 from the $300 she had stolen from Mary Morris. On the night of the fire, this man allegedly promised to give her $25. She does not reveal why she gave him money or why he promised her $25.[35] The fact that money might have exchanged hands between the two suggests either Rose paid this man for something or he paid her.

Although it is not possible to fully untangle truth from fiction more than 200 years later, there are some consistent threads in every version of the account. Rose's multiple confessions all had her desire for revenge as the motivation for the arson. First, in Rose's statements to various people, she consistently declared that she did not like Mary Morris and was "determined to be revenged on her." To Eliza Duell, she explained that she did not like her mistress and decided to seek revenge because she was "always finding fault and scolding at her." She gave the same reason to Rev. Stanford: she told him that she set the fire "for no other cause, than that her mistress was always finding fault with her work and scolded her and that she never did like her mistress."[36] Another element consistent in every version of her accounts is that she had a co-conspirator(s) – a white man/men. The allegations of Mary Morris' unpaid debts from her first husband were yet another element consistent in every version. Finally, Rose mentioned the Hook in at least two versions of her narrative, so perhaps it also factored into the truth in some way. Perhaps the truth was hidden in these consistent elements. What is clear is that Rose buried the truth within an elaborate web of contradictory stories mixed with some fictional details. Each story is complex and reflects that a great deal of intellectual work went into hiding the full truth and the real identities of her co-conspirators.

It should be noted that all Rose's versions of the story bear remarkable similarity to another arson conspiracy in New York City in January of that same year. In that case, an Italian man working in the home of a wealthy family had been terminated from his job for drunkenness. He devised a plan for revenge with an Italian friend and his former employer's cook, an African American woman. According to their plan, the cook was to let the men into the home after the family fell asleep. The men planned to terrorize, rape, and murder the family and steal their valuables. Once done, they planned to torch the home. In exchange for her assistance, the cook was to have been paid $130 after the stolen household goods were sold by the two men. The plot, however, never launched because someone working in the home overheard their plans and alerted the family. The two Italians and the cook were arrested and detained.[37] This story was printed in the local press. There is a small possibility that some of the details of Rose's stories had been copied from this real story.

Rose spent her nineteenth birthday in Bridewell. After eight months, she was finally indicted and tried in New York City's court of oyer and terminer on November 18, 1818. Established in 1788, this court had jurisdiction over criminal cases, including misdemeanors and felonies. Rose's case was presided over by Smith Thompson, the state's chief justice, Cadwallader D. Colden, New York City's mayor, and an alderman.[38] David Graham and John R. Scott served as Rose Butler's defense attorneys. The jury found her guilty of arson of an inhabited dwelling, which brought an automatic death sentence. The court postponed judgment so the state supreme court of judicature could review the case on the question of whether the house burned sufficiently to constitute a capital offense.[39] In New York at that time, "supreme courts" were actually trial-level courts with jurisdiction over civil and criminal cases and lower-level appeals. After a defendant's indictment in an oyer and terminer court, the case was then referred to the supreme court of judicature for final judgment.[40] This is the reason this court would hear Rose's case, but it would not be heard for another six months. Until then, she remained in Bridewell.

Any question about whether Rose Butler would be tried in a just legal system must be considered through the legal context of her day. In the colonial era, New York legislators constructed different and unequal judicial processes for enslaved people. The judicial system codified many of the same approaches used by slaveowners, including extraordinary violence to punish enslaved people for crimes, big and small. Another feature of New York's judicial system in the colonial era as it related to enslaved people is the tendency to subject them to confinement without due process for extended time periods. Moreover, enslaved people accused of committing violent crimes against whites in the colonial era were denied jury trials; their cases were heard by two justices, instead. After the Revolution, things began to change because society changed. Bowing to pressures from the state's free African Americans, antislavery whites in the Manumission Society, and other white allies who lobbied for a reduction of corporal and capital punishments for enslaved people, New York changed these colonial laws. After 1785, enslaved people were guaranteed a jury trial, but only for capital crimes, and by 1800 corporal punishment was abolished in the state.[41]

By the early nineteenth century, New York afforded enslaved people some of the same legal rights as free people. The most significant gain is that they were extended the right to trial by jury for all legal issues in 1813.[42] By then, enslaved people in New York fared better than those in other states. For example, slaveowners did not control or lord over the judicial process from start to finish as they did elsewhere. New York had functioning police departments that did the investigative work; in other states, coroner's inquest juries were made up of slave-holders performing crime scene investigations – often bringing inherent biases to the process. Enslaved and free Black New Yorkers were issued warrants and indictments when suspected of crimes, just like other state residents. Although enslaved people could not testify in court against any free person, white or Black, their testimony against another enslaved person was admissible. They had a right to be represented by an attorney, and if they could not afford the costs, New York guaranteed one appointed by the court. Finally, in New York, enslaved people were not subjected to an accelerated judicial process that arrested, tried, convicted, and executed them in a matter of days like other states with slavery. However, if they were convicted of a capital offense, enslaved people would receive a mandatory death sentence, after which their owners would be compensated for their loss.[43] These were the legal conditions and considerations facing Rose Butler.

On May 14, 1819, Rose Butler's case went before New York's supreme court of judicature on whether her actions satisfied the statutory and common-law definitions of arson and warranted a death sentence. David Graham, Rose's attorney, argued some compelling points about whether the burning of the home had been sufficient to support the indictment for "burning an inhabited dwelling." First, Graham argued that the revision of the 1808 statute distinguished arson of an empty building from arson of "an inhabited dwelling." The latter, he argued, signified that there had to be some personal injury of people in the building. Second, Graham insisted that burning something was very different from setting fire to it. He argued that Rose merely set fire to the home; she did not *burn* it. With just three kitchen stairs burned, the home had not been sufficiently consumed by fire to support the indictment for "burning an inhabited dwelling."[44]

Despite Graham having built what Chief Justice Ambrose Spencer called an "ingenious" case, the justices returned a unanimous decision that the crime had been completed and the burning of the home was sufficient. When rendering the decision, Justice John Woodworth, speaking directly to Rose, said, "Your crime originated in a wicked and depraved heart – you was a servant in the family – confidence was placed in you; you owed fidelity and obedience – their lives and property were in some measure, placed within your power ..." Woodworth, here, resorts to paternalist moralism, insisting Rose *owed* her masters her loyalty and obedience in return for the confidence they placed in her. It is unreasonable to think that enslaved people owed their enslavers anything at all in exchange for their stolen freedom, unpaid labor, denied humanity and personal dignity, fractured families, abuse, and disrupted peace. In a revealing exposé of his own views about justice, Woodworth continued, "You was offended with one of them [Morrises] for having reprimanded you, and for this cause determined on revenge. The remainder of the family had never injured you or given you least provocation, and yet you intended to involve all in one common destruction."[45] He believed Rose's act of revenge was unjustified, disproportionate, and made worse by the possibility that there could have been collateral damage – the innocent other members of the Morris family. His comments reveal a clash of two competing versions of justice. In Woodworth's version, "This system, with all its imperfections, has, on the whole, been consoling to the friends of humanity." Rose, however, operated with a different philosophy and exercised a Black feminist practice of justice, which rejects the idea that the United States judicial system was sound, trustworthy, or "consoling to the friends of humanity". Her version of justice negates the possibility of innocence among slaveowners, their family members, or agents. Rose was fully aware that young children were in the home; she even shared a bedroom with one. To her, the children of her enemy and the woman who had mistreated her were reasonable targets of her lethal resistance. If we analyze Rose's actions as evidence of her views, all those who advance *or benefit* from slavery are complicit and, therefore, parties to it. This is consistent with a Black feminist practice of justice. On May 14, 1819, that same court condemned Rose Butler to death and set her date of execution for Friday, June 11 between 1:00 and 3:00 p.m. When asked if she had reason to object to the sentence, Rose responded in the negative.[46]

She was taken back to Bridewell and placed in the condemned room for the twenty-odd days left in her young life. Baptist minister Reverend John Stanford, the Chaplain to the Public Institutions, was responsible for ministering to her and preparing her soul for the execution. Rev. Stanford bears the distinction of being New York's first paid chaplain for correctional facilities and had been serving in that role since 1812. He earned a nominal annual salary of $250 and his appointment was renewed annually. Stanford ministered to at least ten people who were later executed, including Butler. In fact, he became a pioneer of the "true confession" genre of memoirs of condemned people, printing and selling them for profit. Stanford's *An Authentic Statement of the Case and Conduct of Rose Butler, who was Tried, Convicted, and Executed for the Crime of Arson* is one of many similar pamphlets he produced. Although the sale of these death-row confessions benefited him personally, Stanford also embraced the missionary nature of the job – seemingly committed to saving these souls from eternal damnation and the gallows in equal measure.[47]

Rose also received visits from other clergy – some Black, some white – who counseled and prayed for her. Rose misbehaved terribly during these clergy visits. According to one report, her temper was "violent" and she "threatened vengeance on her prosecutors." She reportedly behaved "in a very insulting manner" and her "perverseness was in the extreme." Dorothy Ripley, who also ministered to Rose while she was in Bridewell also noticed her "perverseness," but did not provide any details about what that meant specifically. The *Evening Post* reported that Rose's "behavior and language were rude and offensive," and mostly directed at the clergy who visited her. Her spirit and conduct, one witness observed, "evinced the callousness of her mind and heart."[48] Rose's behavior may have met severe correction because after April 2, 1819, inmates who misbehaved like Rose could receive corporal punishment.[49] As objectionable as people reported Rose's behavior to be, she is not the only Bridewell inmate who expressed disrespect for clergy. Other inmates resisted the counsel of Rev. Stanford, refusing to speak to him at all or rejecting his message. His own diary reflects that he often became dispirited by those "hardened in iniquity" and indifferent about religion.[50] Perhaps they resented the exploitative financial motivation he had for obtaining their confessions.

A second possible reason for Rose's irreverent protests is that the ministers who visited her kept pressuring her to reveal the identities of her accomplices up to the moment of her execution. Their repeated requests must have been irritating, and perhaps infuriating. According to Eliza Duell, one day Rev. Stanford told Rose that if she "wished to relieve her mind and disclose any facts to him," he would stop by the next day with his notebook. Rose replied that she was ready to disclose information and would do so the following day. Eliza Duell alleged that that night, she overheard Rose rehearsing two different stories that she planned to tell Rev. Stanford about the crime. Given all of his pressure, it is not surprising that Rose rehearsed two versions of her story and later "confessed" to Rev. Stanford on June 2. Her scraggly signature is affixed to the bottom of the page.[51]

Another possible reason she had contempt for the clergy is that one of them told her she was "sure to go to hell," which deeply upset her. She told Ripley, "I do not think he is fit to preach; for he is not a gospel minister," adding, "I like to hear Mr. Strong pray better than him, for he speaks so comfortably to me, and encourages me."[52] Rose clearly had very strong opinions about how she wished people to treat and speak to her. She also had been offended by how Mary Morris spoke to her. By contrast, she did respect Reverend Strong who spoke to her in a pleasant tone with encouraging words. It should come as no surprise that African American women, across time and space, have insisted on such respect regardless of who the person is or what power they hold.

While awaiting execution, Rose gave her final confession during a conversation with Dorothy Ripley. Ripley asked her if she thought her being hanged was just, to which Rose replied, "Yes . . . but I do not think I was so much to blame as them who put me up to it; for I was young and ignorant: but never mind, Justice will find them out as well as me someday, I did set fire to it; I am not going to deny it, and tell a lie about it."[53] This may be the clearest and most direct of all of Rose Butler's confessions. Even then, she still maintained that she had accomplices who had manipulated her to set the fire. Rose, as a practitioner of Black feminist justice, was fully confident that this karmic or retributive "Justice" would give these accomplices their "just deserts." Contemporary people close to the case noted that Rose never showed any remorse for the fire, but had instead "declared and expressed her resentment toward her mistress."[54]

After Rose's sentence (Figure 4.3), Mayor Colden began receiving letters threatening his life should she be executed.[55] She clearly had accomplices who were committed to doing whatever was necessary to stop her execution, even taking the huge risk of committing a felony by sending death threats to a city official. It is unlikely that the author of those threatening letters really intended to murder the New York City mayor. The death threats were one last-ditch effort to get Rose Butler released from Bridewell. This tactic failed.

On June 11, 1819, the date of Rose's execution, newspapers reported a crowd of two or three thousand people at the gallows in Potter's Field to witness her execution. Potter's Field, located in now what is Washington Square Park, was a cemetery for indigent people whose families could not afford a regular burial. The crowd was informed that New York's governor, DeWitt Clinton, had given her a respite until July 9. The two reasons he cited for the respite were her presumed "insanity" and to give Rose enough time to reveal her accomplices. Although this is the first time a question of Rose's mental health had been raised since her arrest, her behavior in Bridewell, including insulting the clergy, gave the governor reason to think mental health might have been a factor. He also was fairly confident that she had accomplices, given that two fires were set after her confinement and the death threats had been sent to the mayor.[56] The governor reasoned that extra time was needed to obtain their identities. In this vein, Rev. Stanford as the Bridewell chaplain was the linchpin to the success of that objective. Surely, as a state employee, he understood his assignment?

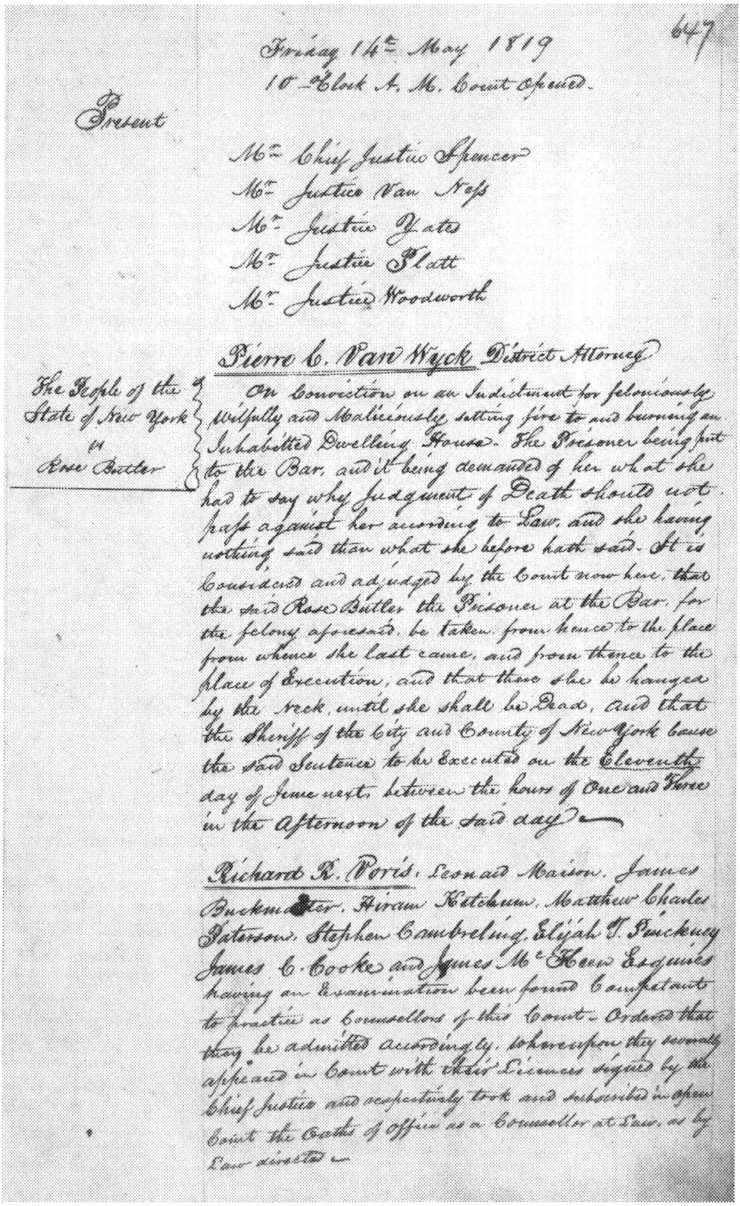

647

Friday 14th May 1819
10 oClock A. M. Court opened.

Present

Mr. Chief Justice Spencer
Mr. Justice Van Ness
Mr. Justice Yates
Mr. Justice Platt
Mr. Justice Woodworth

Pierre C. Van Wyck District Attorney

The People of the State of New York vs Rose Butler

On Conviction on an Indictment for feloniously wilfully and Maliciously setting fire to and burning an Inhabitted Dwelling House. The Prisoner being put to the Bar, and it being demanded of her what she had to say why Judgment of Death should not pass against her according to Law, and she having nothing said than what she before hath said. It is Considered and adjudged by the Court now here, that the said Rose Butler the Prisoner at the Bar, for the felony aforesaid, be taken from hence to the place from whence she last came, and from thence to the place of Execution, and that there she be hanged by the neck, until she shall be Dead, and that the Sheriff of the City and County of New York cause the said Sentence to be Executed on the Eleventh day of June next, between the hours of One and Three in the Afternoon of the said day.

Richard R. Voris, Leonard Maison, James Buckma[illegible]ter, Hiram Ketchum, Matthew Charles Paterson, Stephen Cambreling, Elijah T. Pinckney James C. Cooke and James McKeen Esquires having on Examination been found Competent to practice as Counsellors of this Court. Ordered that they be admitted accordingly. Whereupon they severally appeared in Court with their Licences signed by the Chief Justice and respectively took and subscribed in open Court the Oaths of Office as a Counsellor at Law, as by Law directed.

Figure 4.3 Rose Butler's sentence
Credit: New York State Archives

On the second and final date set for her execution, Rose Butler was taken to the gallows by a carriage and accompanied by two women from the Methodist society, Rev. Stanford, and a physician. It was reported, again, that thousands of people had gathered to see the event at Potter's Field, while thousands more watched from windows, trees, and rooftops. Rev. Stanford delivered a speech in which he declared the offense of arson to be "more malignant than that of murder." The crime of burning, he reasoned, "involves the inconscious [sic], innocent family, in one common conflagration; and ... unfrequently hazards the lives and property of a whole neighborhood."[57] Besides that comment, the rest of Stanford's speech was somewhat sympathetic toward Rose. She was executed on the afternoon of July 9, 1819 – the last person executed in that location and one of the last enslaved women executed in New York. To the disappointment of her executioners, she never disclosed her accomplices. Rose's last words were, "I am satisfied as to the justness of my fate – it is all right."[58] Like so many other women who used a Black feminist practice of justice to resist slavery, Rose was at peace with her death. She was buried in Potter's Field.

It is difficult to understand Rose Butler without understanding the world in which she lived. Slavery was in its last stages in New York, but for her, the prospect of freedom was far away. Each day, she encountered many groups of free people, including free African Americans and immigrants. Yet she belonged to the small group of people who were not free. In 1824, when so many others lived freely, there was little solace in a distant freedom for Rose.

Lethal force was not Rose's first or even second option to deal with slavery and an oppressive mistress. She had resisted for years by stealing and appropriating the Morris' wealth; she also defended herself with words, arguing with her mistress as if they were equals. "Talking back" restored the dignity of the insults thrown at her, but it was not really *enough* to make her whole from the psychological damage slavery caused. None of Rose's verbal resistance could counter the crushing weight of her servitude, unfreedom, and mistreatment.

Rose's many confessions reveal that her singular motivation for lethal resistance was revenge for scolding; but her reason is much more nuanced. Mary Morris' expectations were unrealistic, and she was overly critical of Rose. It is not surprising because mistresses became well versed in psychological and verbal violence inside the home. Since their primary objective was to get enslaved people to work efficiently and submit to their wills, it is reasonable to assume that Mary Morris was willing to do whatever was necessary to effect that, including using verbal abuse and insults, open hand slaps, name-calling, pinches, and denial of food or sleep. Rose's varied forms of resistance and unmanageability likely did not go unchecked, either. Her resistance may have been part of a circular cycle of resistance and punishments that could only be permanently broken with a lethal intervention. Perhaps this is what happened between Rose and Mary Morris. Mistresses could be unjustly cruel to their enslaved women, in particular. And if they were, there was little hope for reprieve, relief, or redress. Although the New York slave code dating back to the colonial era gave enslaved people the right to appeal to authorities if their owners treated them cruelly, very few tried in the state's long history. It was a hopeless proposition. Even Sojourner Truth lamented the lack of options enslaved people had to redress the cruelty of their owners.[59] The only options enslaved women had to get relief was to seize it for themselves.

Rose's desire for revenge for her mistress was deep – beyond one unsuccessful act of arson on March 4, 1818. Burning the woman's home, terrorizing her entire family through multiple acts of arson as they slept, rendering them homeless, and destroying her property, furnishings, belongings, and memories were not enough "just deserts" for her; she wanted nothing less than Mary Morris' peace of mind, or life. As a testament to that, Eliza Duell reported hearing Rose vow that "if she should ever get clear she would have the life of Mrs. Morris in some way."[60]

Consistent with a Black feminist practice of justice, Rose coolly planned and coordinated every detail of the first arson – or *all* of the arsons. Undeniably, the plot and her efforts to deflect suspicion away from herself were intellectual acts. From carefully waiting until everyone was asleep, obtaining the flammable items, and securing the outside door to prevent escape to cutting the door with a knife to pretend someone else had committed the crime, Rose Butler invested much time and thought into planning. She may have recruited accomplices (as opposed to them recruiting her, as she claimed) who were committed to her singularly until the end. Even after Rose had been sent to Bridewell, her accomplices doggedly set additional fires in the Morris' homes. They then had the audacity to send death threats to the mayor on her behalf. Just as she never divulged their identities, they never turned state's evidence on her, unlike other accomplices in this book. Rose and her accomplices' commitment of loyalty and protection was mutual and enduring.

Finally, like other practitioners of this kind of justice in the age of slavery, Rose lacked regret for her actions. She resigned herself to accept her fate before her execution. Her final words: "I am satisfied as to the justness of my fate – it is all right," further underscore this point. She also seemed somewhat fearless about her impending execution. When Dorothy Ripley asked her if she feared being hanged days before her execution, she allegedly responded, "I do not think so much about the hanging as the consequences after." In other words, she feared only God's punishment, not man's.[61] At nineteen, Rose Butler walked to the gallows, resigned to face her fate with the courage of a much older woman.

. . .

Without a doubt, fire was one of the most readily available and thoroughly destructive weapons available to enslaved people. In April 1734 in Old Montréal, a defiant Marie-Joseph Angélique, who also nursed a desire for revenge against her mistress, set fire to her home. The fire quickly spread to forty-six other buildings and homes in Old Montréal, including a hotel, and the merchant sector.[62] This Montréal fire is unmatched in mainland North American history: no enslaved woman on American soil committed an arson of this magnitude.

Closer to home, the list of Black female arsonists across time and space in United States' history is rather long. In the seventeenth century, Maria, who was enslaved to Joshua Lamb, was accused of setting fire to the home of Thomas Swann in Roxbury, Boston, in September 1681. She confessed and implicated Cheffellia (also known as Jack), an enslaved man, as her co-conspirator. Maria also accused Cheffellia of having set fire to the home of Lieutenant William Clark two months prior – a crime for which he had not been arrested before her accusation. A second enslaved man, owned by

James Pemberton, was also convicted of being part of Maria's arson plot. He and Cheffellia were sentenced to transportation out of the country. Of all the so-called co-conspirators, Maria, alone, was executed by hanging. Hers is the first documented case of a legal execution of a Black woman for any crime in United States' history; the first woman executed was Jane Champion, a white woman, in Virginia in the 1630s for infanticide.[63] There may have been other executions of enslaved women before Maria, but those cases did not proceed through the courts, so they are lost to history.

It would be irresponsible not to mention the 1741 fires that burned through New York City, incinerating outhouses, barns, stables, and even the governor's home. Historians have hotly debated whether the fires were the result of a Black rebellion conspiracy, or whether this idea is just white paranoia. Enslaved women Sarah and Diana factored prominently in the presumed plot.[64] A cursory review of the cases in the colonial and early national eras include one based in Anne Arundel County, in the colony of Maryland, in which two enslaved women, Grace and Jennye, were convicted and hanged for arson in 1751. An unknown enslaved woman was executed in Charleston, South Carolina, in 1754, but very few details exist about her case. In 1766, Beck, in Calvert County, Maryland, was hanged for arson. In 1780, Violet was accused and tried in Augusta County, Virginia, for burning down her owner's home. Unlike many of the other accused enslaved women in this book, Violet denied that she had committed the arson. She was convicted regardless and sentenced to death in March 1781. After her hanging execution, Violet's head was cut from her body and placed on a pole at a major thoroughfare in the county as a deterrent to others. In Queens, New York, in October 1788, Nelly set fire to the home of her enslaver, Captain Daniel Braine. After Nelly's confession, a girl named Sarah was charged with being an accessory. Nelly was hanged, but Sarah was given clemency because of her age. That same year, in Somerset County, New Jersey, Dine was hanged for arson. In Albany, New York, in November 1793, Bet and Dean, two enslaved teenaged girls, and an enslaved man named Pomp (short for Pompey) set a fire that consumed twenty-six homes at the intersection of Broadway and Maiden Lane. The property loss was estimated at $250,000 ($7 million today). Bet and Dean were hanged on March 14, 1794, and Pomp a month later.[65] The antebellum era witnessed scores more executions of enslaved women for arson – too many to list here.[66] While some of these cases were brought as the result of whites' exaggerated fears of being burned alive by enslaved people or losing everything they owned, unknown numbers of incendiary acts were acts of revolt executed by enslaved women bent on delivering their own justice.[67]

In the final analysis, fire is *the most* formidable, if not effective, weapon enslaved women wielded to resist slavery because of its capacity to destroy everything their owners valued. A successful arson leaves in its wake economic, emotional, and physical damage for the target. It had the capacity to kill people and livestock and erase homes, barns, businesses, and towns. As Rev. Stanford stated at Rose's execution, arson's potential to harm an entire family, community, or town makes it "worse than murder." If victims escaped with their lives and without injury, destruction of their property brought untold economic devastation. For example, in 1736, slaveowner William Cox of Virginia petitioned the House of Burgesses requesting financial assistance. He told the body that he had been "reduced to poverty" after his enslaved woman had broken into his home, critically wounding his son, burning his tobacco house, and murdering his other slaves, before taking her own life. Although arson was just one element of her destructive attack, Cox's enslaved woman destroyed every bit of his financial wealth, rendering him destitute.[68] White slaveowners who watched their homes, belongings, or businesses burn, lost far more than just property; intentional fire also burned a hole through their sense of safety and peace. And if enslaved women achieved nothing else but that with the fires they set, they returned to their owners the terrorism they experienced on a daily basis.

5 JANE WILLIAMS
"Never Forgets or Forgives Anything"

> *Justice is always uncompromising in its claims and inexorable in its demand*
>
> ~ Frances Ellen Watkins Harper

Between 4:00 and 5:00 a.m. on July 19, 1852, Nelly Scott, an enslaved woman residing at the home of Virginia and Joseph Pendleton Winston on Seventh Street in Richmond, Virginia, rushed into the streets screaming that all the Winstons were dead. Nelly's piercing screams awakened neighbors from their slumber. She was inconsolable. Several neighbors and physicians sprang from their beds and hurriedly followed her back to the Winston home, where she directed them to a horrible scene of mutilation in the couple's bedroom: the young couple and their nine-month-old daughter, Virginia Bell, lay dying from the injuries of a vicious attack with an ax or heavy hatchet as they slept. One person reported "their faces and heads were literally cut and hacked to pieces – Virginia Winston had as many as half a dozen deep cuts about her face and head, out of which her brains were oozing." The blows to the elder Virginia's head had fractured her skull. One cut on her head was so deep that it chipped her skull bone down to her brain matter. Little Virginia Bell had been spared the ax, but apparently had been hit in her head several times with blunt force. One physician on the scene, Dr. T. J. Deane, concluded that the child's skull had been crushed. According to Dr. James Bolton, another physician who tended to the family, when he pressed against her head to ascertain her injuries, he "heard the broken pieces of bones grating against each other." Both mother and child were in "the last struggles and agonies of death" by the time the neighbors arrived. Dr. James Beale concluded there was "no hope" for Virginia Winston – who passed away twenty minutes after the arrival of Dr. Deane – or baby Virginia, who died shortly thereafter. Joseph Winston was more fortunate than his wife and daughter; he survived. He suffered three severe hatchet wounds on the top and back of his head, but none were bone-deep like his wife's. His injuries were significant enough, though, that he slipped into a coma for more than a week. When Joseph Winston recovered, he had no memory of the attack.[1]

. . .

Joseph Pendleton Winston was born on April 5, 1825, in Hanover County, Virginia, as the eighth child of Sarah Madison Pendleton and Philip Bickerton Winston. Philip Winston was a planter who owned fifty-three enslaved people in 1850.[2] Joseph moved to Richmond, in Henrico County, as a young adult.

In 1847, Winston married Virginia Bell Pankey, who was three years his senior. By the 1850 census, the young couple reported having two young children, a two-year-old son named Charles Pankey and a one-year-old daughter, Lavinia Cary, named after Virginia's sister, Lavinia. The Winstons lost Lavinia Cary on Christmas Eve that year, at just thirteen months old.[3] A second daughter, Virginia Bell Winston, was born on September 26, 1851; she was just nine months old when she was murdered in her home on July 19, 1852.[4] Joseph P. Winston became a widower at just twenty-seven years of age after the attack, burying his thirty-year-old wife and their second daughter together (Figure 5.1).

Joseph P. Winston lived a far humbler life than his father in Hanover County. He co-owned the Winston & Powers grocery store located at Fourteenth and Cary streets with W. H. Powers. The duo employed at least five clerks and one salesman. In addition, as was typical of grocers in that era, Joseph also operated a commission merchant business, Nace & Winston. Commission merchants sold goods and products owned by others and reaped a commission from the sales.[5] Despite being entrepreneurs of two business, the Winstons – like Richmond's other traders, merchants, and manufacturers – did

Figure 5.1 Tombstone of Virginia Winston and her daughters
Credit: Hollywood Cemetery, Richmond, VA. Photo by Nikki
M. Taylor

not get wealthy in the business.[6] The couple's real wealth and status
came from the enslaved people they owned.

According to historian Midori Takagi, the majority of
slaveholders in Richmond in 1840 and 1860 owned one or two
people, accounting for 53 and 56 percent of all Richmond slaveholders, respectively. At the other end of the spectrum, those who
owned four or more in those same decades, comprised just 30 and
34 percent of the slaveholding population in Richmond. In 1852, the
couple owned three enslaved people – John and Jane Williams and
their young daughter. As the owner of three enslaved workers, the

Winstons owned one more person than the average slaveholder in antebellum Richmond. In 1840, 16 percent of slaveholders owned three people, like the Winstons. By 1860, eight years after the murders, just 1 percent of all Richmond slaveowners owned three enslaved people.[7] At the time, the Winstons were numbered among the Richmond slaveholding elite.

Slaveholding in Richmond was very different than it had been on Winston's father's plantation in Hanover County. Most Richmond slaveholders owned far fewer enslaved people than those in the countryside. In Richmond, enslaved people did not work in gangs or reside in separate slave quarters, and they had relatively more freedom of movement. Many hired out their own time and were allowed to find their own jobs. Hiring out was accompanied by "living out," a practice whereby enslaved people who hired their time found their own housing. Both hiring out and living out led to a great deal of independence and self-confidence among enslaved people, eroding the bonds of slavery and the authority of owners.[8]

The record is silent on how the Williams family had been acquired or from whom, but they initially belonged to different owners – she to the Winstons and John Williams to John Enders, a Richmond resident who owned 100 enslaved people in 1840. Enders sold John out of state for making death threats to Mr. Rock, his white employee. Threatening a white person was a felony offense for enslaved people in nineteenth-century Virginia. An 1847 Virginia law prohibited them from using "provoking language or menacing gestures to a white person." The punishment for such an offense was thirty-nine lashes, but Enders also sold John out of state – possibly because of his incorrigibility. To appease John Williams' wife, Joseph Winston eventually purchased him from Solomon Davis of South Carolina to reunite the couple.[9]

The Winstons were nearly polar opposites of the enslaved family who lived in their home. By the time of the murders, the Williamses were approximately thirty-five years old, and parents to one child, a daughter. Jane Williams was described as a "yellow," or light-complexioned, woman of ordinary size, with straight hair and one eye.[10] The historical record does not reveal how Jane lost her other eye. Because she was enslaved, it is very possible that it was the result of abuse. It is highly unlikely that Jane and John Williams had been officially married, but they believed themselves to be in a marriage and shared the same surname just the same. Like slave-holders everywhere, the Winstons' wealth would be directly tied to the wombs of their female enslaved workers. Unfortunately for them, Jane Williams, the only woman of childbearing years the couple owned, had given birth to just one child. Already in her mid-thirties in 1852, Jane may not have had any more children in her future, thus diminishing the prospects that the Winstons would ever become wealthier through the natural increase of their enslaved population.

Jane Williams worked as the Winstons' housemaid and child nurse. As the nurse, she tended to the needs of Virginia Winston and her infant daughter virtually nonstop. Jane would have been under the watchful and critical eye of her mistress all day, every day. At least she had a reprieve from Joseph Winston while he worked, but the same was not true of Virginia, her mistress. Jane's workday began when her mistress rang a bell for her very early every morning – before sunrise – and ended twelve hours later at 5:00 or 6:00 p.m.[11] As the only enslaved woman the Winstons owned, they may have given her every household task inside the home, except cooking. She likely cleaned latrines, swept and scrubbed floors, cleaned and dusted furniture, cleaned windows and curtains, and washed, sewed, and ironed all of the family's clothing and linen. Although she was not the family's cook, Jane may have also been obligated to help in the kitchen when the Winstons hosted dinner parties. Her work was unending. After tending to the Winston family all day, Jane had to cook, clean, launder, and sew for her own family in the evenings.

By all appearances, John and Jane Williams may have been literate. Jane Williams had in her possession a letter from her husband written while he was in South Carolina. Of course, it is also possible that they had people writing and reading their letters for them. If they were literate, the record is silent about how they learned to read and write. The state of Virginia did not *explicitly* prohibit teaching enslaved people to read or write like other southern states, but state legislators did deter it. An 1830 Act prohibited any meeting of free Blacks to teach them "reading or writing, either in the day or night, under whatsoever pretext." Such meetings would be con-sidered "an unlawful assembly"; any white person found in such a meeting place for that purpose would receive a $50 fine and be imprisoned for up to two months.[12] However the Williamses learned to read, it had been done at great risk to the person who instructed them.

John Williams was a carpenter by trade – a skill that placed him in the top echelons of the slave community and Joseph Winston allowed him to hire his time. State law prohibited enslaved Virginians from seeking employment and hiring themselves out, but it could not realistically be enforced in Richmond, where tobacco and other manufacturers demanded these contractual enslaved workers. More than half of enslaved people working in Richmond's tobacco industry hired

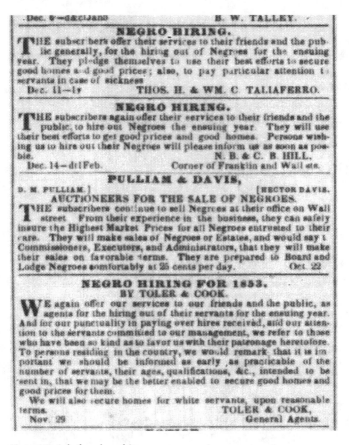

Figure 5.2 Ads for slave hires
Credit: *Alexandria Gazette and Virginia Advertiser*, December 31, 1856.
Library of Virginia

their own time, making the practice very common in the 1850s (Figure 5.2).[13]

In Richmond, hiring season was after Christmas. Then, potential employers and employees roamed the streets searching for one another. Their work terms might be only a few days, but they typically lasted fifty weeks – nearly a year. "Hires," as they were called, could choose their own employers, so naturally they were inclined to choose masters who treated them humanely and offered good wages.[14] For an enslaved artisan like John Williams, employers paid between $120 and $150 per year in 1860. By contrast, free skilled workers could command wages of $197, so there was less incentive to hire them at these higher wages.[15] Enslaved people who hired their own time paid their owners a portion of their wages but were free to keep the rest. This arrangement afforded enslaved people the opportunity to function – more or less – as free people: they chose their employers, negotiated their own contracts and wages, moved about relatively freely, rented their own places, and had disposable income. Some even earned bonuses and payment for extra hours worked.[16] Most used that money efficiently and purchased their own freedom and/or the freedom of loved ones; others, especially those hired out in cities, squandered it on vices.

As a carpenter who hired out his time, John Williams improved his and his family's life circumstances. The Williams family did not eat their owners' leftovers or scraps of stale food. Instead, they went to the market to purchase their own food and had the dignity of choosing what they ate daily. They enjoyed food such as sausage, cabbage, tomatoes, potatoes, soup, apple dumplings, and chitterlings, and sometimes luxuries such as sirloin steak.[17] The diversity of the family's dietary options stands in stark comparison to the weekly ration of a peck of cornmeal and pork lard enslaved people received in rural Virginia. Other proof of their relatively high standard of living is that the couple owned more than two changes of clothing each.[18]

Hiring one's time slowly weakened the hires' ties to slavery; it made them anxious for freedom and increasingly discontented with their enslaved status. With so much at stake, why would slaveholders hire out their enslaved people? Most resorted to this practice because of financial insecurity. Allowing workers to hire their time could bring in additional income when needed. Second, slaveowners whose people hired their own time did not need to provide food, clothing, or medical care for them. Finally, owners could escape taxes during the time their enslaved workers were hired out to others.[19] For families like the Winstons who owned skilled artisans, that ownership could prove rather lucrative in the Richmond market. John Williams worked for other people during the day throughout the week, but lived above the Winston kitchen with his family.[20]

In addition to the Williams family, other enslaved people boarded at the Winston home. This arrangement was not unusual in antebellum Richmond: by 1840, it was common for enslaved people to live separately from their owners.[21] Other enslaved people who resided at the Winston home included Nelly Scott, the Winston's twenty-three-year-old cook who was owned by Lavinia Pankey, Virginia Winston's sister. A slaveowner named Richard Archer owned Nelly's husband, Joseph Scott, who also hired his time to others. He had been hired out to a family in Manchester, Virginia, in northern Chesterfield County at the time of the murders; although he did not live at the Winston home, he spent a great deal of time there visiting his wife. The Scotts' room was located near the kitchen. Anna, another enslaved woman, lived in the Winston home in a room above the couple's bedroom. Her owner was a Mrs. Austin who lived in Buckingham, Virginia. It is not clear why the Winstons boarded these other people in their home, but they possibly earned extra money doing so. Although they did not own Anna or the Scotts, the Winstons, nonetheless, exercised a measure of authority over them, including the right to chastise and whip them.[22]

According to neighbors' accounts, the enslaved people who resided in the home not only did not get along with each other but also some had serious contempt for the Winstons. Nelly indicated that although she and Anna had grown up together in the same household, they did not like one another. Anna revealed that there was bad blood between her and the Williamses. Jane admitted that she "did not approve of all Anna did." The household dynamics between the enslaved people seem to be a mirror reflection of the dynamics between them and the Winstons. There was a great deal of antipathy, hostility, distrust, and ill will all the way around. The enslaved people who resided on the property had frequently resisted the Winstons' authority. They made threats, talked back, refused to be whipped, and ran away. For example, Anna had run away two days before the incident in response to being whipped by Joseph Winston. Jane claimed that Anna had also threated Winston that night before she left. Allegedly, Anna said she would "fix" anyone who "interfered" with her.[23] None of the enslaved people in the household were exempt from this rebellious behavior or animosity towards the Winstons. At the very least, this resistance suggests that the Winstons had problems exerting their authority.

Jane and John Williams' defiant spirits, though, eclipsed those of the others who resided on the property. Nelly indicated that Jane Williams and her husband had "some difficulty" with Virginia Winston. Anna echoed that assessment, saying that she heard Jane say that "she did not like Mrs. Winston and never would." Anna also claimed that John recently told her "he did not like master Joe, and never would."[24] John confirmed that his wife was unhappy in the household and had once requested to be sold. Outsiders confirmed that the Williams couple had problems with their owners. John's multiple employers revealed his long history of defiance. For example, John Wortham, who had hired him in 1851 to work at T. J. Glenn & Co., claimed that he had been difficult and violent for the duration of his employment. Wortham also stated that John had complained to him that Joseph Winston was abusive and gave him "too much work." Wortham said he advised John to speak to Winston to get some relief from the workload. According to Wortham, John replied that he would not speak to his owner, but in veiled terms declared that he would "put an end to it." When Wortham pressed him on what he meant by that comment, Williams said that he "knew and would do it." Wortham concluded that Williams intended to harm Winston. Wortham also testified that he was troubled by John Williams' menacing behavior throughout his employment, testifying that he once had to pull a knife on Williams to prevent him from killing him with a hammer. James Green, another man who hired John Williams, said that he was a "turbulent and refractory," "insolent," and "dangerous man." Green explained that he did not whip Williams out of fear he would burn his house down, so he fired him instead. John Enders, whose father previously owned John, reported that his father sold him because he threatened to kill a white man. Jane's previous resistance was not quite as explicit as her husband's, but seems consistent with other enslaved women – talking back, having a sullen attitude, work slowdowns and so on.[25]

As a literate man who hired his own time, it is not surprising that John Williams was difficult to manage. He had tasted a kind of freedom, which made him discontented with his enslaved status. Another enslaved literate artisan who hired out his time also became discontented with slavery in Richmond five decades earlier. In that case, Gabriel and other enslaved artisans were so discontented that they planned a slave revolt scheduled for August 30, 1800. John Williams did not go that far, but his defiance threatened white men with power, and therefore the social and racial order. His very lengthy history of insubordinate, threatening, and defiant behavior brought a spotlight to bear on him and his wife, casting the mantle of suspicion of murder on to them.[26]

A coroner's inquest began at the Richmond City Hall within hours of the discovery of the gruesome scene. In the nineteenth century, it was customary for a coroner's inquest to be held after a murder. The purpose of the inquest was to gather evidence from the scene and testimony from witnesses. Then, coroners did much of the investigatory work to determine the means and circumstances of the murder and culpable party. Coroners could also impanel a jury to assist in the questioning and cross-examining of witnesses, which is what happened in the Winston case. Physicians, John's former employers, neighbors, and their enslaved people were interviewed about what they had seen that morning and what they knew about the Winston household, in general. John's former employers spoke negatively about his behavior under their employ. As white employers, these witnesses held a great deal of power in shaping how the suspects were viewed by the courts, even in the coroner's inquest jury. Again, the jury already suspected John, which is why they selected these witnesses in the first place. Other people living at the home were questioned and vigorously cross-examined about the Williamses, in particular, their history, and everything they had witnessed since the previous evening.[27]

Beginning with their own preconceived belief about the Williams' guilt and operating on the thinnest circumstantial evidence, the inquest jury concluded that the couple had committed the murders. The Williams' history of alleged verbal threats and comments about not liking their owners made them the likeliest of suspects in the minds of the inquest jurors. Another factor that led the jury to limit their scope was that there was no sign of forcible entry to the home. This led them to conclude that the person or people who committed the murders resided within the home. Thirdly, the jurors believed Jane Williams' behavior that morning to be suspicious: she discovered the couple, but did not sound the alarm. They also found it fishy that she had broken from her usual patterns in the weeks preceding the murders. According to Anna, Jane had changed the time she went into the Winston bedroom each day, going earlier than usual. Jane's established new pattern caused Anna and the inquest jurors to believe it pointed to her guilt. Finally, Nelly testified that although her mistress rang the bell every morning for Jane, that morning she did not – the implication being that Jane had curiously gone to the room despite not hearing the bell.

Other circumstantial evidence that contemporary people assumed indicated guilt was the Williams' demeanor after the Winstons were discovered. By all accounts, the couple lacked human empathy for the Winstons – even as they lay suffering from their injuries. Nelly Scott testified that "Jane did not appear to be much affected by the death[s] ..." Joseph Scott observed that Jane "looked serious, but not distressed" by the scene. A dozen white neighbors who went to the scene were directly asked about Jane's demeanor. Nicholas Wellington noted that she "appeared sullen." William Gwathmey recalled that Jane seemed "unconcerned"; David A. Brown testified that she looked "totally indifferent about the affair," so much so that he did not even know that Jane lived in the Winston home. John Blair testified that Jane "manifested a great want (lack) of feeling," and Joseph's brother, Bickerton, recalled that Jane showed "no sympathy," but added that she and her husband seemed restless. To Lucy Taylor and Anna Smith, owned by Samuel Greenhow, she was "very much composed, and not excited as they expected." Another observer concluded that the couple was "wholly destitute of the ordinary feelings of humanity."[28] For these witnesses, the Williamses lacked appropriate emotions of compassion and empathy for their owners, which was itself proof of guilt.

Jane's testimony before the coroner's inquest jury proved to be her undoing. As the infant's nurse, she routinely entered the Winston bedroom early in the mornings. She testified that when she entered the Winstons' bedroom that morning, she heard belabored breathing in the dark room, but assumed one of the members of the family was just snoring; she claimed she did not immediately suspect anything was wrong. Jane testified that she went to the couple's bed that morning and picked the infant up from between its parents as she usually did, but noticed that the baby was limp. She said that she opened the blinds to see what was wrong with the baby and that was when she saw all the blood on the bed. She put the baby down, went downstairs, and alerted Nelly who had also just begun her chores. Nelly then rushed outside, spreading the alarm through the neighborhood.[29]

Although the circumstantial evidence in the case was built around the Williams' history of resistance and their lack of appropriate affect after the discovery of the family, her lies and the physical evidence pointing to her culpability were insurmountable. When authorities searched the living quarters of the enslaved people, they found a hatchet and pieces of Mrs. Winston's wig – along with what people assumed was brain matter, but was later determined to be only flesh – in a bucket of dirty water in the Williams' room. In the corner of the same room, hidden behind a chest and beneath a pair of boots was another hatchet with "fresh" blood on the handle. When questioned about the hatchet, Jane denied that it belonged to her husband. Yet John Williams and Nelly Scott identified the hatchet as his. Jane claimed the blood on it had come from the sirloin she purchased from the market the previous day. When asked what she had done with the meat, she claimed she cut it up and made soup, which she claimed her husband and another man had eaten the previous evening. Several people who worked at the market were summoned and testified that they never saw a woman fitting Jane's distinctive physical description – a mulatto woman with one eye – at the market that day. Moreover, when asked to point to where she had cut the beef, she pointed to a windowsill, but there were no cut marks in the wood. Additionally, the Scotts testified that they did not see Jane make soup. Even John Williams attested that he never saw his wife go to the market and had not seen or eaten any soup that day. He also testified that he had never seen her use the hatchet to cut meat as she had claimed.[30]

There were additional holes in Jane's testimony. She claimed several windows and the front door were open when she arrived in the main house for work that morning. Everyone else who rushed to the home indicated that all the windows and doors except the one to the dining room were shut and locked when they arrived. Jane's lies were so obvious that police officer John B. Yarrington claimed that while in custody, her own husband remarked that "she did it." When the inquest jury recalled John Williams to explain why he said that, he clarified what he meant, "I never did say that my wife committed the murder. I believe she ought to know of it. She goes into the house early and must have known something of it, if any one on the lot committed the murder. I can't say that she did it or that any one was with her to help her do it." He added, "If I, or my wife had committed the murder, and I knew it, I would tell you."[31] At this point, John Williams had started to realize that his wife was involved.

Using the only "scientific" methodology available in the mid-nineteenth century, investigators determined that the hatchet was the murder weapon by comparing the measurement of the Winstons' wounds with the width of the hatchet blades. There appeared to be a match. Moreover, blood was found on both sides of the stairway leading up to the Williams' room. Finally, they found a striped dress with blood on its sleeve in the couple's living quarters. Jane admitted that the dress was hers and that she had it on when she discovered the Winstons. She explained that she may have gotten blood splatter on the sleeve by ripping the covers off their bodies. To account for why she had changed her clothes, Jane testified that she changed out of that dress before being taken to jail, presumably to be presentable in court.[32]

When the inquest jury re-examined Jane, she added a new element to her testimony. She claimed that she had forgotten about a male visitor Anna had who became upset that Winston would not allow him into his home. According to Jane, Anna's visitor said that if it happened again, he would "knock Winston in the head." This is a pretty significant addition to her testimony and only came after her own husband's damning testimony. Clearly, Jane was attempting to shift the suspicion to Anna's mysterious visitor. One of the inquest jurors must have asked Jane whether she liked the Winston baby and being enslaved to the family because she replied, "The child was a good child – not fretful." She followed with, "I liked my home very well. Sometimes I did ask to her [Virginia Winston] to sell me, but not lately." Although Jane attempted to convince the inquest jury that she was content under the Winstons' authority, asking to be sold certainly reflects some frustration with one's situation.[33] During her final interview with the inquest jury, Jane stated in no uncertain terms, "I have no confession to make, as I have told the truth."[34]

Anna, the last person interviewed by the inquest jury, flatly denied Jane's allegations about her visitor. In fact, she is the first and only person who bluntly told the inquest jury that she believed Jane and John Williams had the motive and the character to have committed the murders, "I strongly suspect John and Jane of committing the murder. I suspect Jane because she always had such bitter feelings toward Mrs. W. and her child. I heard that she was suspected of poisoning the other child of Mr. W's that died. I suspect John because he never liked Mr. Winston. I have not heard that Jane and John had anything to do with the murder. My opinion is formed independent of what I heard in the street." Anna offered the jury a motive: she contended that Jane was upset with the Winstons because they threatened to sell her without her child. She added, "Jane says she never forgets or forgives anything done to her," and that threat of sale was a sore spot. In other words, Jane held grudges.[35]

Not only did Anna implicate the couple in the Winston deaths, but she also accused Jane of poisoning the Winstons' first daughter two years prior – a death that people assumed had been due to natural causes. In many ways, Anna's inflammatory accusations may have been the most damaging to the Williams. After her testimony, the coroner's inquest jury concluded that the deaths of Virginia Winston and her child came by the hands of Jane and John Williams.[36] With her arrest for those murders, Jane became part of a very small group of just thirteen enslaved women ever charged with murder in Richmond. Eleven of those thirteen were accused of murdering an infant; and just a few of those were charged with killing their *owner's* infant.[37]

Although Jane and John Williams were the most obvious culprits, others residing in the Winston home could possibly have committed the murders. Anna also had a motive. She did not like the Winstons, either, and by all accounts resented a recent whipping. Moreover, a huge block of her time was unaccounted for. She had stayed at a white woman's home on Cary Street on Saturday night; this may be understood as a brothel, for these were common on that street – in Richmond in the 1850s, the phrase "Cary Street woman" was a euphemism for prostitutes who worked that street. By Anna's own admission, on Sunday night, she had slept with a white man at a tobacco factory. Afterwards, she claimed she just "walked about" in the wee hours of the morning.[38] Despite the fact that she had been roaming the streets alone precisely at the same time as the murders, the coroner's jury did not consider her a suspect and, therefore, did not ask her to elaborate on her whereabouts; nor did the jury interrogate her thoroughly about her own possible motives. Anna had just as much motive, access, and opportunity to murder as anyone in the home that night. Nelly also had the opportunity to commit the murders. John Williams testified that she had slept in the kitchen that night – unusual for her. He also said that when he came into the kitchen, a healthy fire was going, indicating that Nelly had been awake at least a couple of hours. Nelly also claimed that her husband had gone on errands on the morning of the murders. It is not feasible that Joseph would have gone on errands before 4:00 a.m. so Nelly clearly lied about that. She testified that after his errands her husband went to work. Joseph Scott himself did not testify that he had gone on errands that morning.[39] The inquest jury never explored any of these other people with motive and opportunity. Of course, there is a small possibility that all the enslaved people in the Winston home conspired to kill them together.

Within a few days of the conclusion of the inquest, Jane Williams received a visit from Reverend Robert Ryland, the pastor of the African Baptist Church to which she and her family belonged. The African Baptist Church, established in 1841, was one of four Black churches in Richmond by the time of the Winston murders. The churches were not fully independent, though, because Virginia law required that these bodies be led by white ministers. The white First Baptist Church had appointed Ryland to lead the African Baptist Church. He supported slavery and used the pulpit to indoctrinate his flock not to resist slavery. For example, Ryland preached that enslaved people should be obedient to their masters.[40] In response to Nat Turner's revolt, after 1832, Virginia denied enslaved people accused of murder access to clergy so Ryland's call was unofficial. During Ryland's visit, Jane Williams allegedly confessed to the murders of the Winston mother and child and to inflicting Mr. Winston's injuries.

Despite his using Christianity to keep African Americans compliant under white authority, Reverend Ryland would have enjoyed great deference from his Black parishioners as a man of God. They would have held him in high regard and complied with his directives. It was, perhaps, a little too convenient that Ryland would have elicited a confession. Surely, the news that a member of his congregation murdered her owner's wife and child would have sent alarms through the white parishioners of the parent church and would have caused them to question his capacity to effectively guide Black members. Jane had claimed her innocence up until that visit by Reverend Ryland, suggesting he might have pressured her to confess. He claimed that Jane told him that she wanted to "make . . . peace with God," confessed, and accepted the inevitability that she would be hanged (Figure 5.3). The following day the jailer claimed she also made a full confession to him:

> She said that a little before daybreak, and in advance of her usual hour of rising, she rose without disturbing her husband, procured the broad edged hatchet, entered the house, proceeded to Mr. Winston's room and commenced her fiendish labors by knocking Mr. Winston senseless. He scarcely struggled. On leaving him she stepped around the bed, and commenced cutting into the head of Mrs. Winston. Mrs. W's struggles were so great that Jane said she inflicted stronger and more frequent blows upon her head than she did upon Mr. W's in order to silence her quickly. She then killed the infant, washed off the blood and laid it in the cradle. She then washed the blood off the hatchet, hid it, and then gave the alarm.[41]

Jane's third-party confession reveals that although she hit Joseph first, Virginia Winston received the brunt of the attack. She received more blows than her husband and daughter combined. Jane mutilated her. If Virginia Winston relied on violence to enforce her authority and dominance over Jane, it should not be surprising that Jane spoke that same language.

One wonders if Virginia was the real target and the other two Winstons merely collateral damage? What insults and assaults had Jane suffered at Virginia Winston's hands? Is she the one who

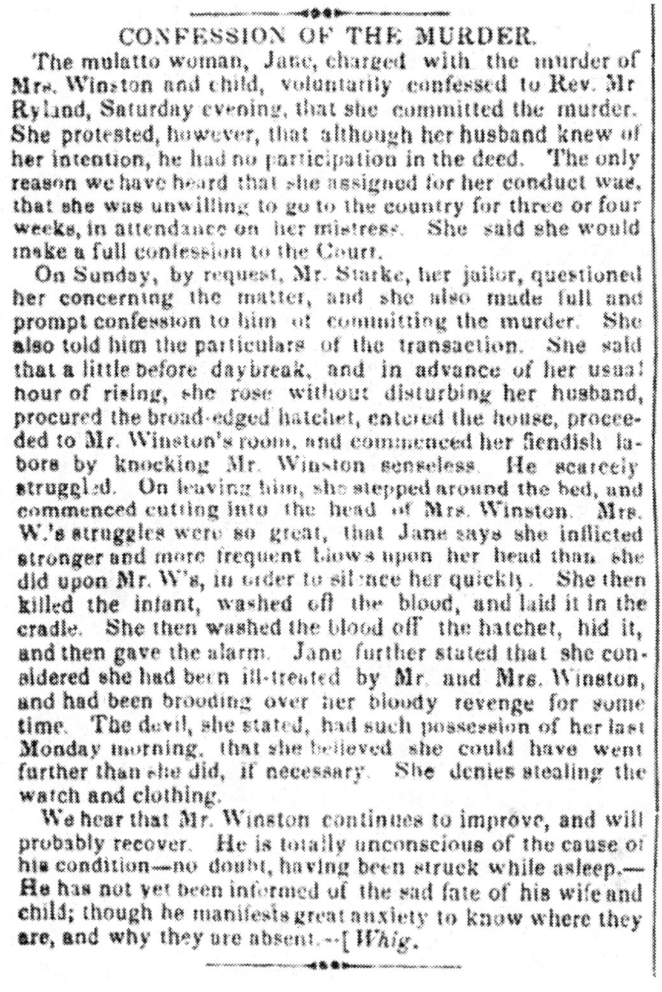

CONFESSION OF THE MURDER.

The mulatto woman, Jane, charged with the murder of Mrs. Winston and child, voluntarily confessed to Rev. Mr Ryland, Saturday evening, that she committed the murder. She protested, however, that although her husband knew of her intention, he had no participation in the deed. The only reason we have heard that she assigned for her conduct was, that she was unwilling to go to the country for three or four weeks, in attendance on her mistress. She said she would make a full confession to the Court.

On Sunday, by request, Mr. Starke, her jailor, questioned her concerning the matter, and she also made full and prompt confession to him of committing the murder. She also told him the particulars of the transaction. She said that a little before daybreak, and in advance of her usual hour of rising, she rose without disturbing her husband, procured the broad-edged hatchet, entered the house, proceeded to Mr. Winston's room, and commenced her fiendish labors by knocking Mr. Winston senseless. He scarcely struggled. On leaving him, she stepped around the bed, and commenced cutting into the head of Mrs. Winston. Mrs. W.'s struggles were so great, that Jane says she inflicted stronger and more frequent blows upon her head than she did upon Mr. W's, in order to silence her quickly. She then killed the infant, washed off the blood, and laid it in the cradle. She then washed the blood off the hatchet, hid it, and then gave the alarm. Jane further stated that she considered she had been ill-treated by Mr. and Mrs. Winston, and had been brooding over her bloody revenge for some time. The devil, she stated, had such possession of her last Monday morning, that she believed she could have went further than she did, if necessary. She denies stealing the watch and clothing.

We hear that Mr. Winston continues to improve, and will probably recover. He is totally unconscious of the cause of his condition—no doubt, having been struck while asleep.— He has not yet been informed of the sad fate of his wife and child; though he manifests great anxiety to know where they are, and why they are absent.—[*Whig.*

Figure 5.3 Confession of Jane Williams
Credit: *Richmond Enquirer*, July 30, 1852. Library of Virginia

had injured Jane so badly that she lost her eye? Had she humiliated and embarrassed Jane as a mother by name-calling, slapping, or whipping her in front of her daughter? How many times was Jane forced to neglect her own daughter in favor of her owners' children? How many times had she left her child alone above the kitchen while tending to countless and endless demands from Virginia Winston?

How many times had Virginia threatened to sell Jane's daughter for one minor infraction or another? Had Virginia already started working, insulting, and beating Jane's daughter – far earlier than enslaved children usually began work? Jane showed the world how much she hated Virginia Winston that fated day. Her hatred was so deep that it reverberates through time and space to shock modern readers.

According to her jailer, Mr. Starke, Jane told him she committed the murders because she had been "ill- treated" by the couple and had been "brooding over her bloody revenge for some time." Jane's tendency to nurse her grievances over long periods of time is consistent with what Anna revealed in her testimony before the coroner's inquest when she said Jane never "forgets or forgives anything." Select newspapers reported that John Williams admitted that Jane had "threatened to murder them [the Winstons] because they intended to send her to the country." The phrase, "send to the country" is a euphemism for returning her to a plantation – possibly the one owned by Joseph's father in Hanover County. The Winstons may have no longer been willing to deal with Jane. According to Wilmington, North Carolina's journal *Tri-Weekly Commercial*, John said he tried to reason with Jane about her plans. On one of the nights preceding the murders, he had been awakened by Jane fumbling around in the room. When he asked what she was doing, she replied, "I am looking for the hatchet."[42] Revenge is a powerful motivator; by all accounts both Winstons had done unforgivable things to her personally.

Jane used what she knew about the Winston household to her advantage in planning their murders. Enslaved women who worked inside homes had a high degree of intimate and personal knowledge of their owners' behavior, likes, and dislikes. They knew their bedtimes and how deeply they slept. They knew where they kept their valuables and their weapons. They knew which sides of the bed the wife and husband preferred. Armed with a desire to right some moral wrong, they could be quite dangerous to sleeping white slaveowners. Jane was familiar enough with the couple's bedroom and their sleeping patterns that she knew Virginia would not awaken easily, giving her time to kill Joseph Winston first.

Consistent with a Black feminist practice of justice, Jane's confession reflects a great deal of forethought and planning – even about details – including the time she would commit the murder, the weapon, and how she might escape suspicion. Jane's washing the baby and the hatchet and then hiding the hatchet afterwards indicates that she hoped to hide all evidence tying her to the crime. But, by hiding the ax in her own apartment and leaving the water she had used to wash it in plain sight, she made critical errors.[43] Regardless, her deliberate efforts to lie and hide evidence suggest that she believed she could get away with murder.

Also consistent with the aspects of a Black feminist practice of justice, Jane alone determined the targets and proportionality of her vengeful act. She allegedly told the jailer that "the devil ... had possession of her that morning" and "she believed she could have gone further than she did, 'if necessary.'" Jane essentially admitted here that she was prepared to inflict worse damage on the couple if they had resisted.[44] The crime scene made it clear that Jane felt no measure of restraint, regret, or mercy, even towards little Virginia: Jane bludgeoned her as if she had been washed in the deeds of her parents and was fully deserving of a share of their "just deserts." The truth is, though, Jane might have seen the little girl as the embodiment of her oppression, given the endless work needed to care for her.

After the coroner's inquest jury charged Jane and John Williams with murder and conspiracy to commit murder, Anna and the Scotts were released from jail and returned home. Jane and John Williams were retained and sent to the mayor's court. The primary objective of the mayor's court was to deter crime. Most enslaved people brought before this court were accused of minor offenses. Richmond's mayor, Joseph Mayo, determined whether they would be punished or have their cases discharged. Those deemed guilty were publicly whipped. In some ways, this court might be considered an extension of the slaveholders' authority. At the very least, it copied their manner of punishment. In murder cases, the mayor would indict the accused and then send the case to the hustings court as Mayor Mayo did.[45]

The hustings court[46] adjudicated criminal cases in Richmond. Enslaved people were tried in special sessions of the court, called oyer and terminer. Instead of juries, enslaved people charged with felonies went before five justices of the peace in Virginia's oyer and terminer courts. As James M. Campbell asserts, these courts institutionalized and codified injustice within their structure. This egregious violation of due process was rare in the rest of the United States at the time. In the antebellum era, only Virginia, South Carolina, and Louisiana denied enslaved people the right to a trial by jury. Other slave states had decades earlier replaced colonial practices that mandated that slaveowners oversee such cases. North Carolina, for one, ceased this practice in 1816.[47]

Other violations of due process were endemic in these courts. Although court-appointed attorneys were assigned to all defendants, the law dictated that the trials be held five to ten days after an indictment, which was not enough time to reasonably prepare a case. Second, these courts allowed confessions of any stripe as evidence. In other words, even confessions obtained through violence were admissible. Moreover, the standard for a guilty verdict was not "beyond a reasonable doubt"; prosecutors only had to prove *probable* guilt. To its credit, Virginia allowed Black people, enslaved and free, to testify in these courts.[48]

Jane Williams' trial began on August 9, 1852, in the hustings court. The justices assigned to the case were Evans, Cowles, Inloes, Bernard, Farrar, Bray, and Wingfield – two more than the five outlined in the law. Her pleading guilty negated the necessity of a trial. No witnesses were called by the prosecution. Her court-appointed defense attorney, J. H. Gilmer, insisted that she had acted alone. Because of her guilty plea, Jane Williams was summarily sentenced to die on September 10, 1852, between 10:00 a.m. and 2:00 p.m. State law mandated that justices of oyer and terminer unanimously condemn enslaved people to death. Jane's death sentence is no surprise in Virginia, which was notoriously hard on enslaved people's misbehavior. Even the crime of assaulting a white person with an *intent* to kill or injure could result in a sentence of death or transportation out of state. In the antebellum era, there were just three ways to escape a death sentence: an 1801 law gave the Virginia governor the option of sale and transportation out of the Commonwealth instead of execution; the governor could grant a pardon in cases involving torture of the defendant; or he could grant a stay of execution. Despite the availability of those options, 454 enslaved people were still condemned to execution.[49]

Jane remained adamant that her husband had not helped her commit the murders and had no advanced knowledge of her doing so. Despite her best efforts, jurors were not inclined to believe that her husband had not been involved. Most men in the mid-nineteenth century would have been unlikely to believe that an enslaved Black woman could plan and execute a double homicide alone and without the knowledge and assistance of a man. They would not expect a Black woman to have the intellect or the strength to execute such a crime. John was charged with murder and conspiracy to commit murder.[50]

On September 10, the morning of Jane's execution, Reverend Ryland met her at her jail cell and prayed with her. Dressed in white, Jane Williams was driven to the gallows in a four-horse wagon at 10:00 a.m. Public executions of enslaved people who killed their owners were performative events with private prayers, processions to the gallows, speeches, public prayers, final public confessions, and sometimes public desecration of the body post-execution (as was done with Mark's body in Charlestown). A crowd of 6,000 went to witness Jane Williams' execution. The large size of the crowd – just as with Phillis and Mark – suggests that there was public thirst for the spectacle of execution of enslaved people who resisted slavery. Many in Jane's crowd were African Americans, though, who may have come out of curiosity or support for her. Reverend Ryland delivered a sermon for the crowd in which he stated, "if she had three lives instead of one, they should all be taken to pay the penalty of her wicked and bloody deeds."[51] Ironically, the minister's words bore an air of condemnation – not the genuine support and absolute forgiveness one would expect from a man of God. They also reflect his own belief in retributive justice. When he finished the sermon, Ryland asked Jane a final question seeking names of accomplices, Jane answered simply, "No one." Jane Williams was hanged at 11:00 a.m.[52]

Apparently, it was rare for enslaved people to be convicted of murder in antebellum Richmond owing to the pressures brought by the slaveowners who did not want to lose them. According to James M. Campbell, between 1830 and 1860, of the thirty-one enslaved people indicted for murder in those years, only sixteen were convicted. Campbell determined that women, who accounted for a higher proportion of enslaved defendants charged with murder in that city, were less likely than men to be convicted. Of the enslaved women indicted on murder charges, most were charged with killing their own children. Only two of thirteen enslaved women were charged with murdering a white person. Black male murderers were considered more threatening than females in antebellum Richmond.[53] Jane was one of the unlucky ones convicted of murder.

Ten days after Jane's execution, Reverend Ryland revealed that she had confessed to him that she had previously killed another Winston infant, Lavinia – just as Anna had claimed. No one had suspected murder in Lavinia's death, so Jane's confession came as quite a surprise in Richmond. Reverend Ryland reported that she confessed to administering bed-bug poison to "hasten the end of the sickly child's life." Jane reportedly told him she wanted to use the infant to test the strength of the poison and its potential effectiveness in killing the entire family. This confession suggests Jane and been actively planning to kill the family longer than anyone had known. The *Richmond Dispatch* reported that the family dog also met an untimely and sudden end after suffering from convulsions. The paper speculated, "it is supposed that Jane tried one of her hellish experiments on [the dog]."[54] For whatever reason, she abandoned poison as a means of killing the family.

Although Jane had been highly forthcoming about why she wanted to kill the Winston couple, both she and the historical record remain silent about why she killed their second daughter, Virginia. After all, during the inquest, she had stated that little Virginia was not a problem: the baby was not fussy and did not require her to wake up too early. Jane found her to be "a good child – not fretful." Given that little Virginia's skull had been crushed, Jane clearly resented both slain daughters, the work required to care for them, and what they represented as the children of her enslavers. Fearing that she would be lynched, Jane reputedly begged Ryland not to divulge her confession until after she had been executed. He honored that promise.[55]

Still, it is unsettling that Ryland bore witness to two separate confessions by Jane Williams. This is not to suggest that she did not authentically confess to him, but to question whether her confession had been coerced by the power imbalance between them. Confessions such as hers, which occur within established power relations – Jane as a Black, enslaved woman and Ryland as the white, male minister of her church – typically benefit the powerful. Still, Jane gained nothing tangible from these confessions: for example, Ryland did not use them to advocate for leniency or to increase public sympathy for either her or John. Instead, these confessions served to reassure white Christians that Ryland was a good minister and that his flock was under control.

Apparently, a significant portion of the Black community supported Jane Williams – long after her execution. The *Richmond Dispatch* editorialized that too many in the Black community had made sympathetic comments about Jane, such as "she has gone home" and "she is in glory." In other words, these people did not think Jane had been condemned to hell for her actions. The editorial also complained that one person had even declared that "her seat is far higher in Heaven than that of Mrs. Winston." This comment is most telling because it implies that Virginia Winston had not been a good person. Unwilling to consider the possibility that Jane had wide support and sympathy after her execution because the Black community felt she had been mistreated, the editorialist concluded, instead, that "there is a better need of religious instruction" for Blacks in the city. The editorial mentions Ryland and the African Baptist Church by name and implores them to correct the prevailing belief that once people are baptized, they are saved from hell regardless of their crimes.[56]

John Williams' trial began on September 14, 1852, just four days after his wife's execution. He faced two charges, including murder and conspiracy to commit murder. Unlike his wife, he never confessed. Instead, when asked for his plea, he firmly responded "Not Guilty."

The state's witnesses included Nelly and Joseph Scott, John's former employers, the Winstons' neighbors, physicians who examined their bodies, and people from the judicial system including the jailer and sheriff. In addition, there were two new witnesses who had never given statements previously – namely, Joseph Winston and his sister-in-law, Lavinia Pankey. Joseph Winston reportedly looked "pale and dejected" as he approached the witness stand. After spending more than a week in a coma, he had learned the details of the murders on June 30. According to the *Richmond Dispatch*, Winston "manifested the utmost astonishment at the conduct of his servants, and protested that they had done this foul deed without cause." By the time he testified at the inquest, he still had no memory of the night in question. He, instead, testified about an incident a week earlier when he heard someone at his back dining room door around midnight. When he raised his bedroom window and looked out, he saw only Jane. When he called down to her, she explained that she had come down to the dining room to lock the door. Winston's testimony implied that Jane (and John) Williams might have been trying to get into the home to kill him and his wife that night. Virginia's sister, Lavinia Pankey, corroborated Winston's testimony because she had been in the home that night and witnessed the exchange. Bickerton L. Winston, Joseph's brother, testified that John Williams' face "exhibited shame and guilt." He also testified that John had failed to clean Joseph's boots on the morning of the murders as he typically had done. He believed that oversight proved John had been otherwise occupied and, therefore, guilty. Bickerton also added that the work clothes John had worn the week prior to the murders were missing. Although neither Bickerton nor Virginia's sister added anything substantive to the state's case against John Williams, their testimony carried a great deal of power as a victim, victim's brother, and sister of the deceased.[57]

More flimsy "evidence" was introduced into this trial, just as it had been in the inquest. John's former employers cast him in a disparaging light. Dr. Bolton and Francis J. Deane, the wife of Dr. T. J. Deane, testified that baby Virginia had been killed with "some broad, blunt weapon," such as a wooden roller. The weapon was never found or identified. Neither witness could definitively say with what the infant had been killed, but they concluded that because John Williams was a carpenter, he must have made a weapon "for some murderous purpose." An early newspaper account of the murder speculated that the infant's injuries could have been done with "the eye and butt end of the hatchet." James Lyons, the prosecuting attorney, then submitted evidence from letters found when searching the couple's room. The letters apparently had been written by John to Jane while he lived in South Carolina. Mr. Lyons read the letters in court, because he believed they included "some ambiguous terms referring to a previous subject of conversation and to some hidden motives." G. W. H. Tyler, a police officer who searched John and Jane's room and found the letters, testified that he asked John what he meant when he wrote the sentence, "think of what he had been talking about." Tyler testified that John replied that it was a private matter. Tyler testified that he then asked John about the phrase "prudent exertion." John told him his friend wrote the letter, implying the words were not even his own. Those letters are a ridiculous body of evidence to our modern sensibilities, but to whites hoping to convict John Williams, the words he used in letters to his wife years earlier were sufficient "evidence." At the very least, they do illustrate that assertive language coming from the hand of an enslaved man was deemed threatening. John did not testify in his own trial.[58]

John Williams was defended by John H. Gilmer, the same court-appointed attorney who had represented Jane. He did not offer much of a defense: Gilmer did not cross-examine *anyone*, protest the inclusion of love letters between the Williamses as evidence, and offered no alternative theory. It is not clear if his failures were owing to a lack of competence or will. Contemporary reports stated that Gilmer "spoke at some length" in his closing statement, but a lengthy close is not a defense. The justices swiftly and unanimously convicted John Williams of murder. When asked whether he had any comments about the death sentence that would be imposed, John Williams "arose and with much agitation, declared that he was innocent of the crime charged against him – said that the [weapons] found in his room, were [tools of] . . . his trade and that he used them for no other purpose." His insistence mattered to no one in that courtroom. Rather than let the state execute him, white male spectators instead "talked strenuously of taking John out and hanging him in advance." The lynching never happened; the execution did.[59]

John Williams met the same fate as his wife on Friday, October 22, 1852.

. . .

In many ways, Jane Williams is the embodiment of centuries of slaveowners' fears that they would be bludgeoned to death in their beds as they slept. She is not the only enslaved woman who used an ax to kill her enslavers this way. One of the earliest instances dates back to colonial New York when an unnamed enslaved woman and Sam, her Native American husband, conspired to kill their owners "because they were restrained from going abroad on Sabbath." In January 1708, in what is now Queens, New York, the couple used an ax to kill their owners, William and Sarah Hallett – who was pregnant – and their five children as they slept.

It was the area's first capital crime and one of the most brutal murders in colonial America, The couple ran to their neighbors and claimed that strangers had murdered everyone in the home, and they had barely escaped the murderers themselves. They eventually confessed. Sam was charged with murder, but his wife was charged with the higher charge of *petit treason*. The reason for these charge differentials may be because of race or because officials believed the woman to be the mastermind. Sam was executed by hanging and placed in a gibbet, but his wife was burned at the stake.[60]

Still others used axes while their owners were awake. Phereby, an Alabama woman living in slavery in Fayette County, Alabama, struck her owner, Elizabeth Sheppard, twice in the back of her head with an ax in January 1849. Sheppard died of her injuries. The following year, in Prince William County, Virginia, Agness, an enslaved woman, was indicted, convicted, and executed for killing her owner, Gerald Mason, with an ax as he slept. By all accounts, Agness had been upset that her owner had ordered his foreman to whip her two weeks earlier. Agness allegedly told other enslaved people that she would kill anyone who attempted to whip her again and would "knock [Mason] in the head with a club" if he "laid hands on her." In other words, the murder had been a premeditated retaliation for physical abuse. In her trial, several white witnesses testified that when they arrived on the scene on the day of the murder, Agness told them Mason had called her a "damned bitch" and had attempted to "turn up her clothes and take privilege with her" – a reference to attempted rape. The multiple motives Agness provided all center on revenge and stopping specific forms of abuse, including rape and beatings. Her self-defense in her trial ended up being an exercise in futility in Virginia slave courts, which were presided over by slaveowners. Agness was executed on July 16, 1850.[61]

That same month and year, in Jasper County, Mississippi, an enslaved woman named Cecily used a broad-ax to attack her owner, Dr. Longon, his wife, and children as they slept. Cecily's blow to Dr. Longon was so hard that she decapitated him. In her matter-of-fact confession to the crime at her execution two years later, Cecily said that when Mrs. Longon awoke and attempted to escape into the yard, she felled her with a "chunk" and then chopped her about her head until she died. She then returned inside, intending to kill both children. One child died, but the second survived her gruesome injuries. Cecily initially told the neighbors a tale about five men entering the home with the intention of robbing Dr. Longon, who ended up killing the family in the process, with her barely escaping with her life. However, Cecily's bloody footprints were found throughout the house, implicating her as the killer.[62] In Dallas in May 1853, Jane (Elkins), an enslaved woman, was indicted, convicted, and executed for bludgeoning her employer, Andrew C. Wisdom, to death with an ax as he slept.[63] In 1857 in Salisbury, North Carolina, John and Fanny Haney were hacked to death with an ax by their enslaved people as they slept. John was discovered in his home with a broken neck and bashed skull. Fanny escaped and ran seventy-five yards from the home when she was felled by an ax, suffering blows to her head and shoulders.[64]

With few exceptions, axes are the deadliest weapons enslaved women used to kill their owners. They inflicted unbearable pain on their victims, face to face. One cannot ignore the gruesome nature of an ax murder, with brain matter, bone fragments, and pieces of flesh scattered through the room. Each blow served as an indictment of these slaveowner's character; each "chunk" was a judgment on their abuse; each bone piece expelled from the victim's body was an execution of "wild justice." Jane Williams and the other enslaved women who bludgeoned their owners with axes as they slept prove that when revenge is the only form of available justice, the disempowered will seize it, without any ethical concern or constraints about the proportionality of the violence, the innocence of the victims, or the optics of the murder scene.

6 NELLY, BETSY, AND ELLEN
"We concluded to get rid of him . . . "

Revenge is simply justice with teeth

~ Simon R. Green

On the evening of December 24, 1856, Dr. Jesse Ewell, acting coroner of Prince William County, Virginia, arrived at George E. Green's farm. Green, a bachelor, had been found dead in his burning home by his neighbors, who then summoned the coroner. Dr. Ewell noted that "all that was visible," or remaining, of Green's body was "the charred spine & pelvis of an adult human body." In other words, Green's clothing, flesh, muscles, and most of his bones had been consumed in the fire by the time Dr. Ewell arrived at the property on Christmas Eve.

The cold weather and time of night prevented Dr. Ewell from doing an investigation that evening, but the following morning, he returned to the Green property to resume his work. Recounting the details of his investigation, he "discovered a spot in the road much trampled & smoothed over, with traces of blood" near the barn. He noted that a trail of blood led from that spot to the house which, to him, appeared to be the result of "a body having been dragged, marked also by spots of blood at intervals." Looking around the property, the coroner found additional clues that illuminated the circumstances leading to Green's untimely demise. He wrote, "The yard gate had one of the slats broken; the ketch which held the latch was split off. The cap of one of the gate posts was broken off and split, & the gate had other marks of violence on it."[1] It was clear to him that someone had murdered George E. Green during a violent struggle in his front yard, dragged his body to his home, and then set it on fire.

. . .

Prince William County, Virginia, was developed on land occupied for centuries by the Anacostan, Doeg, Iroquois, and Piscataway peoples. In 1649, the exiled King Charles II of England granted seven noblemen the "Northern Neck" or "Fairfax Proprietary," which roughly consisted of all Virginia lands from the Potomac to the Rappahannock rivers. More than twenty Virginia counties were carved from that land tract, including Fairfax and Prince William counties. Prince William County – named after King George's son Prince William – was officially established in 1731 on 2,000 square miles in the northeastern corner of the colony, bounded by the Occoquan River in the northeast and the Potomac in the southeast. The county is roughly thirty-five miles south of Washington, D.C.[2]

Prince William's first county seat was Dumfries, Virginia. The sale and shipment of tobacco became central to the booming economy of the town, a port city on the Potomac River. Dumfries' population and prosperity increased until well into the nineteenth century. Haymarket, Occoquan, and Brentsville began to rival Dumfries as high population centers in Prince William County in the early nineteenth century. Their growth coincided with a steady population decline in Dumfries. Consequently, the county seat was moved to the more populous Brentsville in 1822.

Tobacco was king in Virginia in the colonial era. The crop precipitated the economic growth of Prince William County's waterfront communities, generating a great deal of wealth for planters and even those who transported tobacco to other regions or across the Atlantic. Tobacco was so central to the colony's economy that it *became* the economy. At one point, tobacco was even used as currency to purchase goods, pay taxes and salaries, and satisfy other debts.[3] Just as tobacco was central to the regional economy so, too, were the enslaved people who worked the fields.

Tobacco exhausted the rich soil of the Chesapeake region over time. By the early nineteenth century, the effects of soil exhaustion meant a precipitous decline in tobacco farming and production. Many tobacco planters left the region for the virgin soil of lands further west. Others remained and adjusted by switching to different crops – grains. By the nineteenth century, wheat, oats, corn, and other grains replaced tobacco as the primary cash crop in the region. Prince William County farmers also sold hay and butter.[4] By 1850, the county boasted a fledging industry, including nineteen flour, grist, plaster, and sawmills, plus cotton and wool factories. In 1851, a railroad reached the town of Manassas. The county also boasted thirteen churches and educated 316 students in its public schools. In 1850, the population of 8,129 included 5,631 free people, including free Blacks. The enslaved population of Prince William County that same year was 2,498, or 31 percent of the total inhabitants.[5]

A decade later, Prince William County's population of 8,213 included 2,356 enslaved people. Prince William County's 357 slaveholders each owned an average of 6.6 enslaved people in 1860. They were largely small-middle slaveholders who worked alongside of and personally managed their enslaved and hired workers. In addition to the 2,356 regular enslaved people living in the county, Prince William County farmers also hired 202 enslaved workers from other counties. For example, James Havener hired fifteen enslaved people owned by J. B. Robertson of Alexandria to work his farm. Similarly, Alexander Hollyclaw hired all sixteen of his enslaved workers from William Gaines who resided in Warrenton, Virginia.[6]

By far, the biggest slaveholder in the county was William James Weir, who owned eighty people who worked on a nearly 1,600-acre plantation.[7] The second biggest slaveholder in Prince William County in the few years before the Civil War was Edward Berkeley, who owned fifty-two enslaved people.[8] Weir and Berkeley were the exceptions rather than the rule. Prince William County farming was dominated by small slaveholders, many of whom could never hope to become planters – people like George E. Green.

George E. Green had been born in Prince William County in 1802 to Sarah and James Green. He had at least one brother, James, who was nine years younger. George was a farmer and slaveowner, but also a schoolteacher, who held classes at his farm. George owned nine enslaved people, including five males and four females by 1830. Two decades later, in 1850, he and his brother lived together and owned seven enslaved people, which appear to be three generations of one family that included Nelly, aged fifty-four, her husband, aged fifty-three, their thirty-eight-year-old daughter Betsy, and Betsy's children, nine-year-old twins, Ellen and Elias, and eleven-year-old son, James, also known as Jim. There was one other unidentified enslaved twenty-one-year-old male residing on the Green property, who may have been Betsy's oldest son. According to the 1850 census, George owned real estate valued at $3,570 ($121,000 today); his brother James' real estate was valued at $5,000 ($169,000 today). By no means was either brother wealthy. By 1856, George E. Green lived alone on a 238-acre farm, six miles outside of Gainesville, Virginia.[9]

The biographical record of George E. Green before Christmas Eve 1856 is quite thin. He cohabited with his younger brother or lived near him all their lives, much like Henry Ormond. George never married and had no children. Physical descriptions of him indicate that he was fifty-four years old when he was murdered. A neighbor testified that he suffered from diseases, but was a "pretty stout man" who "weighed about 160 pounds." He was described as "tall" with "tolerably good muscles." He had been observed working on his farm regularly "when able."[10] Other than the physical description, Green is more historically invisible than his enslaved people. Ironically, this white slaveholding male only became more visible in the record as a result of the actions of his enslaved people.

The enslaved family Green owned had been with him at least six years, if not longer. They likely worked planting staple crops for their sustenance, such as potatoes and corn. Green also raised peanuts for profit, which the family would have been responsible for planting and harvesting. The women may have also served as house servants. Elias, one of the twins, was described by John B. Grayson as "the most intelligent of the set." He was, perhaps, Green's most trusted worker. Elias had been trusted to drive his owner's four-horse wagon alone to deliver the peanut crops to the railroad station eight miles away.[11] Elias, with his trusted position, enjoyed higher mobility than his family members, but that personal privilege did nothing for his loved ones. And apparently, it did not guarantee his loyalty to Green, either.

Although Green's farm is not listed in the 1850 non-population census, based on an extrapolation from other farmers in his vicinity, it is likely that he grew corn, oats, and wheat. Working on grain farms with few hands, Nelly's kin would have had an exhausting work regime, year-round and from sunrise to sunset, six days a week. Farm work, on the whole, was hard, labor-intensive and seemingly endless for Green's enslaved people.[12] Although large groups of enslaved workers were ideal for growing grains, small farmers such as Green expected his smaller workforce to do the same volume of work.[13] With such a heavy workload, Nelly and her kin would have worked from sunrise to sunset. In the summer, the workday could end as late as 8:00 p.m., which left little time for leisure activities or personal time. The only thing that made the work bearable was that they did it together as a three-generation family.

Nelly claimed that Green refused to allow them to leave his farm. His refusal seems to have been a misguided attempt to stifle any independence, while maintaining total control of his enslaved people. With the exception of Elias, Nelly and her family members were not permitted to leave their farm, which meant they were isolated from the rest of the slave community of Prince William County, Virginia. Green denied them the small privileges that other enslaved people could expect, including the right to visit friends and loved ones on other farms, attend parties and dances, church service, or even go to the market or waterfront. In the trial that was held later, one of Green's neighbors, Luther Lynn, stated that Nelly told him that Green had not let them "go to meeting," a reference to church services.[14] This family was significantly more confined to the farm than other enslaved people in the neighborhood.

Neighbors also observed that "Mr. Green always had his gun convenient where he could put his hand upon it and if any noise occurred at night, he would go out and shoot low on the ground."[15] Surely such behavior was intended to deter his enslaved people from sneaking off the property after dark. Knowing that Green used his gun to deter them from moving around at night underscores the family's grievances about not being free to ever leave the property.

Nelly also complained that her family was not getting enough food to eat. Slaveholders generally gave weekly food rations to their enslaved people, which in northern Virginia in the antebellum era consisted of cornmeal, salted pork, or some other meat and vegetables. Nelly complained that Green did not provide *any* meat, not even the salt pork. Austin Steward, who was born into slavery in Prince William County, Virginia, in 1793, recalled in his autobiography that the weekly food allowances consisted of "one peck of corn, some salt, and a few herrings" per person. Steward wrote that they were given "very little meat," except on special occasions. Smaller slaveholders in Prince William County such as Green gave their people just enough to keep them alive, productive, and fairly healthy.[16] Meat was a luxury most small farmers could not afford to give to enslaved people. Interestingly, though, when the inquest jurors searched the quarters of Nelly and her kin, they found a collection of food including, "two pieces of bacon, two spare ribs, some sausage meat, some lard, right smart sugar and coffee, probably twenty pounds of sugar, some molasses and tea."[17] Obviously, that list of food was far better in quality, quantity, and diversity than even the favored enslaved people of the wealthiest planters possessed, so more than likely Nelly and her family had removed these items from Green's home after his death.

In terms of the work regime in the Upper South states, most enslaved people worked six days a week, Monday through Saturday. Owners released them early on Saturdays so that they could enjoy their Saturday evening and Sunday. Enslaved people looked forward to this time off on the weekend, but Nelly and her kin were denied even that. In addition to carrying the field workload sunrise to sunset, Nelly, her daughter, and granddaughter had additional chores inside Green's home pounding corn to make cornmeal, cooking, cleaning, and washing for the bachelor. Being denied free time was dispiriting for enslaved people. It was one of their most valued things, besides family. With free time and the permission to leave their farms, they could attend parties and dances on Saturday evenings, and religious services on Sunday. Historian Eugene D. Genovese indicated that all except the "most unfeeling masters" threw parties and dances on Saturdays or allowed their enslaved people to attend parties elsewhere in the neighborhood. Because Green did not allow his people to leave the property, they were denied such privileges.[18] This is the world Nelly and her kin inhabited – a very small one, which did not extend past the Green property line and where they had very little to no reprieve from work.

. . .

On Christmas Eve 1856, as he lay in front of his fireplace, George E. Green's home was invaded by unexpected, but familiar, visitors. His visitors were members of the enslaved family he owned: fifteen-year-old twins, Ellen and Elias, their older brother James, their forty-four-year-old mother Betsy, and the family's matriarch, sixty-year-old Nelly. But they did not come bearing Christmas cheer. The family had decided that this Christmas Eve would be Green's last. Considering how Green liked to shoot his gun if anything stirred in his yard at night, it had been a grave risk for the family to attack him. But because they knew about his gun, they made sure he did not have a chance to grab it. After they entered his home, Betsy and her children jumped on him and tried to tie his hands and feet. The children held his legs down: Ellen got one leg and Elias the other. Betsy and James tried to tie his hands, but Green fought back, so they were unable to completely tie them. While her grandchildren and daughter held Green, Nelly struck him with an ax several times. He struggled to get free, caught one of her blows with one of his hands, and wrested the ax from her. He then used the ax to ward off further attacks for a while.[19]

With the ax in hand and bleeding from his injuries, Green managed to flee from his home – running for his life. He was hotly pursued by Nelly's family. They chased their owner to the yard, determined to execute their plan ... and him. Green swung the ax at his pursuers and one of his blows struck James in his head. Another hit the gate. Green then took off running toward his field, but unfortunately for him, at fifty-four years old, he was out-matched by younger, stronger, swifter legs. The family caught him and beat him with "shovels, axe, & sticks" and fence rails, until they killed him. Elias later admitted that he used the shovel to hit his owner and also stabbed him with a piece of a nail. With the exception of the ax, the "weapons" the family used were not things one could reasonably consider deadly weapons, but to enslaved people intent on lethal resistance, any household item could be weaponized. Once Green was dead, Nelly's family dragged his body back to his home. Apparently, they then cleaned up the blood with rags and took meat from Green's icebox and some clothing from his wardrobe, before setting fire to the home. They returned to their quarters, where they removed and hid their bloody clothing, along with the bloody ax and rags, under their beds. By one account the family "pretended to be asleep" when neighbors responded to the fire.[20]

All of Green's neighbors reported that his home was nearly completely consumed by the time they arrived and indicated that it had been burning for a while before anyone outside of the property noticed. Green's neighbors, George B. Tyler, Gustavus A. Hutchinson, Luther L. Lynn and their enslaved people arrived on the scene first at around 8:30 p.m., having noticed the fire. They lived in close proximity to the Green farm and obviously knew him rather well. Tyler's 1,000-acre farm, where he raised wheat, rye, corn, and oats, was located about a half a mile from Green's. Like Green, Tyler was a small slaveholder who owned just eight people. Tyler testified that he had rushed over to Green's after one of his own enslaved women alerted him that Green's house was on fire. By the time Tyler got there, at least a dozen enslaved people from the neighborhood were already present, including three of his own, three of Hutchinson's, and two or three of Lynn's. Tyler reported that when he arrived, he asked Elias about Green's whereabouts. Because Green lived alone on his farm, naturally the only source of information would have been his enslaved people. Elias responded that he was in the house, implying he was in the fire. Tyler then followed that question with another, asking the boy why his owner had not escaped. Elias responded that he "did not know." Tyler stated that he asked about Green's whereabouts again, this time directing his question to the crowd. Peter, one of his own enslaved people, pointed to the fire without any verbal response. Tyler then said he saw Green's body himself. He asked Nelly how the home caught fire and she replied that "she did not know [and] that some of them were asleep & others on the bed and when they came out the house was falling in."[21]

Luther L. Lynn was another of Green's neighbors on the scene after the fire. Like Green and Tyler, Lynn was a farmer who raised wheat and corn on his 429-acre farm. A slaveholder himself, Lynn owned nine people in 1860. He recounted that his wife had first seen the fire and woken him from his sleep to alert him. Lynn dressed immediately, mounted his horse, and rode over to the Green farm. He also asked Green's enslaved people what had happened. At this point, the neighbors' questions were just the normal inquiries curious people make after a tragic death. It was not until Eliza, a woman belonging to Gustavus Hutchinson, was questioned at the scene that anyone explicitly articulated that they believed Green's enslaved people were responsible for their owner's death. Eliza stated that when she went to the Green slave quarters and called for Nelly and her kin to come out, they came "out of the door, looked at the fire & went back [inside]." She implied that they were neither alarmed nor surprised by the fire. According to Eliza, when she asked Nelly and her family why they had not tried to save their owner, they did not respond. Eliza then offered a damning conclusion, "It was my opinion that something wrong had been done."[22] In other words, she believed the family had done something to Green.

According to Tyler, Green's body was "burnt up and the skeleton could not [be] recognized as the body of Mr. Green or tell whether it was a white or black man." Tyler sent his own man, Peter, and Green's Elias to summon the other neighbors and possibly Coroner Dr. Jesse Ewell, who arrived shortly thereafter and began his inquest. Dr. Ewell owned a farm in Green's neighborhood, where his two dozen enslaved people raised corn and oats. He was called because in Virginia, coroners typically carried out investigations, or inquests, when people died under unusual circumstances or when murder was suspected. Dr. Ewell may have been somewhat nervous when he arrived at the Green property, for good reason. This was the first time he had ever acted as coroner.[23]

Coroner Ewell interviewed Nelly's family and walked the property looking for clues he could find in the dark. He then examined Green's remains, which consisted of his charred spine and pelvic bones. Most who saw the scene were shocked by the extent of the disintegration of the body. Normally, a body would need to burn at 1,000°F for two to three hours to cause the majority of the body's bones to disintegrate in this way. The fact that Green's spine and pelvis remained is because bones do not burn evenly; the higher density ones burn last. Given the late hour, darkness on the scene, and frigid temperatures, Dr. Ewell left quickly, intending to conclude his investigation the following day. Tyler, Hutchinson, and Lynn remained on the property for an hour or two and agreed to return at 9:00 a.m. on Christmas morning.

The following morning, Coroner Ewell and Green's neighbors and their enslaved people returned to his farm. By then, Luther Lynn stated that "the dogs or something had turned the remains of the body round some three feet – found his back bone-part of his head – his hips and shoulders and his entrails – all connected together ..."[24] Ewell recruited Green's slaveholding neighbors to serve on the coroner's inquest jury. This action sealed the fate of Nelly and her kin – regardless of their guilt or innocence. Those men could not have acted impartially because they were Green's friends and immediate neighbors. Nonetheless, they immediately got to work investigating, examining the body and scene, and searching for clues about who might have been responsible. The inquest jurors began with what remained of Green's body and found his keys and watch. They determined that he must have still been dressed when the fire began because he clearly was wearing his watch and had his keys in his pocket. They followed the traces of blood leading from the house for about 150–200 yards. On that path, they found evidence of a bloody struggle in one spot, so they concluded Green had been murdered. Tyler testified that when he arrived the previous night all three of the women Green owned had blood on their dresses. In the middle of the investigation, Mr. Norris, a member of the inquest jury, accused James of the murder because he had a fresh, two-inch wound on the crown of his head, that was so deep that it cut to the bone. This impromptu accusation was not unusual for inquest juries. James initially proclaimed his innocence. Lynn, another neighbor-turned-inquest juror, asked Nelly what she had hit her owner with and she responded that she had done it with an ax. Lynn instructed her to retrieve the ax. He claimed that she retrieved the bloody ax from under one of their beds, but Constable Pattie later claimed it was he who had found it when he searched their quarters. Their conflicting statements underscore how little care was taken to record where evidence was found and who found it. Nelly confirmed that the ax belonged to one of her two grandsons. An inquest juror then found a jacket with a hole in it under another one of the beds in their slave quarters. Lynn asked Nelly who the jacket belonged to and she replied that it was James', which he confirmed. James was told to put on the jacket to verify that it fit him. Lynn then matched that hole in the jacket to the wound on his back and concluded he had been injured the previous night while wearing it. Lynn later testified that he had examined the clothing of Nelly and her family, and "they were more or less bloody except Elias – don't think there was any blood on his – there was found a jacket which was said to be his on which there was blood – about the sleeves." After this investigation and evidence collection was completed, Dr. Ewell and the inquest jury then formally interviewed Green's enslaved people.[25]

Dr. Ewell interviewed a total of seven people for his inquest: Nelly; James; Elias; two of Hutchinson's people, Newman and Eliza; George Tyler; and Luther Lynn. Nelly, the sixty-year-old matriarch testified first. After she was sworn in as a witness, Dr. Ewell asked her to tell him everything she knew about Green's murder. She admitted that the family had murdered him. Nelly felt perfectly justified, too, "He (meaning said Green) was a hard master. He would not give us enough meat to eat. He would not allow any of us to go from home, nor give us any of the privileges which other people's servants have. He told us we should stay at home during the Christmas holydays [sic] & work." Three of the four grievances Nelly mentioned are related to personal liberties that made slavery somewhat bearable, especially at that time of the year. Christmas "holidays" included the time off between Christmas and the New Year. This break was not only a festive time, but offered a much-needed mental and physical break from the work schedule. Enslaved people engaged themselves in this festive season by activities such as decorating a tree, having parties, and visiting friends and kin on neighboring farms and plantations. Gift-giving was an essential feature of holidays: owners generally gave their enslaved people Christmas presents, which might include tobacco, ribbons, extra food, or even cash. Holiday parties lasted into the night and featured singing, barbecues, whiskey, dancing, music, and revelry. For those in bondage, although the year brought many denials of their basic humanity and human rights, holidays were a time of restoration for their souls and psyches and reaffirmed their humanity. They eagerly anticipated holidays and the free time with loved ones. Most owners accepted this generations-old tradition. Even brutal owners would at the very least provide a three-day break for these festivities. Depriving enslaved people of their "holidays" altogether was considered cruel and mean-spirited.[26] Denying them their holidays, coupled with denying them the privileges of movement throughout the year, was exceedingly heartless from their perspective. Within this context it is clear why Green's enslaved people found their treatment unjust and opted to exercise their own justice. According to Nelly, "We concluded to get rid of him."[27]

She went on to provide details of *how* they murdered George Green the previous evening. "When I went in the house. The others (meaning Betsy, James, Elias, & Ellen) had him down on the floor; tied, I gave him one crack, (meaning a blow), I believe it was with an axe. I cut one of his hands & he caught the axe & got it away from me. He got out of the house. I did not follow him. The others did. Two of them dragged him back to the house. I do not know which of them."[28] Nelly's confession matched the evidence found on the scene. She was remarkably unflinching and unhesitant in her commitment to the truth, despite the life-or-death consequences for her and her kin. She proceeded to implicate every single member of her family – even the children.

The next person to testify in the coroner's inquest was James, Nelly's oldest grandchild, who was eighteen years old at the time, based on data from the 1850 Slave Schedule. According to James, "He (meaning said Green) was hard upon us & we could [do] nothing to please him." James essentially stated that Green was an exacting and overly critical master. An owner who could not be pleased made it impossible for them to take pride in their work. It was a hopeless prospect. James then repeated the same grievance iterated by his grandmother, Nelly, "He said we should work through Christmas holydays [sic]. We decided to burn him up." According to James, Green was laying in front of the fire when they went inside the home, "... we got on him & tied him. He got out of the house & we struck him with a shovel & pieces of fence rails." Although Nelly said she was unsure about how Green came to his end, James clarifies it for the inquest jury. Elias, the fifteen-year-old twin, echoed the same justification for their owner's murder, "He would not let us have holyday [sic]." The fact that three of Nelly's kin expressed that the denial of holidays was the primary reason for the murder underscores the significance of that season in their lives. Elias also adds a new detail to the murder: he indicated that Green was "knocked in the head" before he was dragged to the kitchen and set afire.[29]

Neighbor George B. Tyler provided the most comprehensive testimony during the inquest. He gave many details about the night of the murder from his perspective as a slaveowner and witness to the events after the fire. He also recounted the confessions of Nelly and her kin. He said that Nelly had admitted that "they had done it – meaning the five prisoners – that he was a hard master & they were tired of living with him." Granted Tyler is the only one to have heard the part of her confession when she stated that they were "tired of living with him," it does have a ring of truth. It is consistent with the spirit of Nelly's own confession. Tyler's testimony provided other essential details about Nelly's confession, "She said [they] went into the house and cussed at him – she said at first she struck with [him] something she did not know what, finally said it was an axe – she then said that the deceased got up and ran off out of the house – they pursued him with shovels, axe & sticks till they killed him – as he was going out of the house he got the axe from her and Elias and struck Jim with the axe – after killing him they dragged him back in the house and set fire to it but said nothing about what occurred in their house." Tyler observed that James and Elias' testimony was "substantially what old Nelly had said." However, he did recall that Ellen and her mother, Betsy, claimed they knew nothing about Green's murder when questioned. It is doubtful they knew *nothing* about it, but perhaps Betsy and Ellen feared that confessing to murder would lead to a death sentence, so they lied to save themselves.[30]

The final person to testify before the inquest jury was Luther Lynn, who testified that on the night of the fire he remembered asking Nelly if she had gone to bed by the time it started. According to him, she responded that she had not noticed the fire until the roof was collapsing. Lynn then asked her if she had heard Green yell for help, to which she responded "No."[31]

At the conclusion of the inquest, Dr. Ewell charged all five of Green's enslaved people with "having willfully, deliberately and with malice and forethought killed and murdered the said George E. Green on the night of the 24th of December 1856." He drafted a warrant for their arrest. Constable B. F. Pattie took the family, the bloody ax, and James' jacket to the county courthouse in Brentsville.[32]

Coroner Ewell's inexperience compromised the integrity of the inquest. In a letter to Phillip D. Lipscomb, the clerk of the court, dated December 26, Dr. Ewell wrote that he hoped "to inquire what else is proper for me to do, besides returning to your office the warrant & verdict of the coroner's jury." Ewell was unsure of the next steps needed for him to conclude his investigation. He outlined many errors he had made in the inquest in his letter to the clerk. First, he mentioned that "there was much confusion & excitement. The negro house was crowded & darkened." Here, he implied that it had been hard to investigate that first night. Second, Dr. Ewell claimed he had been "pressed" for time and wanted to "expedite the proceedings," so that he could "prevent tragic violence, frozen ink, [and] benumbed fingers." Dr. Ewell would have been taking notes using a dip pen which required an ink reservoir to refill, as was common in 1856. Doing so on a cold December night could very well have caused frozen ink and fingers. He also complained that he had no desk or table to write on; in other words, he provided ample justification for the brevity of his notes and a rushed inquest with multiple errors. However, the coroner also made a reference to "prevent[ing] tragic violence," implying that neighbors were inclined to inflict vigilante justice that night. Yet there is no corroborating evidence of these claims of a mob. Ewell acknowledged that he "should have affirmed a scroll to each of the signatures to the verdict, which I believe was neglected." He added, "Perhaps I ought to have recognized the witnesses to appear at court, but the confession of the three culprits caused me to doubt the necessity of so doing."[33] In other words, two days after the murder, the Prince William County coroner admitted that he had grossly failed to do due diligence during the inquest investigation and subsequent legal process. Each one of his mistakes or failures could justify evidence being thrown out and charges dropped for white suspects, but because they were enslaved Black people, no one cared that the investigation consisted of a flurry of errors. Coroner Ewell's mistakes, coupled with his decision to appoint Green's slaveholding neighbors to the inquest jury, created undue prejudice and stacked the case against Nelly and her relatives. With an inquest jury composed as such, they could not hope for leniency.

The trial for Nelly and her family began on January 6, 1857, in the Prince William court of oyer and terminer. Like in so many other southern states, enslaved people charged with capital murder in the Commonwealth of Virginia would not receive a trial by jury. Instead, county justices presided over a court of oyer and terminer for capital cases involving enslaved people. The combination of the justices' ignorance of the law and procedure, coupled with their own bias, nearly guaranteed unfairness. According to prominent jurist and legal scholar A. Leon Higginbotham, Jr., "slaves were doubly damned: not only were they deprived of trial by jury, but, in addition, they were tried by . . . inept and unlearned [justices]."[34] *Commonwealth* v. *Nelly & Others* was no different.

The Prince William County justices for this case were Seymour Lynn, John C. Weedon, William W. Thornton, John Underwood, and John B. Grayson – all of whom were slaveholders. Grayson lived in Green's neighborhood. Underwood owned one slave, Grayson three, and Weedon and Thornton seven each. Seymour Lynn owned twenty-eight enslaved people, making him among the biggest slaveholders in the county. Grayson also served as the county justice of the peace. Even the prosecuting attorney, Eppa Hunton, owned eight enslaved people. Hunton served as the Commonwealth's prosecutor for Prince William County in 1849–1861. In that time, he convicted at least four enslaved women who were subsequently executed, including Agness, who was convicted of the 1850 murder of her owner, Gerard Mason; Nelly and Betsy in 1857; and Lucy, who was convicted of murdering her mistress, Araminta Moxley, in 1859. Hence, Eppa Hunton convicted more cases involving enslaved women who were subsequently condemned to execution than any other prosecutor in American history. The court assigned separate public defenders for each of the accused, Charles E. Sinclair (Nelly), Douglass Tyler (Betsy), Nathaniel Tyler (James), J. M. Forbes (Elias), and John P. Philips (Ellen).[35]

White, slaveholding men – Green's neighbors – were the only witnesses at the trial. Many of them had served on the inquest jury. As Black people, the defendants were not permitted under Virginia law to testify in any trial involving whites, even in their own behalf.[36] George B. Tyler gave the same testimony he had given in the coroner's inquest – mostly about what he had witnessed on the Green farm the night Green was murdered and during the coroner's inquest the next day. According to Luther Lynn's testimony, when he first arrived at the farm on the night of Green's death, it looked as if "something had been butchered" because there was a "good deal of blood" in the yard. Lynn was the only witness to testify that the bloody ax and James' jacket were found under the beds in the slave quarters and that the clothing of Nelly and her family members was "more or less bloody." Lynn also made a point of refuting the claims Nelly made about her owner. Because slaveowners measured the goodness of their peers in terms of what they provided materially for their enslaved people, Lynn set out to prove Green had been a good master by carefully listing the various types of food, snacks, and drinks found in their cabin – clearly hoping to refute Nelly's claim that Green not given them enough food. Lynn also testified that Green's enslaved people were "well-clothed, never saw a more comfortable negro house, it was weather boarded and sealed inside – two beds down stairs and two up stairs all comfortable with an unusual quantity of wearing apparel hanging up on the bedsteads . . ." Based on these observations about their material comfort, Lynn concluded that Green was "one of the best masters" and that his people were "as well taken care of as any slaves in the county." Nelly and her kin thought otherwise. According to Philip D. Lipscombe, the court clerk, when he told Nelly that he believed Green to be a "mild good man," she retorted that "I [Lipscombe] knew nothing about him – that he had taught school up there [on the property] and treated the children so bad [that] none of them liked him." Lipscomb believed these claims to be "damned lies." Nelly's claim about how Green treated free white students is suggestive of how he must have treated his enslaved people.[37] Because Black Americans were prohibited from testifying in court their perspectives were not heard or considered by the justices – just one way that the process created inherent unfairness.

Because they could not testify in court, the confessions of Nelly and her family could only be told through the testimony of whites who heard them confess. Constable B. F. Pattie, who had arrested the family and transported them to jail, claimed that while he was transporting them, "the whole five confessed [to me] an agency in the murder." Lipscombe testified that Nelly and her family members had confessed to him, too. He explained that she told him that Green was a bad owner and explained why they had wanted him dead. Lipscomb is the only person to testify that the defendants told him that before they hit their owner with an ax, they had first begged him to sell them. Green allegedly refused and retorted that "they would all be hung for what they had done." Allegedly, his refusal to sell them led Nelly to follow through on her last best option – to kill him.[38] The principles of the Black feminist practice of justice reveal that enslaved women who took justice into their own hands always tried other options before murder, including everyday resistance or even asking to be sold.

The justices found Nelly and her entire family guilty of murder. When the convicted defendants were asked to offer any

reason "why the court should not proceed to judgment and execution," they did not utter a word. The court summarily scheduled
Nelly, her daughter, and grandchildren to be executed for their
crimes on February 13, 1857, between 10:00 a.m. and 4:00 p.m.
Because Virginia compensated the owners of enslaved people executed by the state, the court had to estimate the worth of each. Nelly,
advanced in age "was said to be worth nothing." Betsy was valued at
$300, James at $800, Elias at $600, and Ellen at $300.[39]

Nelly did communicate how she felt about being executed for
the murder. The last person to testify in *Commonwealth* v. *Nelly &
Others* was R. G. Davis who told the court that when he told Nelly she
"better prepare to meet her God," she replied that she was "all right
on that question."[40] Like many other women featured in this book
who also used a Black feminist practice of justice in the age of slavery,
Nelly did not fear justice on earth or divine justice in the afterlife for
murdering Green. Her declaration that she was "all right on that
question" of meeting her God leaves three possibilities: 1) that Nelly
felt forgiven by God; 2) that she felt her crime was justified because she
believed Green to be truly evil; or 3) that she was reconciled to eternal
damnation. Regardless, hers was a radical mindset in the nineteenth-
century world of Christianity, which conveyed different messages
about murderers. That, plus her seeming fearlessness in readily confessing to every gory detail when questioned by the inquest jury, is
consistent with so many other women in this book when faced with
the inevitably of a death sentence.

Immediately after the sentencing, some people began to
question the ethics of executing Ellen and Elias, who were minors.
An 1801 law gave the Virginia governor the option of sale and
transportation instead of execution.[41] In light of that, the defense
attorneys and others began to petition Governor Wise for a stay of
execution for the minors. Thomas B. Baless, a Prince William County
resident who previously had served as the minister of the
Presbyterian Church of Snow Hill, Maryland, wrote to Virginia
Governor Henry Wise, asking him to stay the executions of the
minor children. In a letter dated January 24, Baless suggested that
Ellen and Elias, who had barely "passed the age of accountability"
might have been pressured to participate by their elders, speculating
that the children might have been threatened "even to the peril of
their lives . . . to take part in the infamous deed." Because of that and

other appeals, Governor Wise granted a stay of execution for Ellen and Elias on February 6, 1857, owing to their "youth and feeble intellects," just one week before their scheduled executions. He postponed their execution until May 22.[42]

Nelly and her family, who were in the same jail cell, spent their last night together singing hymns and praying as a family. Clergy who attended to them up to the date of execution, reported that Nelly and her family expressed "great penitence" for the murder. That report, however, is dubious because clergy were expected to say that. Moreover, there is no other independent evidence that the family articulated any remorse. On February 13, the scheduled date of execution, Nelly, Betsy, and James were escorted from their jail cell at noon, guarded by the Prince William County sheriff, his deputies, and jailer. They must have said their final heartfelt good-byes to Ellen and Elias. They were loaded into a two-horse wagon to be transported to Brentsville, the place of execution. One newspaper reported that the three sang hymns on the journey. A crowd traveling by foot and horseback followed the wagon that carried them to their final destination.[43]

Nelly, her daughter, and grandson arrived to a waiting audience of roughly 1,000 spectators, many of whom were African American. The county had constructed new gallows on an acre of land, which easily accommodated the large crowd. As in the case of Phillis and Mark, Rose Butler, Jane Williams, and others, the executions of the enslaved people who murdered their owners were performative and ritualized spectacles. The *Alexandria Gazette and Virginia Advertiser* reported that Nelly, Betsy, and James mounted the stairs of the gallows "with apparent alacrity," expressing their willingness to pay for their crimes. In one final statement, one of them declared that they "placed their trust in Jesus, and believed that they had so repented as to have secure salvation through him."[44] Clearly Nelly, her daughter, and grandson found a degree of peace in the moments before their executions – a momentary peace in a world without Green. They did not fear death, the pain of the execution, or God's judgment on their souls for the murder. In that way, their last moments are consistent with the Black feminist practice of justice.

The fate of the twins was left to the governor. In Virginia, governors had the power to pardon or stay executions. The most compelling moral imperative to grant clemency was the young age of

Elias and Ellen. The logic behind that is that children have not yet developed independent complex thoughts to understand the life-or-death consequence of their actions. Another factor is that the children could have been coerced to assist by their mother and grandmother. Coercion can mean many things within any family, but at the least, enslaved parents expected their children's emotional support, assistance, and even direct participation in covert and overt community resistance to slavery.[45] Some white Virginians following the case understood coercion as a denial of the children's personal choices. Ellen and Elias never suggested that they had been forced into the violence. In fact, it is the young people in the family who completed Green's murder.

Governor Wise decided to stay Ellen and Elias' executions temporarily, citing their young age as a justification. Some local slaveholders were upset with that decision. John B. Grayson, one of the justices for the case who also lived in Green's neighborhood, wrote to Governor Wise in protest of his decision, "I do not know upon what ground you considered it your duty as Governor of Virginia to respite those negroes ... but I am perfectly certain that no petition has been for respite or pardon circulated for signatures or signed by a single respectable man in this county." Grayson went on to diminish the twins' age as a significant factor in their capacity to make independent, mature decisions. Instead, Grayson tried to use their physical features as a more fitting measure of adulthood, "The woman [note: Grayson referred to Ellen as a woman instead of a girl] is of large size for a woman, and very well developed physically – probably as well developed as she ever would be." He insisted that Elias' intelligence was proven by the fact that Green had trusted him to deliver his peanuts to the train depot. Grayson closed by insisting that the sentence was "perfectly just" and warned the governor that "any further interference ... with [these] execution[s] would be an improper control of our own county business." Grayson ended his letter by telling the state executive that anyone who did not reside in Prince William County had no more of a right to petition about that county's business than "I have to advise that you do not allow your overseer in Accomack to whip one of your negroes there, who disobeyed him."[46] The fact that a justice in the trial was so personally invested that he went to these lengths to ensure the children were executed underscores the bias of justices. Seemingly unmoved by

Grayson's entreaties, Governor Wise reduced Ellen and Elias' sentence to "sale and transport" instead of execution. The twins were subsequently transported from Gordonsville to Richmond (Figure 6.1).[47] The historical record is silent on whether they

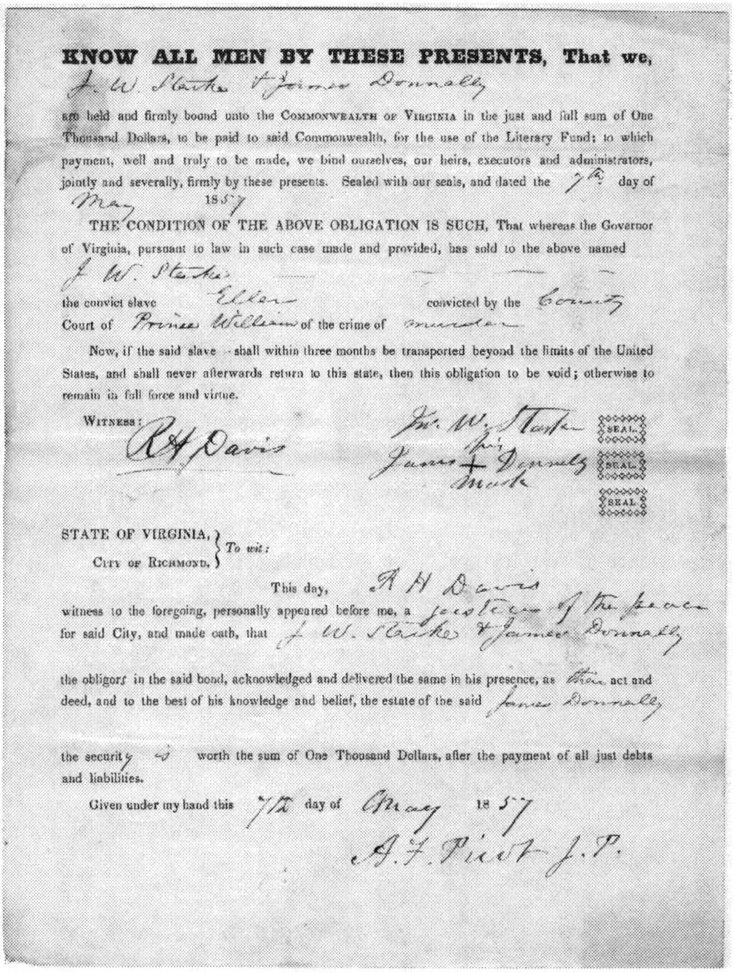

Figure 6.1 Bond for the purchase and transportation of Ellen
Credit: "J.W. Starke Bond for the Purchase and Removal of William and Others," May 7, 1857, *Virginia Untold: The African American Narrative Digital Collection*, Library of Virginia

remained in Richmond or were sold outside the Commonwealth of Virginia.

. . .

History is littered with stories of enslaved Virginia women who resisted slavery. By the time Nelly and her daughter and grandson were hanged for murdering their owner, nearly 100 other enslaved women had been executed before them. Just seven years earlier in the same Virginia county, Agness hacked her owner, Gerard Mason, to death as he slept. In Richmond five years earlier, Jane Williams had done the same to the family who owned her. What makes Nelly, Betsy, and Ellen unique is that none of those other women's resistance was part of a three-generational family plan led by its sixty-year-old matriarch. Nelly is the oldest enslaved woman executed in Virginia.

Nelly and her kin did not intend to end slavery that day. Nor did they seek personal freedom from it. That does not mean that they were not motivated by a revolutionary vision. They wanted the same things other enslaved people had in their neighborhood: a decent owner, Christmas, mobility, leisure time, church, and meat. And from their enslaver's perspective, their desire to ameliorate their condition and demand personal autonomy was radical. What lived at the heart of revolutionary dreams for enslaved women was not violence, but fairness, freedom, sustenance, and humanity.

7 LUCY
"Bad treatment &c."

The day that the black man takes an uncompromising step and realizes that he's within his rights, when his own freedom is being jeopardized, to use any means necessary to bring about his freedom or put a halt to that injustice, I don't think he'll be by himself.

~ Malcolm X

Late Sunday morning, January 3, 1858, Maria Dougherty, operator of the Columbia Hotel in Galveston, Texas, came up missing. Although not alarmed at first, Maria's husband, Joseph *was* perplexed as to his wife's whereabouts. He went looking for her at the Palmetto House, a boarding home on the corner of Tremont and Mechanic streets, owned by Maria's aunt. Dougherty thought his wife might have gone there to visit her aunt, but was told that Maria had not been there at all that day. Out of ideas, Dougherty called for a general search for his wife. By 8:00 p.m., Maria Dougherty's body was found in the brick cistern underneath the Columbia Hotel. Her head had been crushed by at least two blows from a large heavy object that had landed with bloody force in her left temple and middle of her forehead. Either of these blows could have killed her. Maria Dougherty's neck also appeared to have pressure marks indicating she might have been choked, as well.[1] The murder sent shock waves through the community. As the details emerged, it became clear that Maria's murderer was close to home.

. . .

Inhabited by Indigenous people for centuries, the barrier island on which Galveston rests was settled by whites in 1816. Galveston's port, established in 1825, became an important harbor in the Gulf of Mexico and the West, in general. Ships from New Orleans, Europe, the Caribbean, and Latin America were regular visitors to the Galveston port. The city's founders envisioned that it would one day rival New York City as a western commercial hub. That desire became more fantasy than real: Houston's port quickly eclipsed Galveston's in traffic and prominence. Regardless, Galveston remained a consequential city and port. By the Civil War, it was the second largest city in Texas with a population of 7,000 (Figure 7.1). Galveston's port did eventually rival New York City's in one critical way: in the last decades of the nineteenth century, it became a major port of entry for European immigrants.[2]

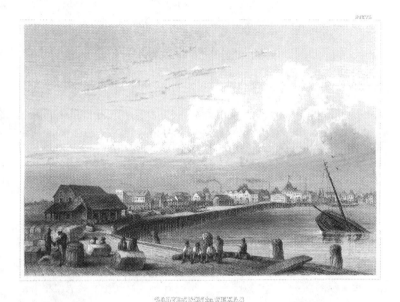

Figure 7.1 Port of Galveston, Texas in the mid-nineteenth century
Credit: "Galveston in Texas," artwork, date unknown. University of North Texas Libraries, The Portal to Texas History: https://texashistory.unt.edu; Star of the Republic Museum

In the antebellum era Galveston was a city of poor and lower-class whites, a large percentage of whom had no skills, worked as casual laborers, and owned either no land or possessed low-valued property. The 1850 census indicates that 45 percent of Galvestonians possessed no property whatsoever. For the state as a whole, only 10 percent of whites owned no property, so Galvestonians were comparatively propertyless. Another 25 percent of Galvestonians owned property valued at $1,000 or less (or the equivalent of $33,800 in today's terms). In other words, 70 percent of them owned either no property or less than $1,000 worth of property. By comparison, in the rest of the state only 42.7 percent of Texans owned less than $1,000 of property. So Galvestonians were not only comparatively propertyless but also relatively poor compared to other Texans.[3] In sum, the majority of white Galvestonians was of modest means.

In 1860, only 17 percent of Galvestonians owned enslaved people, which was significantly below the 25–30 percent average in the Deep South. That same 17 percent of Galvestonians, though, owned 64 percent of the city's real estate as well. Property ownership was required to hold political office in Galveston. For example, anyone hoping to run for mayor had to own at least $1,000 worth of real property. The majority of white residents were automatically excluded from holding office because they owned no, or too little, property. Consequently, slaveholders held 100 percent of elected political offices and appointments.[4]

Joseph Dougherty first appears in the Galveston historical record in 1853. His occupation then is difficult to determine, but in the one extant city directory from that era his occupation is listed as "Oysters" and "Mechanic," suggesting he made a living as an oyster fisherman/salesman and manual laborer or machine operator.[5] Dougherty owned taxable property in block 567, lots 1 and 2 – which was between avenues C (also known as Mechanic Avenue) and D (Market Avenue) and between Twenty-Seventh and Twenty-Eighth streets. In 1853, that property was worth $800. Dougherty's property increased in value annually; by 1855, it was worth $1,500. By then, he owned additional property worth $800, but quickly disposed of it. Two years later, Dougherty's lots on block 567 were valued at $2,000 ($63,943 today).[6]

Joseph Dougherty married Maria Hays in 1856, when she was twenty-one years old. The couple had one child, Hugh, who was still an infant when he lost his mother to murder. The Doughertys operated the Columbia Hotel on the corner of Strand (Avenue B) and Twenty-First streets, across from the Galveston waterfront. The hotel had previously been owned by a B. McDonnell, who was married to Maria's aunt, Winneford, a woman thirteen years his junior. Irish immigrants, the McDonnells owned and operated at least one other Galveston hotel, the Palmetto House. In 1850, their real estate was valued at $2,500.[7]

When the McDonnells owned the Columbia Hotel, it was located on Strand and Twenty-Fourth streets. An 1851 advertisement illuminates the quality of the hotel, noting that it had been recently renovated and "newly furnished throughout." The ad states that the proprietors – the McDonnells – would spare no effort to "render this Hotel one of the most desirable in the city." Through the McDonnells' efforts, the Columbia Hotel became a well-known institution on the Galveston waterfront. In 1854 they began leasing the hotel to others – F. Harrison in 1854, and Joab H. Banton two years later.[8]

The McDonnells may have leased the Columbia Hotel to their niece and her new husband because by 1858, the Doughertys were managing it. Under the Doughertys' management, the hotel boasted a restaurant and bar and offered rooms to visitors, as well as housing to long-term boarders. The Doughertys were of modest means and owned no enslaved people initially, but they did employ at least two servants – two German women – who helped with chores around the home and hotel.[9] As white immigrants, these employees would not have been inclined to forge a relationship with enslaved people, lest they risk their own upward mobility.

Perhaps the responsibility of managing the hotel grew too heavy, so Joseph Dougherty decided to purchase an enslaved worker to help with the workload. On October 10, 1857, he purchased Lucy for $460, from Captain John H. Sterrett. Sterrett operated *Island City*, a vessel that transported people between the ports of Houston and Galveston. Both cities hosted substantial slave markets.[10] The bill of sale describes Lucy as forty-five years old, dark-complexioned, and 5ft 2in in height (Figure 7.2). Apparently, she had been sold in the domestic slave trade that relocated enslaved people from the

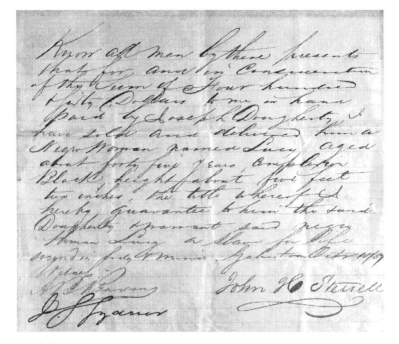

Figure 7.2 Bill of sale for Lucy
Credit: "Dougherty, Joseph A. Bill of Sale for Slavewoman," October 10, 1857. Texas State Library and Archives Commission

eastern seaboard states to states further south and west. She indicated that she had been born in North Carolina and sold and transported to Georgia. From there, she was sold and likely transported to New Orleans initially and then on to Houston, where she was placed in an auction again.[11] In all, Lucy had traveled more than 1,200 miles from her place of birth to what would be her place of death. In the antebellum era, the internal slave trade typically pulled enslaved people from the Upper South, where there was a labor surplus, to the Lower South, where the demand was high. Between 1790 and 1860 more than a million enslaved African Americans made such a journey.[12] Unlike them, Lucy did not journey between the Upper and Lower South. Her most immediate place of origin was Georgia, which is in the Lower South. Her being sold and transported from one Lower South state to another defies typical patterns of the domestic trade, suggesting she was sold from Georgia to Texas for a non-economic reason. That, coupled with her personality, makes it highly possible that Lucy had been transported between Lower South states because of her recalcitrance – although there are no records to prove this.

When Lucy arrived in Galveston in 1857, Black residents comprised 10 percent of the total population. Most enslaved Galvestonians worked at the port, or in businesses that catered to wharf traffic, including hotels, restaurants, shops, bars, brothels, and saloons near the waterfront. Many hired their own time, rented their own places, and lived separately from their owners. In their free time, they went to saloons, shopped, and hosted parties. This relative independence and freedom irritated white Galvestonians, many of whom were poor, unskilled workers who lost their whiteness – the presumed superiority it offered – by working and living alongside enslaved people. In 1857, the Galveston city government passed stricter regulations in order to tighten the reins on the Black population. New local slave codes prohibited enslaved people from a range of nightlife activities, including traveling at night, drinking liquor, playing cards, and associating with whites. These regulations also aimed to curb Black resistance by prohibiting them from owning weapons or "striking any white person."[13] Lucy arrived in Galveston just as the stricter regulations on enslaved people were being enacted.

Purchasing an enslaved person was a monumental step for the Doughertys. But at forty-five years old, Lucy was considered old for an enslaved woman. At that time, the average life expectancy of enslaved people was twenty-five years. Enslaved people under thirty were in their prime and their prices reflected that. Those older than forty years old were considered "elderly" and cost less. This was even more true of women, once they matured beyond childbearing years. Enslaved "elderly" women beyond childbearing years cost between $268 and $433. With a price of $460, the Doughertys paid more for Lucy than they should have, especially given their financial outlook.[14] They may have figured she was worth the price, though, because by purchasing her they believed they could be masters. Lucy had other ideas.

Lucy's sale to new owners in a new state would have been emotionally difficult. She had been ripped from the home, family, and friends – everyone she loved; perhaps, she had even left her children or a spouse behind. A small clue emerges in the 1856 ship manifests from New Orleans bound for Texas, which lists an enslaved woman named Lucy who matches her description. This Lucy was dark-complexioned, fifty years old, 5ft 3in in height. Based on the similar descriptions (only the age differed), it is possible that this is the same Lucy who was purchased by the Doughertys a year later. This Lucy is grouped on the same manifest line as another enslaved woman named Nancy, suggesting that they had been sold together or were related. Nancy's age is listed as twenty-six years old. Given the age difference, it is possible that Nancy could have been Lucy's daughter.[15] If so, the two were separated after arriving in Texas. If Nancy and Lucy were mother and daughter, it only compounded the trauma of having been brought to Texas.

Lucy's advanced age also factored into her experience with her new owners. People her age were considered elderly by all standards. The market value of most enslaved people older than forty years old had declined enough for them to be deemed "worthless," reducing the probability of sale. Despite being devalued by the market, enslaved elders like Lucy were revered and respected by their own communities for their wisdom and experience. For example, elders gave younger generations advice on everything from medicinal remedies for illnesses to giving birth and child-rearing, to dealing with slaveowners. Elderly enslaved people did not expect the same degree of reverence – or any at all – from their white enslavers, but at the very least they did not expect to be worked hard or mistreated. The historical record is full of examples of enslaved people speaking out against enslavers who mistreated or overworked the old and infirm among them. Nor did they expect to be sold away from their kin after their prime.[16] Lucy experienced all of those things.

People new to slave-owning and unable to purchase additional people tended to be highly abusive of their enslaved workers in order to establish mastery. Enslaved people concluded that no enslavement experience was as bad as being owned by poor whites because they were more violent than wealthy planters. According to one formerly enslaved person interviewed by the Works Progress Administration, being sold to or hired out to poor whites was akin to "damning" a person's soul. Not only did poor whites tend to be overly violent, but the workload they gave was also unrelenting, and they also failed to provide adequate sustenance.[17] The Doughertys

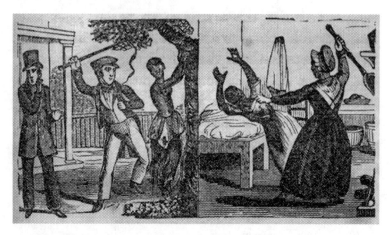

Figure 7.3 Enslaved woman being beaten by her mistress
The scene on the right is a typical scene of the discipline to which enslaved women were subjected at the hands of their mistresses inside their owners' homes.
Credit: Henry Bibb, *Narrative of the Life and Adventures of Henry Bibb, An American Slave, Written by Himself. With an Introduction by Lucius C. Matlack* (New York: Henry Bibb, 1849), 113. Library of Congress, Rare Book and Special Collections Division

matched that typification. They tried to assert their dominance over Lucy shortly after the sale that transferred ownership to them. The couple did what they thought they needed to do to be effective masters, namely breaking Lucy's will through violence in order to force her into submission (Figure 7.3). In 1858, one year later, Texas would enact legislation against "unreasonable abuse" or "cruelly treating a slave," but that was too late to protect Lucy from the Doughertys' cruelty in 1857. In Galveston, she would get no empathy from city officials, because here, slaveowners held all the levers of power.[18] The only relief she would get from her owners' attempt at mastery is what she seized through her own resistance.

It is in this context that Lucy responded negatively to her new owners. Not only had she been ripped her away from her community in her twilight years but they also worked her hard and beat her. This treatment is a terrible departure from what enslaved people would expect in their late forties. It did not help that Maria was half Lucy's age and new to owning enslaved people. Perhaps the

Doughertys were too heavy with the lash. Perhaps they did not understand that it was not necessary to beat an older woman for every minor transgression. Almost from the moment they had purchased her, Lucy reportedly felt "dissatisfied" with her new owners; perhaps the feelings were mutual. Her first acts as a Galvestonian were of resistance. She reportedly ran away and hid from the Doughertys for several days after they brought her home. Lucy was insolent and determined to "act as rebellious as possible." Sometime after Christmas 1857, she disappeared and hid in a crawlspace underneath the hotel. When Joseph reached in after her, she swung at him with a thick piece of wood. Lucy was punished – likely beaten – for this attempted assault. She retaliated by setting fire to her owners' business and home, the Columbia Hotel. The arson, however, was discovered and controlled in enough time to prevent significant damage. When questioned about why she had set the fire, Lucy "refused to answer."[19] Her silence was itself a form of resistance. Lucy refused to give the Doughertys the satisfaction of an explanation. They knew *exactly* why she had set the fire.

As punishment for arson, Lucy was "severely" beaten and placed in stocks – two wooden boards hinged together that confined a person's ankles and wrists. She remained in stocks every night for a week as a punishment and a means of restraining her from committing similar acts. Putting a person in stocks was a medieval punishment that was more common in the sixteenth, seventeenth, and eighteenth centuries than in the nineteenth century. Enslaved people were not the only people placed in stocks in antebellum Galveston; whites convicted of adultery, domestic abuse, theft, public intoxication, and other crimes could also be subjected to this punishment. Enslaved people were typically whipped after being placed in stocks. If Lucy had been whipped, the restraints would have rendered her unable to shield herself or mitigate the impact of the lash. Located in public squares, stocks added another component of punishment – public humiliation. Those placed in stocks could be taunted, spat upon, verbally assaulted, kicked, whipped, or beaten by strangers. Rotten food, dead rodents, street filth, excrement, and stones were typically thrown at those in stocks.[20] As an enslaved woman left in the stocks overnight, Lucy also faced a particularly heightened sexual vulnerability.

The stock experience was humiliating and unjust enough in Lucy's mind that she vowed vengeance against her mistress. Lucy's decision to target Maria Dougherty for revenge illuminates that she held her responsible for her abuse. Slaveholding women – far from being passive and powerless observers – were active participants in the violence of slavery; as historian Thavolia Glymph asserts, "their power was neither invisible nor insignificant" as it related to enslaved people. Mistresses beat, slapped, spit on, threw objects at the heads of, name-called, and whipped enslaved women – sometimes for minor infractions, such as breaking a dish. These women wielded violence on demand and had no problem using it as often as possible. From the perspective of enslaved people, mistresses sometimes created trauma for them through inhumane, petty, hateful, and brutal treatment.[21] It is highly likely that Maria was this type of mistress. After being placed in stocks, Lucy reportedly was "sullen" and "uncommunicative" for the week after her being released from the stocks. Her silent treatment gave her the time and clarity to plan her last and final act of resistance. Because Lucy was attentive to her work, Maria Dougherty had no cause for alarm. Then Maria came up missing.[22]

After searching for his wife at her aunt's hotel, Joseph Dougherty asked Lucy where his wife was. She is said to have replied "with perfect indifference" that she did not know. He suspected that she had something to do with his wife's disappearance. Local journalists who covered the story insisted that Lucy's short history of "general bad conduct" led people to suspect her. When officials went to find Lucy, she could not be found. It did not take them long to find her hiding in an outhouse. She was arrested and lodged in the jail, based on suspicions that she has done something to her mistress.[23]

Maria Dougherty's body was found in the cistern under the hotel around 8:00 p.m. that day. The coroner was immediately called to the scene. He began a coroner's inquest and impaneled a jury to determine the cause of death and collect evidence and witness testimony about the murder. The jury not only examined the body but also visited the scene of the crime. The coroner's inquest jury determined that the blows to Maria's head had been delivered with a hatchet. Either blow would have been enough to cause her death. The jury also noticed that the slaveowner's neck had bruises, indicating she may have been choked. The jurors interviewed all the parties who knew Maria Dougherty or the circumstances of her disappearance. The Doughertys' servants testified that they had left their employer in the kitchen with Lucy that morning. They heard the two women arguing, then after a few minutes there was a thud, as if someone had fallen. As the primary workspaces for enslaved domestic workers, kitchens functioned as sites of work, negotiation, and resistance, so it is no surprise that arguing and a physical altercation would happen there.[24] The servants testified that when they returned to the kitchen after doing their chores, Maria was not there. In other words, they inferred that Lucy had been the last one to see her alive. The jury also examined physical evidence at the scene, which left little doubt of Lucy's guilt. Several spots of blood were found on her dress. In addition, pieces of that same dress and its hook-and-eye fasteners had been found near Dougherty's body, indicating that she and Lucy had had a pretty brutal fight before Lucy bludgeoned her to death. When examining the hotel, the juror had found blood leading from the kitchen to the pump room above the cistern.[25]

Lucy was called to testify at the inquest, but refused to cooperate or answer any questions. Instead, she maintained a "dogged [sic] silence" when questioned by the coroner's inquest jurors. She allegedly admitted her guilt privately to several people and defiantly indicated that she was "willing to be hung." The inquest jury concluded that Maria Dougherty had been murdered by Lucy with a hatchet. The theory of the crime was that the two women had gotten into an altercation in the kitchen and Lucy began choking Maria. Lucy then grabbed a hatchet and hit her mistress in the head twice, causing her immediate death. Lucy may then have dragged the body to the pump room and thrown it into the cistern below.[26] Again, this was something she had planned after being placed in stocks.

Lucy was indicted by a grand jury for first-degree murder, a charge to which she pled "not guilty." The murder trial began on January 18, 1858. The 1845 Texas Constitution guaranteed enslaved people charged with capital crimes the right to an "impartial trial" by a jury.[27] The state also tried them in regular criminal courts and allowed them to testify in court in their own defense. The state also appointed them defense attorneys. Hence, Texas proved far more progressive that the eastern and older southern states when it came to fair and equal trials for enslaved people. The judge appointed a defense attorney for Lucy. It was only during that trial that Lucy articulated a motive. She told the court that she had killed

Maria Dougherty because of "bad treatment &c."[28] The ampersand followed by the c. means that the person who recorded the details of what Lucy conveyed about her bad treatment chose to abbreviate her comments. It is a type of archival silencing. Lucy's statement in court about poor treatment may have been the most forthcoming and revealing about what she had endured in the few months she had been enslaved by the Doughertys but the failure to record those details obfuscates it, effectively silencing her and denying the reality of her experiences. Judge Peter W. Gray told Lucy and the court that "even if what she said was true, it could be no justification for the great crime she had committed."[29] His editorializing from the bench was not helpful. An all-white, all-male jury of free citizens found Lucy guilty of first-degree murder.

A reporter from the *Civilian and Gazette* spoke with Lucy after the verdict. He reported that she was "without remorse" and insisted to him that the murder had been a matter of life or death, and that she killed Maria Dougherty before she could kill *her*.[30] To the reporter, she insisted the murder was self-defense. Interestingly, she had not pursued a self-defense plea in court, which may suggest her attorney realized that self-defense plea would not work in a judicial system in which slaveholders held the power. Lucy's refusal to speak in court at all, but her comparative alacrity about speaking to a reporter suggests that her silence in court was an act of resistance to the judicial system.

Lucy was brought to the court for sentencing on January 23, 1858. Judge Gray asked Lucy if wanted to make a statement about why the sentence should not be imposed, but again, she chose silence. He sentenced her to die on March 5, 1858. *The Colorado Citizen* noted that "she received her sentence with apparent composure, being doubtless fully prepared for it, and being naturally a woman of desperate and hardened character." Between January 23 and March 5, Lucy remained in jail awaiting her execution. Father Louis Claude Marie Chambodut counseled her and spiritually prepared her for death. On March 5, Lucy spoke for one last time, expressing a "perfect willingness to die" and hope for forgiveness in the next life. She was then hanged at 2:00 p.m. It was reported that the executioner hanged Lucy "delicately," which implies that his sympathy led him to treat her humanely.[31]

Like most of the other slave states, Texas compensated owners for executed enslaved people. A year later, Joseph Dougherty petitioned the legislature to reimburse him $460 for the loss of Lucy, which also happens to be exactly what he paid for her.[32] With that reimbursement, Dougherty's brief episode in slaveholding came to a close. He never again purchased another person. And that lesson came at the hands of an enslaved woman named Lucy who enacted her power to avenge the "bad treatment &c."

. . .

New slaveowners Maria and Joseph Dougherty injured Lucy's body and dignity in multiple ways in their few months of ownership. First, they purchased her late in her life and attempted to exert mastery over her, with physical and verbal abuse. The couple also publicly humiliated Lucy by placing her in stocks overnight. Consistent with a Black feminist practice of justice, Lucy avenged all of this abuse and mistreatment, by refusing to work, running away, trying to strike Joseph Dougherty, and setting the hotel on fire. Each effort she made to resist the abusive treatment was met with a humiliating and disproportionately punitive response. Given those considerations, murdering her mistress was the last of several attempts to obtain relief and personal justice. When confronted with Dougherty's body and asked bluntly if she had murdered her, according to one source, Lucy boldly replied, "Yes, and I would do it again."[33] Echoing Annis in North Carolina in 1770 and Nelly in Virginia a year earlier, Lucy's undaunted response reveals that she did not fear the consequences of her actions one bit. Lucy never denied her crime and did not try to escape punishment, despite the fact that she faced a certain execution if convicted. In one final act of defiance to the racial order that governed the courtroom, Lucy maintained a deafening and defiant silence during her trial. Newspaper reporters concluded that she had an air of "stolid indifference and refused to speak concerning the murder."[34] Lucy's actions, though, screamed in thunder tones that she operated with a Black feminist philosophy and practice of justice and was content with the outcome.

Lucy was the second woman to be executed by the state of Texas. Five years earlier in Dallas, on May 27, 1853, Jane (Elkins) earned the designation as the first woman executed in the state for murdering Andrew C. Wisdom with an ax as he slept. Although America Elkins of Dallas was Jane's owner, she had hired her out to Wisdom, a widower living with his two young children just outside of the city. Wisdom hired Jane to help with housework and caring for his children. At fifty-three years old, Jane, like Lucy, was considered an elderly enslaved woman, but that job should have been easy enough for her. She obviously endured abuse that transcended what she ever had experienced in her fifty-three years as an enslaved person. We may never know definitively why she killed Wisdom or, *if* she killed him. Jane never confessed to the murder and nor did she ever articulate a reason for bludgeoning Wisdom in his sleep. The night of the murder, Jane had claimed a prominent man had killed Wisdom, but that seems highly unlikely. During her trial, she opted for silence when questioned by the judge and while facing a jury comprised of thirty-six white men.[35] By then, though, she had received her justice; there was nothing more these thirty-six white jurors could give her that she had not already seized herself.

CONCLUSION

Violence, especially lethal violence, was considered the prerogative of white men in the slave era. They claimed the authority to kill, mortally injure, or maim their wives, servants, employees, and even other white men. Yet none of that societal white-on-white and free-on-free violence could ever trump what was required to maintain slavery. That violence was unparalleled, incomparable, and incomprehensible in the history of human relations in the United States and beyond. White men, their wives, parents, siblings, overseers, and even their minor children often delivered inhumane and even merciless "discipline" to their enslaved people. As one historian wrote, the violence used to maintain slavery was "an obscene violence ... of murders, mutilations, beatings, and rapes ... of husbands forced to see their wives abused, and of wives forced to do unspeakable things."[1]

Unspeakable things were also *done* to enslaved women ... daily. They were wronged, mistreated, exploited, abused, raped, subjugated, oppressed, maligned, and damaged inside and out by their owners and their agents – not just once, but repeatedly. Those who worked inside their owners' homes were spat upon, slapped, burned, name-called, pinched, cursed at, damned, starved, and humiliated regularly. These are deeply traumatic experiences, done to real-life, flesh-and-blood women, which beg for redress. Given what they endured, lethal force *is* a legitimate response to the abuse, violence, and indignity of enslavement.

Even within the Black community/ies, violence is understood to be the prerogative of Black men. These patriarchal ideas about who can wield violence make some uncomfortable with the idea of women exercising lethal resistance to injustice, and even affects how we do the work as historians. Jettisoning these ideas provides room for us to properly analyze women who chose lethal resistance to slavery.

My framework for understanding this is just one approach. Without the framework of a Black feminist practice of justice, these acts seem impulsive, motivated by anger, irrational, disproportionate, and disorganized. To the contrary, the case studies in this book suggest that enslaved women took great pains to plan the act, recruit other hands to assist, assign their collaborators specific duties, and even work out how they would escape suspicion. Driven to revolt and lethal resistance by different things than enslaved men, women did not always strive to destroy slavery or the power structure; instead, they were motivated *to destroy the person in power*. Women's motives are no less consequential than those of the men who have dominated the pages of history books and no less worthy of being classified as revolt.

Using these case studies as a guide, enslaved women were very effective at executing their plans and actualizing their goals. All of the women except Rose Butler succeeded in ending the lives of their owners or members of their owners' families, just as they planned. They produced deeply rational, organized, and contemplative intellectual plots that included acting, storytelling, problem-solving, and critical thinking skills in every stage of their plans. Interestingly enough, too, they devised well-conceived alibis and alternative suspects and theories to ensure they were not suspected of the crime. If the women who used lethal force to resist slavery acted in concert with others at all, they tended to recruit only people close to them, such as spouses, friends enslaved alongside of them, or their own children. Unlike the men who led their own plots, none of these women were betrayed by their co-conspirators before they completed the task. This is largely owing to the fact that women only recruited people they personally deeply trusted. Their efficacy at planning and leading slave revolts cannot be ignored.

We tend to think of revolts as being organized by field slaves. Field slaves did prove among the most reliable recruiters of uprisings. But what did revolt look like in the rural North? What did it look like inside the enslavers' homes? All of the women in this book were enslaved inside their owners' households, or on smaller farms. All of the lethal resistance in this book happened inside the homes, kitchens, and bedrooms of minor slaveowners. These women killed their mistresses or single men – bachelors or widowers – who owned just one to a few people. Many were first-time slaveowners. Yet, these minor slaveowners all strove for mastery and total dominance over their enslaved people – mind, body, and soul – and tended to be punitive and brutal. They denied their enslaved workers personal time and space and attempted to work them perpetually, around the clock and all year round. Their enslaved women complained that they had gone too far, and they initially used non-lethal resistance to express their dissent, to little or no avail. Their isolation from other enslaved people, coupled with unresolved feelings about the injustice they suffered, proved deadly for their owners. This area begs more scholarly attention.

Enslaved women's definition of justice is starkly different from how the concept was defined by owners and local whites. Their philosophy of justice was practical and boiled down to a sense of fairness, decency, and humane treatment. It was a powerful current flowing within them. And their owners had no clue that they harbored such strong views about justice, which was a serious misstep. Justice was so important to the women in this book that they were willing to risk their own lives to obtain it. In fact, they were more willing to die for justice than for freedom.

The burning question that remains is: Did bringing one slaveowner to justice disrupt slavery? The answer is a resounding yes. These women did more than that: they also disrupted slavery where they lived – on their farms, and in their communities, districts, and towns, and cities. Local slaveowners could not have viewed the mutilated bodies of their neighbors and friends through their service as inquest jurors and court justices or listened to the gory details of how they died without being nervous about the possibility of being murdered in the same way themselves. Such a crime in their neighborhood would naturally have led all slaveowners to be distrustful of their own enslaved people. In many ways, these women's actions surely destroyed slaveowners' sense of peace and safety inside their homes. Enslaved people, too, felt the effects of a murdered slaveowner in their neighborhood or vicinity. For one, when an enslaved person murdered an enslaver, the power of all slaveowners was diminished in the eyes of the slave community; certainly, they no longer loomed quite as large, and they were no longer so formidable or invincible. No example inspired enslaved people more than someone who killed his or her owner without being discovered for the crime. In colonial Massachusetts, a successful prior poisoning murder in their Charlestown neighborhood made Phillis and Phoebe more courageous to try the same means to kill their owner, Captain Codman. So, in that way, there was a possibility that successful murders could inspire copycat murders of other enslavers.

There were more than a hundred years between the cases of Phillis (1755) and Lucy (1858). Although Black women's enslaved condition and its subsequent vulnerability to abuse and injustice had not changed much in that century, a few things did improve. For one, by 1858, enslaved women convicted of capital crimes were no longer being burned at the stake like Phillis and Annis. In that way, their executions became less barbaric. By the time of Lucy's trial, enslaved women would benefit from a jury trial. The jury was not a jury of their peers, but at least it was not a tribunal of slaveholders. They also could expect court-appointed defense attorneys and, in some states, they had the right to appeal their cases to the state supreme courts. The one thing that had not changed is the fact that they had to seize justice for themselves.

Enslaved women who rose up in revolt were not too different or politically disconnected from free Black women involved in deadly political violence during slavery. In the 1851, Edward Gorsuch, a Maryland slaveowner had come to Christiana, Pennsylvania to reclaim fugitives Noah Bailey, Nelson Ford, George Ford, and Joshua Hammond under the 1850 Fugitive Slave Law. Once in town, Gorsuch went to the home of William Parker, a free African American, who he believed to be harboring his enslaved people. As historian Kellie Carter Jackson has asserted, Eliza Parker, William Parker's wife, is one of the Black heroines of this story. Upon Gorsuch's arrival to her doorstep, she blew a horn that, at once, alerted the Black Self-Protection Society that slave catchers were in the area and summoned their assistance. Eighty African Americans – men and women – arrived to assist, with protection in mind. Carter Jackson emphasizes that the collective effort made that political resistance against Gorsuch significant.[2] Gorsuch was shot and killed, and his son, Joshua, was badly wounded. Black women's contributions to this Christiana resistance are well-documented in primary sources.

William Parker said that at one point during the standoff, his wife Eliza grabbed a corn cutter and declared that she would cut off the head of the first person who tried to surrender. Dr. Willis Foulkes, a white witness, reported seeing Hannah Decker, an African American woman, with a 2–2½ft stick in her right hand. Samuel Smith saw another Black woman, Elizabeth Boon, wielding a club. Another witness saw Susan Hunter with stones in her hand. Witnesses stated that as Gorsuch lay mortally wounded from a gunshot, "the [African American] women, put an end to him." After he died, they reportedly mutilated his body by hacking it to a "bloody pulp" with corn cutters. Of the more than three dozen people arrested for treason for this crime, six included African American women. Unlike their enslaved counterparts, the free Black women who assisted in the resistance against Edward Gorsuch were never brought to trial because there was not enough evidence against them.[3] And as Carter Jackson has shown us, lethal force against powerful people is in and of itself loaded with social and political meaning and significance.

The legacy of these enslaved women is even found in the twentieth century, although not perfectly paralleled. In 1912, the relationship between a young Black laundress and her wealthy white employer would end in violence in Hampton, Virginia. Early that year, fifty-one-year-old Ida Virginia Belote accused her sixteen-year-old Black laundress, Virginia Christian, of stealing a skirt. Christian stopped washing for Belote after that accusation. Unlike during the slave era, Black women such as Christian had some freedom to choose not to work for employers who mistreated them. Ida Belote found her skirt and decided to try to get Christian back in her employ, so she visited the girl's home and spoke to her mother. She admitted that she had found her skirt and regretted that she may have said something offensive to Virginia that stopped her from washing for her. Christian's mother encouraged her daughter to work out the dispute with Belote and return to work; Virginia Christian arrived at the Belote residence on March 18, 1912, but instead of the resolution Belote promised, she accused her of a second theft, this time of a gold locket. Belote confronted Christian, and berated her, demanding that the locket be returned, but Christian declared her innocence. Belote, who had a reputation of not paying or underpaying her employees, threw a spittoon at her, which hit her laundress in the shoulder. Clay spittoons were heavy, so the blow likely physically hurt, but the fact that they were used for spitting tobacco made the injury offensive, as well. Belote then picked up the broken pieces of the spittoon and threw them at Christian, piece by piece. Christian grabbed a broom to defend herself and used it to strike her employer. She beat Belote in the head and face and with the broom and then stuffed a towel into her mouth to muffle her screams. The towel eventually suffocated Belote to death. Christian left her employer's beaten, battered, and bloodied body on the floor of the Belote home. Virginia Christian was arrested and charged with first-degree murder. She confessed to the crime, but claimed that she had never intended to kill Mrs. Belote, and had only intended to defend herself and silence the woman's screams. But Christian's actions were so much more complicated than self-defense. As historian Lashawn Harris has so brilliantly concluded, Christian's act that day was a "conscious act of self-preservation and survival and arguably a direct challenge to race oppression, labor exploitation, and white brutality." She seized her own brand of justice for the wrongful theft accusations, insults, and physical assaults. Like so many enslaved women centuries earlier, the cards were stacked against Christian in the judicial system of Jim Crow-era Elizabeth City County, Virginia. Her claim of self-defense was not accepted by the court and her counsel failed to get her charges reduced, which would have spared her life. At the height of this era, Blacks who killed powerful whites in the South were certain to meet death by state execution or lynching. The jury returned a guilty verdict after just twenty-three minutes of deliberation. Virginia Christian was executed by electric chair on August 16, 1912, the day after her seventeenth birthday. She was the first woman to die by electric chair in Virginia.[4]

In August 1952 in Live Oak, Florida, Ruby McCollum, an African American woman, shot Dr. Leroy Adams, a white physician and state senator-elect four times in his medical office. He did not survive. According to Ruby, who was pregnant and married, the doctor had been raping her for some time and would not leave her alone. She told officials that the doctor fathered the child she was carrying plus her youngest child. Although whites in Live Oak would have preferred to think the two had some sinister business dealing or even an actual affair, Ruby stated in no uncertain terms that she had been repeatedly raped by this doctor. Rapes done to Black women by powerful white men are an uninterrupted and essential feature of

Black women's experiences in America. As a southern Black woman with no education, Ruby was rendered impotent to stave off his sexual abuse given the compounded power Adams embodied as a wealthy white man with social, economic, and political status.

In 2018, seventeen-year-old Chrystul Kizer was arrested for shooting and killing Randall P. Volar III, a thirty-four-year-old white man who had trafficked her since she was sixteen. Apparently, the teen drove from Milwaukee to Kenosha, Wisconsin, to kill her trafficker. After she murdered him, she set his house on fire, and stole his BMW. Chrystul claims that she killed Volar because he was sexually abusing her and other underage girls. In other words, she believed she was avenging the wrongs done to them and liberating these girls from their enslaver forever. Wisconsin prosecutors ignored these facts and charged Kizer with first-degree intentional homicide. According to one advocate for Kizer, "That lack of protection from the systems we claim keep us safe required that she act in self-defense to survive."[5] And similar to the women in this book, Chrystul Kizer is receiving little sympathy from the Kenosha judicial system. The prosecutors do not see her as Volar's victim, but instead paint him as her victim, thereby willfully ignoring his actions as an enslaver, sexual predator, and trafficker. The prosecution challenged Chrystul's defense team's efforts to build her defense using a 2008 Wisconsin law that allows survivors of child sex trafficking such as Chrystul to use an affirmative defense. An affirmative defense would allow her to claim she acted in self-defense. If permitted to use this defense, her attorneys could then discuss Volar's history of sex trafficking of minors, which is an important part of the context of this case and the reason he was killed. Kenosha County Circuit Court Judge David Wilk sided with the prosecution and denied Chrystul's team the right to use an affirmative defense, underscoring the state's willful refusal to see her as a victim and its intention to prevent the jury from seeing her as Volar's victim as well. Judge Wilk's decision was later overturned by an appellate court. The prosecution persisted even after that decision and requested that the state's supreme court weigh in on whether Chrystul's team could use an affirmative defense. In 2022, the court ruled in Kizer's favor.[6]

Cyntoia Brown Long is another Black woman who survived sex trafficking as a teen. In 2006, when she was just sixteen years old, she was convicted of murdering a man who was there to have sex with her.

Because the judicial system would not see her as a victim, she was sentenced to life in prison. Cyntoia did fifteen years in prison before she obtained clemency in 2019. Now an activist for judicial system reform, she commented on the Kizer case – specifically, the Kenosha prosecution's efforts to deny her an affirmative defense:

> I think another thing it's really important to note is that this is not saying that this is just a get out of jail free card. It's just saying that I have the right to present [my side of the story]. ... I find it disturbing that the prosecution doesn't want her to be able to tell her story. They don't want her voice to be heard. And that's something that we really struggle with in the justice system.
>
> Instead of seeking to punish girls who react out of trauma, who react to protect themselves in the only way that they know how, instead of seeking to throw them in prison, we try to figure out what's going on with them and help them to really uncover all of that trauma and heal from that and learn how they can live a normal life.[7]

Cyntoia Brown Long lays bare the effects of slavery and trauma, and how the judicial system tries to silence and prosecute survivors of modern slavery who take justice into their own hands by killing their enslavers. The irony is that the modern judicial system that she and Chrystul Kizer navigated had many of the same pitfalls that enslaved women stumbled into hundreds of years earlier – specifically, judges that ignored what they had endured at the hands of cruel and abusive enslavers.

These women who utilized a Black feminist practice of justice in the modern era not only find much in common with one another but are also linked to the women in this book and countless other unnamed examples across the long arc of American history. The lesson we can all take from Charlotte, Phoebe, the two Phillises, Annis, the two Lucys, Cloe, Rose Butler, Jane Williams, Nelly, Betsy, Ellen, Ruby McCollum, Cyntoia Brown Long, and Chrystul Kizer is that their stories are cautionary tales of what happens when slavery and its associated injustice and inhumanity is continually heaped upon powerless Black women, to no end.

NOTES

Introduction

1. *Scioto Gazette*, February 15, 1812; *Gleaner*, March 27, 1812; *Commonwealth of Kentucky* v. *Charlotte*, 1812; Probate County Records, Order Book 4, 496–98, and Order Book 5, 2–5, Clark County, Kentucky Public Library.

2. Condemned people often sought to delay their executions. Using pregnancy as a reason was a gendered option used by only women. For more on efforts to delay, see Stuart Banner, *The Death Penalty: An American History* (Cambridge: Harvard University Press, 2002), 18; *Scioto Gazette*, February 15, 1812; *Gleaner*, March 27, 1812; *Commonwealth of Kentucky* v. *Charlotte*, 1812.

3. Even Ann Jones in her feminist classic, *Women Who Kill*, dedicates just three pages to enslaved women. See Ann Jones, *Women Who Kill* (New York: The Feminist Press, 2009), 65–69; Melton A. McLaurin, *Celia, A Slave: A True Story* (New York: Avon Books, 1991); Nikki M. Taylor, *Driven Towards Madness: Fugitive Slave Margaret Garner and Tragedy on the Ohio* (Athens: Ohio University Press, 2016). Other articles about enslaved women and violence include Wilma King, "'Mad' Enough to Kill: Enslaved Women, Murder, and Southern Courts," *Journal of African American History* vol. 92, no. 1 (Winter 2007): 37–56; Rebecca Hall, "Not Killing Me Softly: African American Women, Slave Revolts, and Historical Constructions of Racialized Gender," *Freedom Center Journal* vol. 2 (2010): 1–47; Deborah A. Lee and Warren R. Hofstra, "Race, Memory, and the Death of Robert Berkeley: A Murder ... of ... Horrible and Savage Barbarity," *The Journal of Southern History* vol. 65, no. 1 (February 1999): 41–76.

4. David V. Baker, "Black Female Executions in Historical Context," *Criminal Justice Review* vol. 33, no. 1 (March 2008): 66.

5. Philip J. Schwarz, *Twice Condemned: Slaves and the Criminal Laws of Virginia, 1705–1865* (Union: The Lawbook Exchange, Ltd., 1998), 30.

6. Baker, "Black Female Executions in Historical Context," 66.
7. Glenn McNair, "Slave Women, Capital Crime, and Criminal Justice in Georgia," *The Georgia Historical Quarterly* vol. 93, no. 2 (Summer 2009): 140, 144, 145.
8. Darlene Clark Hine, "Female Slave Resistance: The Economics of Sex," Darlene Clark Hine, ed., *Hine Sight: Black Women and the Re-Construction of American History* (New York: Carlson, 1994), 27–47; Amrita Chakrabarti Myers, "'Sisters in Arms': Slave Women's Resistance to Slavery in the United States," *Past Imperfect* vol. 5 (1996): 144; Deborah Gray White, *Ar'n't I a Woman? Female Slaves in the Plantation South* (New York: W. W. Norton & Company, 1999), 77, 78–79, 81–84; Thavolia Glymph, "Fighting Slavery on Slaveholders' Terrain," *OAH Magazine of History* vol. 23, no. 2 (2009): 39; Stephanie M. H. Camp, *Closer to Freedom: Enslaved Women & Everyday Resistance in the Plantation South* (Chapel Hill: The University of North Carolina Press, 2004), 3, 50–1.
9. Myers, "'Sisters in Arms,'" 148–49.
10. Herbert Aptheker includes almost no women in his discussion of 250 major American slave plots and rebellions in his seminal study, *American Negro Slave Revolts*. See Herbert Aptheker, *American Negro Slave Revolts* (New York: International Publishers, 1943). Douglas R. Egerton, author of *Gabriel's Rebellion*, dismisses women's roles as in the "periphery." He also concludes that women's nominal participation in slave rebellions is owing to their relative lack of mobility. See Douglas R. Egerton, *Gabriel's Rebellion: The Virginia Conspiracies of 1800 and 1802* (Chapel Hill: The University of North Carolina Press, 1993), 22, 53, 68. Similarly, Kenneth S. Greenberg, who edited Nat Turner's *Confessions*, contends that Nat Turner's rebellion had an "exclusively male nature." See his discussion on this, Kenneth S. Greenberg, ed., *The Confessions of Nat Turner and Related Documents*(New York: Bedford/St. Martin's Press, 1996), 12. For more on the masculine sphere of insurrections, see James Sidbury, *Ploughshares Into Swords: Race, Rebellion, and Identity in Gabriel's Virginia, 1730–1810* (New York: Cambridge University Press, 1997), 90, 92. In his recent monograph on Nat Turner, historian Patrick H. Breen, like so many who do acknowledge women's participation, focus on women as wives to rebels. In that vein, Breen focuses on three women who have been presumed to be Turner's wife: Fanny, Cherry, and Mariah. He is mostly concerned with Turner's wife's true identity and not with the material and tactical assistance or moral support she may have given Turner. To his credit, he does a good job illuminating the contributions of two other women

with more clarity: Lucy and Beck. See Patrick H. Breen, *The Land Shall Be Deluged in Blood: A New History of the Nat Turner Revolt* (New York: Oxford University Press, 2015), 18, 47, 117, 125, 133. For other discussions of Turner's wife, see Greenberg, *Confessions of Nat Turner*, 12; and Scot French, *The Rebellious Slave: Nat Turner in American Memory* (Boston: Houghton Mifflin, 2004), 226–28, 450–51; Albert E. Stone, *The Return of Nat Turner: History, Literature, and Cultural Politics in Sixties America* (Athens, GA: University of Georgia Press, 1992), 327; Winthrop D. Jordan, *Tumult and Silence at Second Creek: An Inquiry into a Civil War Conspiracy* (Baton Rouge: Louisiana State University Press, 1993), 176; Edward A. Pearson, ed., *Designs Against Charleston: The Trial Record of the Denmark Vesey Slave Conspiracy of 1822* (Chapel Hill: The University of North Carolina Press, 1999), 129, 130, 131. The primary sources are the basis of many of these conclusions. For example, Ben Woolfolk told a co-conspirator in Gabriel's plot to "keep the business secret ... [do] not divulge to a *woman*." Historian James Sidbury, instead of assuming that the comment was a reflection of Woolfolk's personal, misguided views about women, contends that the rebels as a group may not have trusted Black women as a policy.One of the conspirators in Denmark Vesey's 1822 plot in Charleston insisted that "no woman knows anything about it." Alfred, an organizer of the 1861 Adams County, Mississippi, conspiracy, indicated that women heard about the plan, but had no direct involvement. "The plan," he said, "was men's work." In their defense, these men may have been trying to protect the women by insisting they had no role in their plots. After all, protecting Black women from punishment just might be the ultimate expression of Black masculinity during the age of slavery. We would be remiss to take their views at face value and assume enslaved women were purely pacifists and did not play central roles in collective resistance.

11. Vanessa M. Holden, *Surviving Southampton: African American Women and Resistance in Nat Turner's Community* (Urbana: University of Illinois Press), 7, 9.

12. Eugene D. Genovese, *From Rebellion to Revolution: Afro-American Slave Revolts in the Making of the Modern World* (Baton Rouge: Louisiana State University Press, 1979), xiv. On Hall's definition of revolt see, Hall, "Not Killing Me Softly," 4, 33; Also see Rebecca Hall's imaginative graphic memoir about her difficulties finding material on the topic of women and revolt, *Wake: The Hidden History of Women-Led Slave Revolts* (New York: Simon and Schuster, 2021). Herbert Aptheker defines an insurrection as "a minimum of ten slaves

involved; freedom as the apparent aim of the disaffected slaves; contemporary references labelling the event as an uprising, plot, insurrection, or the equivalent of these terms". See Aptheker, *American Negro Slave Revolts*, 162.

13. The full Bacon quote: "Revenge is a kind of wild justice; which the more man's nature runs to, the more ought the law to weed it out." See Francis, Bacon, *The Essays, or Councils, Civil and Moral of Sir Francis Bacon ... With a Table of the Colours of Good and Evil and a Discourse of the Wisdom of the Ancients* (London: George Sawbridge, 1696), 9–10; for another example of retributive violence used by indentured workers in colonial Fiji in response to cruel acts by the plantation owners, see Robert Nicole, *Disturbing History: Resistance in Early Colonial Fiji* (Honolulu: University of Hawai'i Press, 2010), 159–64; Nietzsche quoted in Guy Elgat, "Nietzsche on the Genealogy of Universal Moral Justice," *History of Philosophy Quarterly* vol. 33, no. 2 (April 2016): 160–61; Ted Peters and Martin E. Marty, *Sin Boldly: Justifying Faith for Fragile and Broken Souls* (Minneapolis: Media, 2015), 93.

14. Scholar-activist and law professor Gloria J. Browne-Marshall's primer *She Took Justice* is a sweeping overview of how Black women have historically pursued justice in spite of debilitating legal obstacles and impediments. Black women emerge defiant and triumphant in her book. Gloria J. Browne-Marshall, *She Took Justice: The Black Woman, Law, and Power 1619–1969* (New York: Routledge, 2021).

15. Genovese, *From Rebellion to Revolution*, xiv.

16. Hall, "Not Killing Me Softly," 33. I reject Elizabeth Fox-Genovese's rationale for the gender differentiation in violent slave resistance. She contends that women, with less physical strength and greater reproductive burdens were less able to participate in organized, collective action. See Elizabeth Fox-Genovese, "Strategies and Forms of Resistance: Focus on Slave Women in the United States," *Black Women in United States History*, Darlene Clark-Hine, ed. (New York: Carlson, 1990), 421–22. *Brooding Over Bloody Revenge* illustrates that women *did* participate in organized and collective slave resistance.

17. According to Stuart Banner, capital punishment served three primary purposes: deterrence, retribution, and repentance. See Banner, *The Death Penalty*, 22.

18. Hammurabi's Code dates back to Babylon 4,000 years ago. The Babylonian *Talion*, or law of retribution, states that retribution must be proportional to the injury. It established the concept of "an eye for an eye." The Pentateuch and the Bible also have the same principle. See

Leviticus 24:17–20 and Exodus 21:22–25, which states "if there is serious injury, you are to take life for life, eye for eye, tooth for tooth, hand for hand, foot for foot, burn for burn, wound for wound, bruise for bruise." In the Quran, the concept of "equal for equal," or *quisas*, can be found in 5:45, which reads, "and We ordained for them therein a life for a life, an eye for an eye, a nose for a nose, an ear for an ear, a tooth for a tooth, and for wounds is legal retribution. But whoever gives [up his right as] charity, it is an expiation for him. And whoever does not judge by what Allah has revealed – then it is those who are the wrongdoers [i.e., the unjust]." However, the Quran and the New Testament also encourage forgiveness of those who cause injury. In terms of philosophers, Immanuel Kant wrote extensively about retributive justice and "just deserts." In his warning against stealing, he wrote "that person deprives himself (by the principle of retribution) of security in any property . . . . [and if] he has committed murder he must die." See Immanuel Kant, *The Metaphysics of Morals*, trans. Mary Gregor (New York: Cambridge University Press, 1991), 142. A more recent philosopher, Ayn Rand, advocated retaliation, especially in defense of one's rights. She wrote, "The necessary consequence of man's right to life is his right to self-defense. In a civilized society, force may be used in retaliation and only against those who initiate its use." See Ayn Rand, *The Virtue of Selfishness: A New Concept of Egoism* (New York: Signet, 1961), 103.

19. Matthew Haist, "Deterrence in a Sea of 'Just Deserts': Are Utilitarian Goals Achievable in a World of 'Limiting to Retributivism'?," *The Journal of Criminal Law and Criminology* vol. 99, no. 3 (2009): 800; Mark R. Fondacaro and Megan J. O'Toole, "American Punitiveness and Mass Incarceration: Psychological Perspectives on Retributive and Consequentialist Responses to Crime," *New Criminal Law Review: An International and Interdisciplinary Journal* vol. 18, no. 4 (Fall 2015): 481, 484.

20. Aline Helg, *Slave No More: Self-Liberation Before Abolitionism in the Americas* (Chapel Hill: University of North Carolina Press, 2016), 108–09; George M. Stroud, *A Sketch of the Laws Related to Slavery in the Several States of the United States of America* (Philadelphia: H. Longstreth,1856), 86, 87, 105; Banner, *The Death Penalty*, 75.

21. Frantz Fanon, *The Wretched of the Earth* (New York: Grove Press, 1963), 51.

22. Thomas D. Morris, "Slaves and the Rules of Evidence in Criminal Trials – Symposium on the Law of Slavery: Criminal and Civil Law of Slavery," *Chicago-Kent Law Review* 68 (June 1993): 1210, 1229, 1230; Helg, *Slave No More*, 85; Schwarz, *Twice Condemned*, 3.

23. In Spanish territories, the slave code was called *siete partidas*; the French called it the *code noir*. Helg, *Slave No More*, 85.
24. Not to be confused with the legal doctrine that allowed clergy to avoid prosecution for minor crimes. More on the benefit of the clergy, see Banner, *The Death Penalty*, 62–63.
25. Stroud, *A Sketch of the Laws*, 77–80, 86–87; "Codification of the Statute Law in Georgia": https://academic.udayton.edu/race/02rights/slavelaw.htm#1.
26. Banner, *The Death Penalty*, 8; A. Leon Higginbotham, Jr., and Anne F. Jacobs, "The Law Only as an Enemy: The Legitimization of Racial Powerlessness through the Colonial and Antebellum Criminal Laws of Virginia," *North Carolina Law Review* vol. 70, no. 4 (1992): 977, 978, 979; Helg, *Slave No More*, 85.
27. Banner, *The Death Penalty*, 18–20.
28. Morris, "Slaves and the Rules of Evidence," 1227, 1230, 1231; *The Charleston Daily Courier*, January 27, 1842; *State v. Billy Williams*, 1842; Randolph B. Campbell, *Empire of Slavery: The Peculiar Institution in Texas, 1821–1865* (Baton Rouge: Louisiana State University Press, 1989), 107.
29. Higginbotham Jr. and Jacobs, "The Law Only as an Enemy," 986, 1011, 1013–14.
30. Marvin L. Michael Kay and Lorin Lee Cary, "'The Planters Suffer Little or Nothing': North Carolina Compensations for Executed Slaves, 1748–1772," *Science & Society* vol. 40, no. 3 (1976): 291.
31. James M. Campbell, *Slavery on Trial: Race, Class, and Criminal Justice in Antebellum Richmond, Virginia* (Gainesville: University Press of Florida, 2007), 81, 106; Stroud, *A Sketch of the Laws*, 92.
32. Higginbotham Jr. and Jacobs, "The Law Only as an Enemy," 986, 997, 998, 1003.
33. Nancy Marder, "The Changing Composition of the American Jury," *Scholarly Commons* (2013): 67–68: https://scholarship.kentlaw.iit.edu/docs_125/5; James Forman, Jr., "Juries and Race in the Nineteenth Century," *Yale Law Journal* vol. 113, no. 4 (January 2004): 910.
34. Higginbotham Jr. and Jacobs, "The Law Only as an Enemy," 1003; Stroud, *A Sketch of the Laws*, 92.
35. Banner, *The Death Penalty*, 16; McLaurin, *Celia, A Slave*, 101, 102, 106; Schwarz, *Twice Condemned*, 240–44.
36. Daniel J. Flanigan, "Criminal Procedure in Slave Trials in the Antebellum South," *The Journal of Southern History* vol. 40, no. 4 (1974): 544–46 *passim*, 550; Banner, *The Death Penalty*, 56; Glenn McNair, *Criminal Injustice: Slaves and Free Blacks in*

Georgia's Criminal Justice System (Charlottesville: University of Virginia Press, 2009), 119, 120; Higginbotham Jr. and Jacobs, "The Law Only as an Enemy," 997, 999, 1003; Campbell, *Slavery on Trial*, 77, 96–97. An 1801 law gave the Virginia governor the option of sentencing enslaved people to sale and transportation to another country, instead of execution; Stroud, *A Sketch of the Laws*, 92.

37. Campbell, *Slavery on Trial*, 80.
38. Kay and Cary, "'The Planters Suffer Little or Nothing,'" 291.
39. Banner, *The Death Penalty*, 16.
40. By 1821, though, every state prohibited murdering an enslaved person. See Stroud, *A Sketch of the Laws*, 20–21.

1 Phillis and Phoebe

1. _____.*A Few Lines on Occasion of the Untimely End of Mark and Phillis, Who Were Executed at Cambridge, September 18th for Their Master, Capt. John Codman of Charlestown* (Boston: 1755): www.loc.gov/resource/rbpe.03501 50a.
2. *Boston Evening Post*, July 7, 1755.
3. Abner Cheney Goodell, *The Trial and Execution for Petit Treason, of Mark and Phillis, Slaves of Capt. John Codman: Who Murdered Their Master at Charlestown, Mass., in 1755; For Which the Man was Hanged and Gibbeted, and the Woman Was Burned to Death* (Cambridge: John Wilson and Son, 1833): www.loc.gov/resource/llst.023; Mark, *The Last & Dying Words of Mark, Aged about 30 years, A Negro Man Who Belonged to the Late Captain John Codman, of Charlestown; Who Was Executed the 18th of September, 1855 for Poysoning his Above said Master* (Boston: np, 1755): www.masshist.org/database/viewer.php?item_id=4231&mode=large&img_step=1&.
4. Mark Peterson, *The City-State of Boston: The Rise and Fall of an Atlantic Power, 1630–1865* (Princeton University Press, 2019), 266.
5. Lorenzo Greene, *Negro in Colonial New England* (New York: Columbia University Press, 1942), 82; Chernoh M. Sesay "The Revolutionary Black Roots of Slavery's Abolition in Massachusetts," *The New England Quarterly* vol. 87, no. 1 (2014): 104. For the 1754 census, see: https://primaryresearch.org/slave-census/?town=&county=Middlesex. Charlestown, however, did not submit a census for its enslaved residents in 1754; "An Overview of Massachusetts to 1820": www.colonialsociety.org/node/1120.
6. African American Trail Project: https://africanamericantrailproject.tufts.edu/18th-century-sites.

7. Calvin Hurd, ed., *New England Library of Genealogy and Personal History: This Volume of the New England Library Containing Genealogy and History of Representative Citizens of the Commonwealth of Massachusetts* (Boston: New England Historical Publishing Company, 1902), 12; Cora Codman Wolcott, *The Codmans of Charlestown and Boston: 1637–1929* (Brookline: Thomas Todd Company, 1930), 6; Stella P. Bruce, ed., *The Ancestry of Rev. John Codman of Boston and Dorchester, Massachusetts* (Leucadia: Stella P. Bruce, 1990), 8, 9, 10; Greene, *Negro in Colonial New England*, 355. For currency converter, see Eric W. Nye, "Pounds Sterling to Dollars: Historical Conversion of Currency": www .uwyo.edu/numimage/currency.htm; Zechariah G. Whitman, *The History of the Ancient and Honorable Artillery Company, From its Formation in 1637 and Charter in 1638, to the Present Time; Comprising the Biographies of the Distinguished Civil, Literary, Religious, and Military Men of the Colony, Province, and Commonwealth* (Boston: John H. Eastburn Printer, 1842), 284, 403: https://archive.org/details/historyofancientoowhit/page/436/mode/2up? q=codman/; "A Complete History of Colonial and Early American Wars Fought on American Soil": www.americanwars.org/ma-ancient-artillery-company/commissioned-officers-1700-1799.htm.

8. The names Phoebe, Quacoe, Kerr and Robbin have the alternate spellings of Phebe, Quaco, Carr, and Robin in the historical record. I use the versions most often used in the inquest proceedings.

9. Goodell, *The Trial and Execution for Petit Treason, of Mark and Phillis*; Commonwealth of Massachusetts, Probate Court (Middlesex County), *Probate Records 1648–1924: Middlesex County* (Middlesex, Massachusetts, 1965): www.ancestry.com; Mark, *The Last & Dying Words of Mark*.

10. Marjoleine Kars, *Blood on the River: A Chronicle of Mutiny and Freedom on the Wild Coast* (New York: The New Press, 2020), 116–17.

11. Jared Ross Hardesty, *Unfreedom: Slavery and Dependence in Eighteenth-Century Boston* (New York University Press, 2016), 12–13, 25–29.

12. Mark, *The Last & Dying Words of Mark*; Goodell, *The Trial and Execution for Petit Treason, of Mark and Phillis*; Whitman, *The History of the Ancient and Honorable Artillery Company*, 429. Commonwealth of Massachusetts, *Probate Records 1648–1924*. Mark spelled Plympton, Massachusetts, phonetically and wrote "Plimtown"; James Oliver Horton and Lois E. Horton, *In Hope of Liberty: Culture, Community, and Protest Among Northern Free*

Blacks, 1700–1860 (New York: Oxford University Press, 1997), 25. For more information on what Mark's early childhood as a slave in Barbados would have entailed, see Hardesty, *Unfreedom*, 23–25.

13. Hardesty, *Unfreedom*, 44, 112.

14. Commonwealth of Massachusetts, *Probate Records 1648–1924*.

15. Mark, *The Last & Dying Words of Mark*; Goodell, *The Trial and Execution for Petit Treason, of Mark and Phillis*.

16. Kelly A. Ryan, *Everyday Crimes: Social Violence and Civil Rights in Early America* (New York University Press, 2019), 129–30; Goodell, *The Trial and Execution for Petit Treason, of Mark and Phillis*; Hardesty, *Unfreedom*, 68–69.

17. Mark, *The Last & Dying Words of Mark*; Goodell, *The Trial and Execution for Petit Treason, of Mark and Phillis*.

18. *The New-York Evening Post*, June 19, 1749.

19. Mark, *The Last & Dying Words of Mark*; Goodell, *The Trial and Execution for Petit Treason, of Mark and Phillis*.

20. For more biblical statements prohibiting murder, see Genesis 9:6, Proverbs 6:16–19, Deuteronomy 19:10, 27:24, and 27:25, Exodus 20:13 and 23:7.

21. *Ibid.*

22. *Ibid.*

23. Mark, *The Last & Dying Words of Mark*; Goodell, *The Trial and Execution for Petit Treason, of Mark and Phillis*.

24. Raw cashews must be boiled or roasted to release the toxic urushiol before they can be eaten. Mark, *The Last & Dying Words of Mark*; Goodell, *The Trial and Execution for Petit Treason, of Mark and Phillis*.

25. David V. Baker, *Women and Capital Punishment in the United States: An Analytical History* (Jefferson, NC: McFarland & Company, 2016), 115; "The Database of Executions in the United States of America": https://files .deathpenaltyinfo.org/legacy/documents/ESPYyear.pdf; Harriet Smither, ed., "The Diary of Adolphus Sterne," *The Southwestern Historical Quarterly* vol. 32 (July 1928–April 1929): 166; "Jimson Weed": www .rxlist.com/jimson_weed/supplements.htm; Sharla M. Fett, *Working Cures: Healing, Health, and Power on Southern Slave Plantations* (Chapel Hill: University of North Carolina Press, 2002), 72, 81.

26. Chelsea Berry, "Poisoned Relations: Medicine, Sorcery, and Poison Trials in the Contested Atlantic, 1680–1850" (PhD diss., Georgetown University, 2019), 55, 116, 153, 170: https://repository.library .georgetown.edu/bitstream/handle/10822/1054953/Berry_george town_0076D_14194.pdf?sequence=1&isAllowed=y; Fett, *Working Cures*, 70–71, 142–43, 159–60.

27. The Louisville Daily Courier, May 31, 1849.

28. *Alexandria Gazette and Virginia Advertiser*, September 19, 1859, and *Richmond Dispatch*, September 19, 1859; "Oxalic Acid": www .cdc.gov/niosh/idlh/144627.html; J. Wang, and B. Kan et al., "Esophageal Mucosa Exfoliation Induced by Oxalic Acid Poisoning: A Case Report," *in Experimental and Therapeutic Medicine* vol. 11, no. 1 (2016): 208–12. The ultimate fate of this girl is unclear. The timing of this case near John Brown's trial likely diminished its significance in the press.

29. Goodell, *The Trial and Execution for Petit Treason, of Mark and Phillis*; Mark, *The Last & Dying Words of Mark*.

30. Mark, *The Last & Dying Words of Mark*; Goodell, *The Trial and Execution for Petit Treason, of Mark and Phillis*; "Abigail Paine Greenleaf to Robert Treat Paine," July 1, 1755, Robert Treat Paine Papers, vol. I, Massachusetts Historical Society: www.masshist.org/pub lications/rtpp/index.php/view/RTP1d234.

31. "Heavy Metal Poisoning": https://rarediseases.org/rare-diseases/ heavy-metal-poisoning/; "Lead Poisoning": www.healthline.com/ health/lead-poisoning#symptoms.

32. Mark, *The Last & Dying Words of Mark; Boston Gazette*, July 1, 1775.

33. Goodell, *The Trial and Execution for Petit Treason, of Mark and Phillis;* R. M. S. McConaghey, "Sir George Baker and the Devon shire Police": http://citeseerx.ist.psu.edu/viewdoc/download?doi= 10.1.1.284.8714&rep=rep1&type=pdf.

34. Mark, *The Last & Dying Words of Mark*; Goodell, *The Trial and Execution for Petit Treason, of Mark and Phillis*.

35. Ichiro Yajima et al., "Arsenic-mediated hyperpigmentation in skin via NF-kappa B/endothelin-1 signaling in an originally developed hairless mouse model" in *Archives of Toxicology* vol. 91, no. 11 (2017): 3507–16: doi:10.1007/s00204-017-1975-0; Hongbo Zhai, Klaus Peter Wilhelm, and Howard I. Maibach, *Marzulli and Maibach's Dermatotoxicology* (Boca Raton: CRC Press, 2007), 877; *Boston Evening Post*, July 7, 1755. Also see *Boston Gazette*, July 7, 1755.

36. The coroner's jury consisted of Richard Phillips, Samuel Kettell, John Larkin, Samuel Larkin, Jr., William Thompson, Thomas Larkin, Richard Devens, Josiah Whittemore, Samuel Hendly, Mitchell Brigden, Nathaniel Brown, David Cheever, Samuel Larkin, Benjamin Brazier, Barnabas Davis, Samuell Sprague, and Edwin Goodwin. Goodell, *The Trial and Execution for Petit Treason, of Mark and Phillis*.

37. Goodell, *The Trial and Execution for Petit Treason, of Mark and Phillis.*

38. *Boston Gazette,* July 7, 1755; Mark, *The Last & Dying Words of Mark*; Goodell, *The Trial and Execution for Petit Treason, of Mark and Phillis.*

39. Mark, *The Last & Dying Words of Mark*; Josiah Bartlett, *An Historical Sketch of Charlestown, in the County of Middlesex and Commonwealth of Massachusetts Read to the Assembly of Citizens at the Opening of Washington Hall* (Boston: John Eliot Printers, 1814), 6.

40. *Boston Evening Post,* July 7, 1755; Goodell, *The Trial and Execution for Petit Treason, of Mark and Phillis.*

41. Goodell, *The Trial and Execution for Petit Treason, of Mark and Phillis.*

42. Goodell, *The Trial and Execution for Petit Treason, of Mark and Phillis*; Helg, *Slave No More,* 83.

43. Harvard-educated, Chief Justice Stephen Sewall was the nephew of judge, Samuel Sewall, who had served as a justice in the Salem Witch Trials (1692–93). Sewall apologized for his role in the trials five years later. Notably, too, Samuel Sewall authored the first abolitionist tract, *The Selling of Joseph* (1700). Stephen Sewall had served on the Superior Court since 1739 and as chief justice since 1752. Benjamin Lynde, Jr., was the son of the well-known chief justice with the same name. Lynde served the court in 1746–71 and presided over the trials of the Boston Massacre. Neither John Cushing nor Chambers Russell had formal legal training. Russell began his career as a justice of the peace in 1740 and served as justice for the Superior Court in 1752–66. For details on Lynde, see *Diary of Benjamin Lynde and Benjamin Lynde, Jr.,* 179: https:// archive.org/stream/diariesbenjaminoolyndgoog/diariesbenjaminoo lyndgoog_djvu.txt; "The Massachusetts Bench and Bar: Biographical Register of John Adam's Contemporaries": www .masshist.org/publications/adams-papers/index.php/view/ADMS-05-01-01-0012; Ibram X. Kendi, *Stamped from the Beginning: The Definitive History of Racist Ideas in America* (New York: Nation Books, 2016), 66–67.

44. Goodell, *The Trial and Execution for Petit Treason, of Mark and Phillis.*

45. *Boston Evening Post,* August 25, 1755; Goodell, *The Trial and Execution for Petit Treason, of Mark and Phillis*; Annette Louise Bickford, *Southern Mercy: Empire and American Civilization in Juvenile Reform 1890–1944* (University of Toronto Press, 2016), 68.

46. Mark, *The Last & Dying Words of Mark*.

47. *Boston Evening Post*, September 22, 1755; *Boston Gazette*, September 22, 1755; *Boston Weekly News-Letter*, September 25, 1755. For more on gibbeting, see Andy Wright, "The Incredibly Disturbing Historical Practice of Gibbeting," Atlas Obscura, October 11, 2016: www.atlasobscura.com/articles/the-incredibly-disturbing-medieval-practice-of-gibbeting. Gibbeting was a gendered practice in that only men were subjected to it.

48. William Blackstone, *Analysis of the Laws of England* (1766), 119; Sarah Tarlow and Zoe Dyndor, "The Landscape of the Gibbet," *Landscape History* vol. 36 (2015): 72, 75.

49. Tarlow and Dyndor, "The Landscape of the Gibbet," 76, 78, 79.

50. *Ibid.*, 76, 83.

51. Caleb Rea, "The Journal of Dr. Caleb Rea, Written During the Expedition Against Ticonderoga in 1758," June 1, 1758, *Essex Institute Historical Collections* vol. XVIII (April, May, June 1881): 88–89; "Paul Revere to Jeremy Belknap," circa 1798, Massachusetts Historical Society: www.masshist.org/database/viewer.php?item_id=99&img_step=1&mode=transcript#page1.

52. Quito Swan, "Smoldering Memories and Burning Questions: The Politics of Remembering Sally Bassett and Slavery in Bermuda," *Politics of Memory: Making Slavery Visible in the Public Space*, Ana Lucia Araujo, ed. (New York: Routledge, 2012), 81.

53. For examples of works that relegate Phillis and Phoebe to accomplices, see Shane White, "Slavery in the North," *OAH Magazine of History* vol. 17, no. 3 (2003): 17–21. White credits Mark exclusively with planning the murder. White does not even consider that the women may have been the ones who conceived of the murder and the means. Another scholar who depicts Mark and Quacoe as the leaders is Jared Ross Hardesty. See his *Unfreedom*, 23–28, 66–69 and "'The Negro at the Gate:' Enslaved Labor in Eighteen-Century Boston," *The New England Quarterly* vol. 87 (March 2014): 77; Also see, Alan Rogers, *Murder and the Death Penalty in Massachusetts* (Amherst: University of Massachusetts, 2008) and Horton & Horton, *In Hope of Liberty*, 25. Also see, Alan Rogers, *Murder and the Death Penalty in Massachusetts* (Amherst: University of Massachusetts, 2008). Kelly A. Ryan, however, presents Phoebe, Phillis, and Mark as co-equal conspirators. See Ryan, *Everyday Crimes*, 77, 92.

54. *Boston Evening Post*, September 25, 1755; *Boston Gazette*, September 22, 1755; Goodell, *The Trial and Execution for Petit Treason, of Mark and Phillis*; "Paul Revere to Jeremy Belknap," circa 1798; *Boston Evening Post*, September 22, 1755; Wendy Warren,

New England Bound: Slavery and Colonization in Early America (New York: Liveright Publishing Corporation, 2016), 199; Helg, *Slave No More*, 108; Adalberto Aguirre and David V. Baker, "Slave Executions in the United States: A Descriptive Analysis of Social and Historical Factors," *Social Science Journal* vol. 36, no. 1 (January 1999):1–9; M. Watt Espy and John Ortiz Smykla, "Executions in the United States, 1608–2002: The ESPY File," Inter-university Consortium for Political and Social Research, 2016: https://doi.org/10 .3886/ICPSR08451.v5. In the Espy index, long considered the most comprehensive database on executions in the USA, 100 percent (59/59) of the people executed for poisoning before 1865 were Black. Of these 59 people executed for poisoning in the USA before 1865, 42 – or 71 percent – were men. The ESPY record, though comprehensive, is not exhaustive and omits many execution cases, including the Phoebe, Phillis, and Mark case. The death penalty database at www .deathpenaltyusa.org is comprehensive and more exhaustive, but lacks details about each case including the name of the victims, specific nature of the crime, or the dates of the crime or conviction. It also would be helpful if the sources of the information were included for each case. The most thorough of the state records are Maryland's database on slave executions 1726–75, which includes the names of the accused and the victims, date of alleged crime, type of crime committed, and dates of conviction and execution. This database also includes the sources.

55. Jennifer Harris, "Offering Nothing: Phillis Hammond and the 'Bitter Effects of Sin,'" *Early American Literature* vol. 55 (November 2020): 401–02; *Boston Evening Post*, January 21, 1751, March 4, 1751, and April 22, 1751; *The Boston Post-Boy*, April 8, 1751.

56. Fielder M. M. Beall, ed., *Colonial Families of the United States Descended from the Immigrants who Arrived Before 1700, Mostly from England and Scotland, and who are now Represented by Citizens of the Following Names, Bell, Beal, Bale, Beale, Beall* (Washington, D.C.: C. H. Potter, 1929), 172; Maryland, "Hanged Slaves By Date": https://msa.maryland.gov/megafile/msa/speccol/sc2900/sc2908/ 000001/000819/pdf/chart28.pdf; Joseph E. Holloway, "Slave Insurrections in the United States: An Overview": http://slaverebellion .info/index.php?page=united-states-insurrections; Espy and Smykla, "The ESPY File"; "The Database of Executions in the United States of America": https://files.deathpenaltyinfo.org/legacy/documents/ ESPYyear.pdf.

57. *Proceedings of the Council of Maryland, 1732–1753* vol. 28 (Virginia: Samuel Ogle, Governor, nd), 137. Archives of Maryland

Online: https://msa.maryland.gov/megafile/msa/speccol/sc2900/
sc2908/000001/000028/html/am28--137.html; *Proceedings of the
Council of Maryland, 1753–1761* vol. 31 (Virginia: Horatio Sharpe,
Governor, nd), 182. Archives of Maryland Online: https://msa.mary
land.gov/megafile/msa/speccol/sc2900/sc2908/000001/000031/
html/am31--182.html; Maryland, "Hanged Slaves By Date": https://
msa.maryland.gov/megafile/msa/speccol/sc2900/sc2908/000001/
000819/pdf/chart28.pdf; Holloway, "Slave Insurrections in the
United States: An Overview": http://slaverebellion.info/index.php?
page=united-states-insurrections; Espy and Smykla, "The ESPY
File"; John Pendleton Kennedy, ed., *Journals of the House of
Burgesses 1761–1765* vol. 10, 5th of November. 5 *Geo. III* 1764
(Richmond, 1907): 237; "The Database of Executions in the United
States of America": https://files.deathpenaltyinfo.org/legacy/docu
ments/ESPYyear.pdf; Maryland, "Hanged Slaves By Date": https://
msa.maryland.gov/megafile/msa/speccol/sc2900/sc2908/000001/
000819/pdf/chart28.pdf.

58. *Race and Slavery Petitions Project.* Petition 11279304, December 7,
 1793 and Petition 11382911, October 24, 1829; *Louisiana Executions
 1722–2010*: http://files.usgwarchives.net/la/state/court/lagniappe/
 prison/executions.txt; Espy and Smykla, "The ESPY File";
 Alexandria Gazette and Virginia Advertiser, January 1, 1857.

59. *Alexandria Gazette and Virginia Advertiser*, February 12, 1859; Prince
 William County Minute Book, 1856–61, CR 1859 Record 18435,
 315–16; *Louisville Daily Courier*, November 16, 1860; *Thibodaux
 Minerva*, September 9, 1860.

60. John Spencer Bennett, *Slavery in the State of North Carolina*
 (Baltimore: The Johns Hopkins Press, 1899), 95–96; Wayne County
 Historical Association and the Old Dobbs County Genealogical
 Society, *The Heritage of Wayne County, North Carolina, 1982*
 (Winston-Salem, Wayne County Historical Association, 1982);
 Joseph Cephas Carroll, *Slave Insurrections in the United States
 1800–1865* (Boston: Dover, 2004), 70; Margaret Hindle Hazen and
 Robert M. Hazen, *Keepers of the Flame: The Role of Fire in American
 Culture* (Princeton University Press, 1992), 99.

61. Baker, *Women and Capital Punishment in the United States*, 115; Fred
 L. Borch, "Legal Lore: The Killing of a Master by His Servant,"
 Litigation vol. 37, no. 4 (2011): 7. For the effects of consuming raw
 milk, see the CDC website: www.cdc.gov/foodsafety/rawmilk/raw-
 milk-questions-and-answers.html#:~:text=Raw%20milk%20and%
 20raw%20milk,coli%2C%20Listeria%2C%20and%20Salmonella;
 William Wallace Scott, *A History of Orange County, Virginia From Its*

Formation in 1734 to the End of Reconstruction in 1870 (Richmond: E. Waddey, 1907), 135.

62. Espy and Smykla, "The ESPY File." See Maryland, "Hanged Slaves By Date": https://msa.maryland.gov/megafile/msa/speccol/sc2900/ sc2908/000001/000819/pdf/chart28.pdf; Fett, *Working Cures*, 164.

63. Statistics calculated from data on "The Database of Executions in the United States of America": https://files.deathpenaltyinfo.org/legacy/ documents/ESPYyear.pdf and Maryland, "Hanged Slaves By Date": https://msa.maryland.gov/megafile/msa/speccol/sc2900/sc2908/ 000001/000819/pdf/chart28.pdf; Stephen Berry, "Coroners of the Enslaved," "CSI: Dixie": https://csdixie.org/exodus/coroners-enslaved.

64. Baker, *Women and Capital Punishment in the United States*,115.

2 Annis, Phillis, and Lucy

1. Bea Latham, "Bath: North Carolina's First Town," reprinted from the *Tar Heel Junior Historian* (Spring 2006): www.ncpedia.org/ geography/bath; Jaquelin Drane Nash, "Charles Eden," *Dictionary of North Carolina Biography*, William S. Powell, ed. (Chapel Hill: University of North Carolina Press, 1986): www.ncpedia.org/ biography/eden-charles; C. Wingate Reed, *Beaufort County: Two Centuries of Its History* (np: C. Wingate Reed, 1962), 50.

2. Herbert R. Paschal, Jr., *A History of Colonial Bath* (Raleigh: Edwards & Broughton Co., 1955); Bryan Grimes, *Abstract of North Carolina Wills Compiled From Original and Recorded Wills in the Office of the Secretary of State* (Raleigh: E. M. Uzzell & Co, State Printers and Binders, 1910), 20, 34, 52, 80; Yancy T. Ormond, "Some Methodist History Along the Lower Neuse and Contentnea," *Historical Papers of the North Carolina Conference Historical Society and the Western North Carolina Conference Historical Society* (Greensboro: North Carolina Christian Advocate, 1925), 6: https://archive.org/stream/historicalpapers00 nort/historicalpapers00nort_djvu.txt; Reed, *Beaufort County*, 81.

3. North Carolina Secretary of State, Land Grant Office, *Warrants, Surveys, and Related Documents, circa 1735–1957*. North Carolina Department of Cultural Services, Division of Archives and History: www.ancestry.com/

4. "A Declaration and Proposals of the Lord Proprietors of Carolina (1663)": www.ncpedia.org/anchor/declaration-and-proposals/. The formula was 100 acres for every head of household; fifty for every male servant and thirty for every female servant; North Carolina, *Land Grant Files 1693–1960*, no. 388, book 10, 116; North Carolina

Secretary of State, Land Grant Office, *Warrants, Surveys, and Related Documents, circa 1735–1957*, no. 68, book 4, 118. North Carolina Department of Cultural Services, Division of Archives and History; Grimes, *Abstract of North Carolina Wills*.

5. The 1755 tax list records only enumerated white males aged sixteen or above and slaves above twelve years of age; _____. *1755 List of Taxables Beaufort County, NC*, 16–30.

6. Francis Hodges Cooper, *Some Colonial History of Beaufort County, NC* (Raleigh: Edwards and Broughton Printing Company State Printers, 1916), 40, 44: https://digital.lib.ecu.edu/text/16949; *Report by the Committee of Both Houses of North Carolina General Assembly Concerning Public Claims* vol. 22 (November 27, 1766): 841: https://docsouth.unc.edu/csr/index.php/document/csr22-0631#p22-841; William and Wesley Ormond Bible: http://files.usgwarchives.net/nc/greene/bibles/ormondbible.txt; Wyriot Ormond, *1764 List of Taxables Beaufort County, NC*: www.ncgenweb.us/beaufort/census_tax/b01764.htm; "Beaufort Regiment": www.rafert.org/colonial/StateMilitia1767.htm.

7. Phillis' name is sometimes spelled Phyllis. I use the same spelling used in the court record.

8. Wyriot Ormond, *1764 List of Taxables Beaufort County, NC*, page 4, column 1: www.ncgenweb.us/beaufort/census_tax/b01764.htm; "Beaufort Regiment": www.rafert.org/colonial/StateMilitia1767.htm.

9. In the age of slavery, only unmarried white men were designated as bachelors; unmarried enslaved men, who depended on their owners for food, clothing and shelter, were never called bachelors: John Gilbert McCurdy, *Citizen Bachelors: Manhood and the Creation of the United States* (Ithaca: Cornell University Press, 2009), 3–4, 57, 161, 195. In his discussion on the sexual life of bachelors, McCurdy does not consider the possibility that some of them used their enslaved women to satisfy their sexual needs.

10. Wyriot Ormond, *1764 List of Taxables Beaufort County, NC*, page 4, column 1: www.ncgenweb.us/beaufort/census_tax/b01764.htm.

11. *Acts of the North Carolina General Assembly* vol. 23 (March 1741), 174.

12. Jennifer Higginbotham, *The Girlhood of Shakespeare's Sisters: Gender, Transgression, Adolescence* (Edinburgh University Press, 2013), 22–23, 37; Kathleen M. Brown, *Good Wives, Nasty Wenches, and Anxious Patriarchs: Gender, Race, and Power in Colonial Virginia* (Chapel Hill: University of North Carolina Press, 1996), 9, 101, 175; Sue Kozel, "Why Wench Betty's Story Matters – The Murder of a NJ Slave in 1784," *New Jersey Studies: An Interdisciplinary Journal* vol. 6 (2020): 6.

13. For the purposes of this project, I will use the spelling contained in the records.

14. Alan D. Watson, "Impulse Toward Independence: Resistance and Rebellion Among North Carolina Slaves, 1750–1775," *Journal of Negro History* vol. 63, no. 4 (October 1978): 317; "The Growth of Slavery in North Carolina": www.ncpedia.org/anchor/growth-slavery-north; Samantha Winter, "A Brief History of Slavery in North Carolina": http://libcdm1.uncg.edu/cdm/history/collection/RAS.

15. Watson, "Impulse Toward Independence," 318; "The Growth of Slavery in North Carolina": www.ncpedia.org/anchor/growth-slavery-north; Winter, "A Brief History of Slavery"; The 1755 tax list records only enumerated white males aged sixteen or above and slaves above twelve years of age; _____. *1755 List of Taxables Beaufort County, NC*, 16–30; Alan D. Watson, "North Carolina Slave Courts, 1715–1785," *The North Carolina Historical Review* vol. 60, no. 1 (January 1983): 29.

16. Ernest James Clark, "Aspects of the North Carolina Slave, 1715–1860," *The North Carolina Historical Review* vol. 39, no. 2 (April 1962): 156, 158, 160; Watson, "North Carolina Slave Courts, 1715–1785," 27, 32, 34; "The Growth of Slavery in North Carolina: Colonial Legacies": www.ncpedia.org/anchor/growth-slavery-north; Watson, "Impulse Toward Independence," 320.

17. *Rinds Virginia Gazette*, September 6, 1770; *New York Journal*, September 27, 1770; *New-Hampshire Gazette and Historical Chronicle*, October 26, 1770; *Connecticut Gazette*, October 12, 1770; The North Carolina Society of the Daughters of the Revolution, ed., "Historic Homes and People of Old Bath Town," by Lida Tunstall Rodman *The North Carolina Booklet* vol. 2 (Raleigh: Capital Printing, 1903), 4: www.archive.org/details/northcarolinaboo1902 nort; Certificate of Special Court for the Trial of Annis, a Negro Wench, 21 July 1770, folder "Magistrates and Freeholders Courts 1770–1779," series 11 box 2. SR.12.11.4.2, Secretary of State Papers, North Carolina State Archives, Raleigh; Certificate of Special Court for the Trial of Cuffy, 21 July 1770, folder "Magistrates and Freeholders Courts 1770–1779," series 11 box 2. SR.12.11.4.2, Secretary of State Papers, North Carolina State Archives, Raleigh.

18. *Rinds Virginia Gazette*, September 6, 1770; *New York Journal*, September 27, 1770; *New-Hampshire Gazette and Historical Chronicle*, October 26, 1770; *Connecticut Gazette*, October 12, 1770.

19. *New York Journal*, September 27, 1770.

20. *The Wheeling Daily Intelligencer*, June 4, 1859.

21. *New York Journal*, September 27, 1770.

22. C. Wingate Reed, *Beaufort County: Two Centuries of Its History* (np : C. Wingate Reed, 1962), 54, 94.

23. Kay and Cary, "The Planters Suffer Little or Nothing," 291; James M. Campbell, *Slavery on Trial: Race, Class, and Criminal Justice in Antebellum Richmond, Virginia* (Gainesville: University Press of Florida, 2007), 81, 106; Stroud, *A Sketch of the Laws*, 92; Watson, "Impulse Toward Independence," 320.

24. Morris, "Slaves and the Rules of Evidence,"1216, 1217; *Acts of the North Carolina General Assembly* (March 1741), 202–03; John Spencer Bassett, "Slavery and Servitude in the Colony of North Carolina," Herbert B. Adams, ed. (Baltimore: The Johns Hopkins Press, 1896), 28–30 *passim*; Watson, "North Carolina Slave Courts, 1715–1785," 25–27 *passim*; Clark, "Aspects of the North Carolina Slave, 1715–1860," 150, 151.

25. Watson, "North Carolina Slave Courts, 1715–1785," 31, 34; Certificate of Special Court for the Trial of Annis, a Negro Wench, 21 July 1770; Certificate of Special Court for the Trial of Cuffy, 21 July 1770.

26. Certificate of Special Court for the Trial of Cuffy, 21 July 1770.

27. Watson, "North Carolina Slave Courts, 1715–1785," 31, fn 27; Certificate of Special Court for the Trial of Annis, a Negro Wench, 21 July 1770; Certificate of Special Court for the Trial of Cuffy, 21 July 1770.

28. *Acts of the North Carolina General Assembly* (March 1741), 202–03; Watson, "Impulse Toward Independence," 320–21, 323; Watson, "North Carolina Slave Courts, 1715–1785," 32. Watson also states that the rising costs of the French and Indian War was another factor that led the colony to try to save money.

29. Watson, "Impulse Toward Independence," 320–21; Her words were quoted in Milton Ready, *The Tar Heel State: A New History of North Carolina* revised edition (Columbia: The University of South Carolina Press, 2020), 63. I was unable to locate the source of these words myself so their veracity cannot be verified.

30. *Connecticut Gazette*, October 12, 1770; *Rinds Virginia Gazette*, September 6, 1770; *New York Journal*, September 27, 1770; *New-Hampshire Gazette and Historical Chronicle*, October 26, 1770; "The Database of Executions in the United States of America": https://files .deathpenaltyinfo.org/legacy/documents/ESPYyear.pdf; Marvin Michael Kay and Lorin Lee Cary, Slavery in North Carolina 1748–1775 (Chapel Hill: University of North Carolina Press, 1995), 79.

31. Certificate of Special Court for the Trial of Annis, a Negro Wench, 21 July 1770; Certificate of Special Court for the Trial of Cuffy, 21 July 1770; North Carolina General Assembly, *Report by the Committee of Both Houses of the North Carolina General Assembly Concerning Public Claims* vol. 22 (January 18, 1771), 856, 857: https://docsouth.unc.edu/csr/index.php/document/csr22-0634#p22-862; Walter Clark, ed., *The State Records of North Carolina* vol. 22 (Goldsboro, NC: Nash Brothers, 1907), 856; Kay and Cary, *Slavery in North Carolina 1748–1775*, 78–79.

32. Daina Ramey Berry, *The Price for Their Pound of Flesh: The Value of the Enslaved, From Womb to Grave, in the Building of a Nation* (Boston: Beacon Press, 2017), 114, 131, 132, 134, 136.

33. *An Act to Repeal the Several Acts of Assembly Respecting Slaves Within This State, as far as the Same Relates to Making an Allowance to the Owner or Owners for any Executed or Outlawed Slave or Slaves* (1786), *Acts of the North Carolina General Assembly, 1786–1787* vol. 24, 809: https://docsouth.unc.edu/csr/index.php/document/csr24-0017.

34. *The Commonwealth v. Gus Depp's Jane*, Powhatan County (1852), Library of Virginia, Record 000382370; Holden, *Surviving Southampton*, 36, 37. Holden highlights the yard, kitchen, and front porch as sites of Black women's daily labor and confrontation. It is suggested that historians begin considering bedrooms the same way.

3 Cloe

1. Cloe's name is alternatively spelled Chloe. I have gone with Cloe, because that is how it is spelled in the earliest records about her.

2. *Carlisle Gazette*, June 24, 1801; *The Times; and District of Columbia Daily Advertiser*, September 1, 1801; *Windham Herald*, August 27, 1801; *Columbian Minerva*, September 8, 1801; *Political Repository*, October 13, 1801; *Federal Gazette*, October 2, 1801.

3. *Carlisle Gazette*, June 24, 1801.

4. *Carlisle Gazette*, June 24, 1801.

5. "An Act for the Gradual Abolition of Slavery": www.ushistory.org/presidentshouse/history/gradual.php.

6. Gary B Nash and Jean R. Soderlund, *Freedom By Degrees: Emancipation in Pennsylvania and Its Aftermath* (New York: Oxford University Press, 1991), 137.

7. Peter P. Hinks, "Gradual Emancipation Reflected in the Struggle of Some to Envision Black Freedom," (January 2, 2020): https://connecticuthistory.org/gradual-emancipation-reflected-the-struggle-of-some-to-envision-black-freedom/; Leslie M. Harris, *In the*

Shadow of Slavery: African Americans in New York City, 1626–1863 (Chicago: The University of Chicago Press, 2003), 11; *An Act Authorizing the Manumission of Negroes, Mulattoes and others, and for the Gradual Abolition of Slavery*, February 1784.

8. David Menschel, "Abolition without Deliverance: The Law of Connecticut Slavery 1784–1848," *The Yale Law Journal* vol. 111, no. 1 (October 2001): 183–84.

9. "An Act for the Gradual Abolition of Slavery": www.ushistory.org/presidentshouse/history/gradual.php.

10. Michael B. McCoy, "Forgetting Freedom: White Anxiety, Black Presence, and Gradual Abolition in Cumberland County, Pennsylvania, 1780–1838," *The Pennsylvania Magazine of History and Biography* vol. 136 (April 2012): 147, 149.

11. "Slave Returns": http://ccweb.ccpa.net/archives/inventory?PSID=541; McCoy, "Forgetting Freedom," 149, 151–52.

12. 1788 Amendment to the Gradual Abolition Act, sec. IV: www.ushistory.org/presidentshouse/history/amendment1788.php.

13. *Carlisle Gazette*, June 24, 1801; *Political Repository*, June 30, 1801; *Philadelphia Gazette*, June 17, 1801.

14. Cumberland County, Clerk of Courts, *Slave Returns, 1780, 1789, 1814*: www.phmc.state.pa.us/bah/dam/rg/di/r47-SlaveRecords/r47-SlaveRecords-Cumberland/cumberland2%20228.pdf; McCoy, "Forgetting Freedom," 149.

15. *Columbia Minerva*, September 8, 1801; *Windham Herald*, August 27, 1801; *Political Repository*, October 13, 1801; "Register of Negro and Mulatto Slaves and Servants, 1780," reprinted in part in William Henry Egle, *History of the County of Dauphin in the Commonwealth of Pennsylvania: Biographical and Genealogical* (Philadelphia: Everts and Peck, 1883), 104; "Slave Transfer from Rebeckah Kelso to John Harland," July 17, 1794, Cumberland Historical Society, box 9, folder 15.

16. "Slave Transfer from Rebeckah Kelso to John Harland," July 17, 1794.

17. *The Times; and District of Columbia Daily Advertiser*, September 1, 1801; *Windham Herald*, August 27, 1801; *Columbian Minerva*, September 8, 1801; *Political Repository*, October 13, 1801; *Federal Gazette*, October 2, 1801.

18. McCoy, "Forgetting Freedom," 161; Rev. Horace Edwin Hayden, *Pollock Genealogy: A Biographical Sketch of Oliver Pollock, Esq. of Carlisle, Pennsylvania, United States Commercial Agent at New Orleans and Havana, 1776–1784 with Genealogical Notes on His Descendants* (Harrisburg, Lane S. Hart, 1883), 15, 17, 19.

19. *The Times; and District of Columbia Daily Advertiser*, September 1, 1801; *Windham Herald*, August 27, 1801; *Columbian Minerva*, 8 September 1801; *Political Repository*, October 13, 1801; *Federal Gazette*, October 2, 1801; Hayden, 19.

20. "Slave Transfer from Rebeckah Kelso to John Harland," July 17, 1794.

21. Pennsylvania, US, Septennial Census, 1779–1863, "East Pennsboro Taxables": www.ancestry.com; Pennsylvania, United States Direct Tax Lists, 1798: www.ancestry.com.

22. "Andrew Carothers Will, July 17, 1817," Register of Wills,Probate Place: Cumberland, Pennsylvania.

23. Jean R. Soderlund, "Black Women in Colonial Pennsylvania," *The Pennsylvania Magazine of History and Biography* vol. 107, no. 1 (1983): 52–53.

24. Stephanie E. Jones-Rogers, *They Were Here Property: White Women as Slave Owners in the American South* (New Haven: Yale University Press, 2019), xii.

25. Jean R. Soderlund found that in rural Pennsylvania Black women were more likely to live with their families than in Philadelphia. This, however, was not true for Cloe. Soderlund, "Black Women in Colonial Pennsylvania," 57, 68.

26. Jones-Rogers, *They Were Here Property*, 7, 11.

27. *The Times; and District of Columbia Daily Advertiser*, September 1, 1801; *Windham Herald*, August 27, 1801; *Columbian Minerva*, September 8, 1801; *Political Repository*, October 13, 1801; *Federal Gazette*, October 2, 1801.

28. *The Times; and District of Columbia Daily Advertiser*, September 1, 1801; *Windham Herald*, August 27, 1801; *Columbian Minerva*, September 8, 1801; *Political Repository*, October 13, 1801; *Federal Gazette*, October 2, 1801.

29. *The Times; and District of Columbia Daily Advertiser*, September 1, 1801; *Windham Herald*, August 27, 1801; *Columbian Minerva*, September 8, 1801; *Political Repository*, October 13, 1801; *Federal Gazette*, October 2, 1801.

30. *The Times; and District of Columbia Daily Advertiser*, September 1, 1801; *Windham Herald*, August 27, 1801; *Columbian Minerva*, September 8, 1801; *Political Repository*, October 13, 1801; *Federal Gazette*, October 2, 1801.

31. *The Times; and District of Columbia Daily Advertiser*, September 1, 1801; *Windham Herald*, August 27, 1801; *Columbian Minerva*, September 8, 1801; *Political Repository*, October 13, 1801; *Federal Gazette*, October 2, 1801.

32. *Carlisle Gazette*, June 24, 1801; *The Times; and District of Columbia Daily Advertiser*, September 1, 1801; *Windham Herald*, August 27, 1801; *Columbian Minerva*, September 8, 1801; *Political Repository*, October 13, 1801; *Federal Gazette*, October 2, 1801.

33. *Carlisle Gazette*, June 24, 1801.

34. *Ibid.*

35. *The Times; and District of Columbia Daily Advertiser*, September 1, 1801; *Windham Herald*, August 27, 1801; *Columbian Minerva*, September 8, 1801; *Political Repository*, October 13, 1801; *Federal Gazette*, October 2, 1801.

36. Paul Crawford, "A Footnote on Courts for Trial of Negroes in Colonial Pennsylvania," *Journal of Black Studies* vol. 5, no. 2 (1974): 168, 169, 170.

37. *Respublica v. Negroe Cloe*, 1–2–3, 11–13; Cumberland County oyer and terminer, March 4, 1801; *Kline's Carlisle Weekly Gazette*, March 10, 1802.

38. *Adams Sentinel (Gettysburg)*, March 25, 1801; *Savannah Georgia Gazette*, April 16, 1801; *Carlisle American Volunteer*, December 23, 1869; *Respublica v. Negroe Cloe*, 1–2–3, 11–13, Cumberland County oyer and terminer, March 4, 1801.

39. *Oracle of Dauphin*, June 15, 1801; *Political Repository*, June 30, 1801; *Mercantile Advertiser*, June 20, 1801.

40. *The Times; and District of Columbia Daily Advertiser*, September 1, 1801; *Windham Herald*, August 27, 1801; *Columbian Minerva*, September 8, 1801; *Political Repository*, October 13, 1801; *Federal Gazette*, October 2, 1801.

41. *Independent Gazette*, September 8, 1801.

42. Thavolia Glymph, *Out of the House of Bondage: The Transformation of the Plantation Household* (Cambridge University Press, New York, 2008), 33, 34, 44.

43. *The Times; and District of Columbia Daily Advertiser*, September 1, 1801; *Windham Herald*, August 27, 1801; *Columbian Minerva*, September 8, 1801; *Political Repository*, October 13, 1801; *Federal Gazette*, October 2, 1801.

44. *The Times; and District of Columbia Daily Advertiser*, September 1, 1801; *Windham Herald*, August 27, 1801; *Columbian Minerva*, September 8, 1801; *Political Repository*, October 13, 1801; *Federal Gazette*, October 2, 1801.

45. *The Times; and District of Columbia Daily Advertiser*, September 1, 1801; *Windham Herald*, August 27, 1801; *Columbian Minerva*, September 8, 1801; *Political Repository*, October 13, 1801; *Federal Gazette*, October 2, 1801.

46. Harris, "Offering Nothing," 401–02; *Boston Evening Post*, January 21, 1751, March 4, 1751, and April 22, 1751; *The Boston Post-Boy*, April 8, 1751.
47. Wilma King, *Stolen Childhood: Slave Youth in Nineteenth-Century America* second edition (Bloomington: Indiana University Press, 2011), 269.
48. *State of Missouri* v. *Mary, A Slave*, Crawford County Circuit Court, 1837; *Mary, A Slave* v. *State of Missouri*, Supreme Court of Missouri Historical Records, Missouri State Archives, box 067, folder 12: www.sos.mo.gov/Images/Archives/SupremeCourt/B067F12.pdf; *The Baltimore Sun*, June 15, 1837; *Crawford Mirror*, August 18, 1904; Helen Tunnicliff Catterall and James J. Hayden, *Judicial Cases Concerning American Slavery and the Negro* vol. 5 (Washington, D.C.: Carnegie Institution of Washington, 1937), 152; Harriet C. Frazier, *Slavery and Crime in Missouri* (Jefferson, NC: McFarland & Co., 2001), 170–73.

4 Rose Butler

1. Composed for Rose Butler, by Dorothy Ripley, July 9, 1819, in Dorothy Ripley, *An Account of Rose Butler: Aged Nineteen Years, Whose Execution I Attended in the Potter's Field on the 9th of 7th Mo. For Setting Fire to Her Mistress' Dwelling House* (New York: John C. Totten, 1819), 12. This epigraph is only a small portion of the poem.
2. *New York Gazette & General Advertiser*, March 25, 1818; *Columbian*, May 19, 1919; *American & Commercial Daily Advertiser*, May 24, 1819; *The Long-Island Star*, May 26, 1819.
3. *The Long-Island Star*, May 26, 1819.
4. Several different washing machine inventions were patented in the late eighteenth century. The machines were designed to save labor, time, and water and were slightly more sophisticated than the usual tub and scrubber variety. Only the wealthiest families had washing machines in 1818.
5. Ripley, *An Account of Rose Butler*; Rev. John Stanford's *An Authentic Statement of the Case and Conduct of Rose Butler, who was Tried, Convicted, and Executed for the Crime of Arson* (New York: Broderick and Ritter, 1819); Eliza Duell's statement and Rose Butler's own confession in Rose Butler *Statements of Confession* (New York Historical Society Museum & Library, 1819).
6. For data on the number of African Americans in Westchester, New York see: https://nesri.commons.gc.cuny.edu/dashboardresult/?CountyBoro=westchester&Locality=.

7. Other scholars have erroneously spelled the surname of her first owner as Straing. There was no such family in the archival record; Harris, *In the Shadow of Slavery*, 113.

8. Westchester County (New York): Surrogate's Court. Probate Place, Westchester, New York, *Wills and Letters, 1777–1983*: www .ancestry.com. *New York, Wills and Probate Records, 1659–1999*, Lehi, UT, USA: www.ancestry.com.

9. According to historian Graham Russell Hodges, the first of these bills failed because of "noxious clauses" attached by slaveowners. They included revoking the rights of suffrage for African Americans and the right to testify in court against whites. The bill initially passed, but the Council of Revision rejected it. The second time, it failed in committee. See Graham Russell Hodges, *Root & Branch: African Americans in New York and East Jersey 1613–1863* (Chapel Hill: The University of North Carolina Press, 1999), 168–69, 170; David N. Gellman, "Race, the Public Sphere, and Abolition in Late Eighteenth-Century New York," *Journal of the Early Republic* vol. 20, no. 4 (2000): 613–14.

10. An Act for the Gradual Abolition of Slavery, New York Archives Trust: www.nysarchivestrust.org/education/consider-source/ browse-primary-source-documents/slavery/act-gradual-abolition-slavery-1799.

11. New York State Senate, *Documents of the Senate of the State of New-York* vol. 13 (New York: E. Croswell, 1903), 295; An Act Relative to Slaves and Servants (1817): https://digitalcollections .archives.nysed.gov/index.php/Detail/objects/10817.

12. Ryan, *Everyday Crimes*, 261; Nell Irvin Painter, *Sojourner Truth: A Life, A Symbol* (New York: W. W. Norton & Company, 1996), 23.

13. Sarah L. H. Gronningsater, "Born Free in the Master's House: Children and Gradual Emancipation in the Early North," Anna Mae Duane, ed., *Child Slavery Before and After Emancipation: An Argument for Child-Centered Slavery Studies* (New York: Cambridge University Press, 2017), 135–37.

14. An Act Concerning Slaves and Servants (1813) in William Peter Van Ness and John Woodworth, eds., *Laws of the State of New-York Revised and Passed at the Thirty-Sixth Session of the Legislature, with Marginal Notes and References, Furnished by the Revisors* (Albany: H. C. Southwick & Co., 1813), 201–02, 207; Jill Lepore, *New York Burning: Liberty, Slavery, and Conspiracy in an Eighteenth-Century Manhattan* (New York: Knopf, 2005).

15. Hodges, *Root & Branch*, 193.

16. Irma and Paul Milstein Division of United States History, Local History and Genealogy, The New York Public Library. *New York*

City Directory 1817–18 New York Public Library Digital Collections: https://digitalcollections.nypl.org/items/8e1ed570-12ac-0137-9f2b-055502cc8899; John Stanford, *An Authentic Statement of the Case and Conduct of Rose Butler, Who was Tried, Convicted, and Executed for the Crime of Arson* (New York: Broderick and Ritter, 1819); *The Long-Island Star*, May 26, 1819; *New York Daily Advertiser*, May 17, 1819; *American & Commercial Daily Advertiser*, May 24, 1819.

17. Butler, *Statements of Confession*, 1819; Stanford, *An Authentic Statement*; Stephanie M. H. Camp, *Closer to Freedom: Enslaved Women & Everyday Resistance in the Plantation South* (Chapel Hill: University of North Carolina Press, 2004), 89–91; Harris, *In the Shadow of Slavery*, 114–15.

18. "Historical Currency Conversion": https://futureboy.us/fsp/dollar.fsp.

19. Hodges, *Root & Branch*, 179; Longworth, *New York City Directory 1818–19*; Butler, *Statements of Confession*; Stanford, *An Authentic Statement*.

20. Camp, 68, 78–87, *passim*.

21. White, *Ar'n't I a Woman*, 123.

22. Butler, *Statements of Confession*.

23. *Ibid*.

24. Ripley, *An Account of Rose Butler*; Stanford, *An Authentic Statement*; Butler, *Statements of Confession*, 1819. Bridewell was then considered as the "nursery" of criminals who would one day graduate to the state prison. The conditions were poor and over-crowded. Edwin Olson, "The Slave Code in Colonial New York," *The Journal of Negro History* vol. 29, no. 2 (1944): 165; New York City, District Attorney Files, *People* v. *Rose Butler* "Indictment for Arson," March 1818, New York City Municipal Archives.

25. William Johnson, *Reports of Cases Argued and Determined in the Supreme Court of Judicature, and in the Court for the Trial of Impeachment and the Correction of Errors, in the State of New York* vol. XV (New York: Banks & Brothers Law Publishers, 1883), 163. *Philadelphia Gazette*, May 18, 1819; *Daily Advertiser*, May 19, 1819; *Columbian*, May 19, 1819; Stanford, *An Authentic Statement*.

26. Butler, *Statements of Confession*.

27. *Ibid*.

28. *Ibid*.

29. *Ibid*.

30. *Ibid*.

31. *Columbian*, May 19, 1919; Butler, *Statements of Confession*.

32. Butler, *Statements of Confession*.

33. Stanford, *An Authentic Statement*.
34. "Statement of Eliza Duell" in Butler, *Statements of Confession*, 1819.
35. Stanford, *An Authentic Statement*.
36. "Statement of Eliza Duell" in Butler, *Statements of Confession*; Butler, *Statements of Confession*.
37. *The Evening Post* (New York City), January 27, 1818.
38. George Ticknor Curtis, Theron Metcalf, and Jonathan Cogswell Perkins, eds., *U.S. Digest: Digest of the Decisions of the Courts of Common Law and Admiralty in the United States* vol. 4 (New York: Little, Brown, and Company, 1851), 464. New York City's 1686 charter set up the structure of this court. The mayor, alderman, or recorder were authorized to preside over this court; Historical Records Survey, *Inventory of the County and Borough Archives of New York City* (New York: Historical Records Survey, 1939), 25, 204. New York's oyer and terminer courts were typically presided over by one supreme court justice and two associate judges from the common pleas court. In New York City, one associate judge plus two aldermen or the mayor and one alderman could also hold court, as was the case in Rose's trial.
39. *National Advocate*, November 20, 1818; *Baltimore Patriot & Mercantile Advertiser*, November 23, 1818; *Boston Daily Advertiser*, November 23, 1818; *The Charleston Daily Courier*, December 1, 1818; *Yankee*, December 3, 1818; *The Long Island Star*, May 26, 1819; *The People v. Rose Butler*, 16 J.R. 203 (May 1819).
40. Jill Paradise Botler, M. Christine DeVita, Stephen John Kallas, and William J. Ruane, "The Appellate Division of the Supreme Court of New York: An Empirical Study of Its Powers and Functions as an Intermediate State Court," *Fordham L. Rev.* vol. 47, no. 929 (1979), 933.
41. Ryan, *Everyday Crimes*, 277, 280, 281.
42. An Act Concerning Slaves and Servants (1813) in Van Ness and Woodworth, eds., *Laws of the State of New-York*, 207.
43. Olson, "The Slave Code in Colonial New York," 148, 149, 150; Mike McConville, and Chester L. Mirsky et al., *Jury Trials and Plea Bargaining: A True History*, (Oxford: Hart Publishing, 2005), 148–50, 159–60.
44. The New York supreme court judges were Hon. Ambrose Spencer, Hon. Peter Van Ness. Hon, Joseph Yates, Hon. Jonas Platt, Hon. John Woodworth. New York Supreme Court of Judicature, *Minutes and Proceedings*, 647: https://acrobat.adobe.com/link/track?uri=urn:aaid:scds:US:4ffc6af6-ee66-4c1d-81ca-9baffb9e8dc8; Johnson, *Reports of Cases Argued and Determined in the Supreme Court of Judicature*, 163–64.

45. *The People* v. *Rose Butler*, 16 J.R. 203 (May 1819); *New York Daily Advertiser*, May 17, 1819; *Philadelphia Gazette*, May 18, 1819; *Columbian*, May 19, 1819; *The Long-Island Star*, May 26, 1819.

46. New York Supreme Court of Judicature, *Minutes and Proceedings*, 647: https://acrobat.adobe.com/link/track?uri=urn:aaid:scds:US:4ffc 6af6-ee66-4c1d-81ca-9baffb9e8dc8.

47. _____, "Rev. Stanford: U.S. and New York's First State-Hired and Paid Prison Chaplain Wasn't Passive" (2013): www.correctionhistory.org/ html/chronicl/nycdoc/NY&US-1st-Prison-Chaplain-Rev-John-Stanford/ Rev-Stanford-1st-NY&US-Prison-Chaplain-Part2.html

48. Stanford, *An Authentic Statement*; Ripley, *An Account of Rose Butler*, 4, 5, 6; Butler, *Statements of Confession*, 1819; "Statement of Eliza Duell" in Butler, *Statements of Confession*, 1819; *The Evening Post*, June 11, 1819.

49. Jonathan Nash, "'The Prison Has Failed': The New York State Prison, In the City of New York, 1797–1828," *New York History* vol. 98, no. 1 (2017): 77.

50. Nash, "'The Prison Has Failed,'" 84–85.

51. "Statement of Eliza Duell" in Butler, *Statements of Confession*.

52. Stanford, *An Authentic Statement*; Ripley, *An Account of Rose Butler* 4, 5, 6; Rose Butler, *Statements of Confession*; "Statement of Eliza Duell" in Butler, *Statements of Confession*; *The Evening Post*, June 11, 1819.

53. Ripley, *An Account of Rose Butler*, 4–5.

54. *The Long-Island Star*, May 26, 1819; *Columbian*, May 19, 1819.

55. *The Evening Post*, June 11, 1819; *Columbian*, May 19, 1819.

56. *Columbian*, May 19 and June 12, 1819; *Columbian Centinel*, May 22, 1819; *The Long-Island Star*, May 26, 1819; *The Evening Post*, June 11, 1819; *Baltimore Patriot & Mercantile Advertiser*, June 15, 1819; *National Messenger* (Georgetown, D.C.), June 16, 1819; Stanford, *An Authentic Statement*.

57. *Lancaster Intelligencer*, July 16, 1819; *Poulson's American Daily Advertiser*, July 23, 1819.

58. Ripley, *An Account of Rose Butler*, 6. *Niles' Register*, July 17, 1819; *Poughkeepsie Journal*, July 21, 1819; *Pennsylvania Correspondent and Farmers' Advertiser*, July 20, 1819.

59. Jones-Rogers, *They Were Here Property*, 62; Glymph, *Out of the House of Bondage*, 33, 35.

60. "Statement of Eliza Duell" in Butler, *Statements of Confession*, 1819.

61. Ripley, *An Account of Rose Butler*, 10–11; *Niles' Register*, July 17, 1819; *Poughkeepsie Journal*, July 21, 1819; *Pennsylvania Correspondent and Farmers' Advertiser*, July 20, 1819; *The Columbian* May 19, 1819.

62. Afua Cooper, *The Hanging of Angélique: The Untold Story of Canadian Slavery and the Burning of Old Montréal* (Athens, GA: The University of Georgia Press, 2006), 193.

63. Colonial Society of Massachusetts, *Publications of The Colonial Society of Massachusetts* vol. VI (Boston: The Colonial Society of Massachusetts, 1904), 324–33 *passim*. Kathleen A. O'Shea, *Women and the Death Penalty in the U.S. 1900–1998* (Westport: Praeger, 1999), 4, 5.

64. T. J. Davis, *A Rumor of Revolt: The "Great Negro Plot" in Colonial New York* (Amherst: University of Massachusetts Press, 1985), 82, 83, 99, 101; Richard E. Bond, "Shaping a Conspiracy: Black Testimony in the 1741 New York Plot," *Early American Studies* vol. 5, no. 1 (2007): 64, 65, 66, 85.

65. Baker, "Slave Executions in the United States"; Espy and Smykla, "The ESPY File"; Maryland, "Hanged Slaves By Date": https://msa .maryland.gov/megafile/msa/speccol/sc2900/sc2908/000001/000819/pdf/ chart28.pdf; Joseph Addison Waddell, *Annals of Augusta County, Virginia, From 1726 to 1871* second edition (Staunton, VA: C. Russell Caldwell, 1902), 177; *Staunton Spectator*, September 18, 1866; "Historical and Genealogical Notes and Queries," *The Virginia Magazine of History and Biography* vol. 16, no. 1 (1908): 94, 95; Olson, "The Slave Code in Colonial New York," 160; David Levine, "An Inside Look at the Most Devastating Fire in Albany's History," *Hudson Valley*, December 2, 2021: https://hvmag.com/life-style/history/albany-fire-1793/; Don R. Gerlach, "Black Arson in Albany, New York: November 1793," *Journal of Black Studies* vol. 7, no. 3 (March 1977): 301–12.

66. Two antebellum cases include: in Vicksburg, Mississippi, an enslaved woman confessed to burning Calvin Beacham's gin house in 1856. Four years later, in Texas, the enslaved woman of Dr. D. W. Snell confessed to burning down his home. The estimated loss of property was $4,000. *Vicksburg Daily Whig*, December 16, 1856; *The Weekly Telegraph*, July 31, 1860.

67. Stacy Groening, "Pyrophobia: Euro-American Fear of Slaves and Fire in Charleston, South Carolina, 1820–1860," (M.A. Thesis, University of Calgary, 2009).

68. Virginia House of Burgesses, *The Journal of the House of Burgesses. At a General Assembly* vol. 6, Henry Read McIlwaine, ed. (Richmond: The Colonial Press, E . Waddey Co., 1910), 254.

5 Jane Williams

1. Thomson's Mercantile and Professional Directory, Virginia 1851: Henrico County: www.newrivernotes.com/topical_business_thomsons_

mercantile_directory_virginia_1851.htm; John D. Hammersley, *Particulars of the Dreadful Tragedy in Richmond, on the Morning of the 19th July 1852, Being a Full Account of the Awful Murder of the Winston Family: Embracing All the Particulars of the Discovery of the Bloody Victims, The Testimony Before the Coroner's Jury, and the Evidence on the Final Trials of the Murderess and Murderer, Jane and John Williams: Their Sentence, Confessions, and the Execution Upon the Gallows: Together With the Funeral Sermon of the Rev Mr. Moore, on the Death of Mrs. Winston and Daughter, and the Sermon of the Rev Robert Ryland on the Subject of the Murders* (Richmond: John D. Hammersley, 1852), 5–7. This eyewitness account is the most comprehensive and accurate. The *Richmond Dispatch* indicated that it was recorded by an "accomplished" stenographer and determined to be "perfectly accurate": *Richmond Dispatch*, July 20, July 21, and October 25, 1852.

2. United States, *Seventh Census of the United States, 1850: Slave Schedule: Virginia, Hanover, West District*, 191–92, Record Group: *Records of the Bureau of the Census*: www.ancestry.com.

3. *United States Federal Census*: www.ancestry.com. Year 1850, Census Place: *Richmond, Virginia*, roll 951, page 324b. Biographical data about the Winston children, including full names, birthdays, and dates of death can be found in Figure 5.1; Hammersley, *Particulars of the Dreadful Tragedy in Richmond*, 5.

4. "Joseph Pendleton Winston Family Tree": www.ancestry.com; Ancestry .com/family-tree/person/tree/86934030/person/180046103569/facts.

5. *Richmond Dispatch*, July 20, 1852; Richmond Hill, *Hill's Richmond City Directory, Chesterfield and Henrico Counties, Virginia*, (Richmond: Hill Directory Company, 1855), 102, 125, 132, 154, 156, 174, 175: https://babel.hathitrust.org/cgi/pt?id=hvd .hn4hge&view=1up&seq=1; M. Ellyson, *The Richmond Directory & Business Advertiser for 1856: Containing the Names, Residences, Occupations, and Places of Business of the Inhabitants of Richmond; Also A Variety of Other Useful Information* (M. Ellyson Printer: Richmond, 1856), 245.

6. James M. Campbell, *Slavery on Trial: Race, Class, and Criminal Justice in Antebellum Richmond Virginia* (Gainesville: University Press of Florida, 2007), 2.

7. Midori Takagi, *Rearing Wolves to Our Own Destruction: Slavery in Richmond Virginia, 1782–1865* (Charlottesville: University of Virginia Press, 1999), 87.

8. Takagi, *Rearing Wolves*, 22–24; Campbell, *Slavery on Trial*, 16, 17.

9. 1840, Census Place: *Richmond Ward 1, Henrico, Virginia*, roll 561, page 144, Family History Library Film 0029687: www.ancestry.com; Hammersley, *Particulars of the Dreadful Tragedy in Richmond*, 16, 19; *Richmond Dispatch*, July 21, 1852.

10. Hammersley, *Particulars of the Dreadful Tragedy in Richmond*, 23–24.

11. *Richmond Dispatch*, July 22, 1852.

12. Hammersley, *Particulars of the Dreadful Tragedy in Richmond*, 26–27; *An Act to Amend the Act Concerning Slaves, Free Negroes and Mulattoes* (1830): https://heinonline.org/HOL/LandingPage?handle=hein.slavery/ssactsva0415&div=1&src=home; *Acts of the General Assembly of Virginia Passed at the Session Commencing December 6, 1847*, 120.

13. *Acts of the General Assembly of Virginia Passed at the Session Commencing December 6, 1847*, 117; Campbell, *Slavery on Trial*, 16.

14. Takagi, *Rearing Wolves*, 77–78; *An Act to Prevent Further the Practice of Slaves Going at Large, or Hiring Out Themselves* (1807).

15. Takagi, *Rearing Wolves*, 80.

16. *Ibid.*, 40, Campbell, *Slavery on Trial*, 16–17.

17. Takagi, *Rearing Wolves*, 42; Hammersley, *Particulars of the Dreadful Tragedy in Richmond*, 11, 14.

18. *Richmond Dispatch*, July 20, 1852.

19. John J. Zaborney, *Slaves for Hire: Renting Enslaved Laborers in Antebellum Virginia* (Baton Rouge: Louisiana State University Press, 2012), 1, 12–14 *passim*, 48; Takagi, *Rearing Wolves*, 38.

20. Hammersley, *Particulars of the Dreadful Tragedy in Richmond*, 6, 10; *Richmond Dispatch*, July 20, 1852.

21. Hammersley, *Particulars of the Dreadful Tragedy in Richmond*, 9, 10, 18; Takagi, *Rearing Wolves*, 38.

22. Hill, *Hill's Richmond City Directory*, 19; Hammersley, *Particulars of the Dreadful Tragedy in Richmond*, 10, 18; *Richmond Dispatch*, July 20 and July 22, 1852.

23. Hammersley, *Particulars of the Dreadful Tragedy in Richmond*, 8, 10, 12, 17, 18; *Richmond Dispatch*, July 20 and July 22, 1852.

24. Hammersley, *Particulars of the Dreadful Tragedy in Richmond*, 17, 18; *Richmond Dispatch*, July 22, 1852.

25. Hammersley, *Particulars of the Dreadful Tragedy in Richmond*, 2, 10, 12, 13, 16; *Richmond Dispatch*, July 21, 1852.

26. Hammersley, *Particulars of the Dreadful Tragedy in Richmond*, 15; *Richmond Dispatch* July 21, 1852.

27. Campbell, *Slavery on Trial*, 91; *Richmond Dispatch*, July 21, 1852.

28. Hammersley, *Particulars of the Dreadful Tragedy in Richmond*, 3, 9, 12, 13, 14, 15; *Richmond Dispatch*, July 21, 1852.

29. Hammersley, *Particulars of the Dreadful Tragedy in Richmond*, 8; *Richmond Dispatch*, July 21, 1852.

30. Hammersley, *Particulars of the Dreadful Tragedy in Richmond*, 11, 14, 15–16; *Richmond Dispatch*, July 20 and July 21, 1852.

31. Hammersley, *Particulars of the Dreadful Tragedy in Richmond*, 17; *Richmond Dispatch*, July 20, July 21, and July 22, 1852.

32. Hammersley, *Particulars of the Dreadful Tragedy in Richmond*, 8, 15–16; *Richmond Dispatch*, July 20 and July 21, 1852.

33. Hammersley, *Particulars of the Dreadful Tragedy in Richmond*, 17; *Richmond Dispatch*, July 20, 1852.

34. *Richmond Dispatch*, July 22, 1852.

35. Hammersley, *Particulars of the Dreadful Tragedy in Richmond*, 18; *Richmond Dispatch*, July 22, 1852.

36. Hammersley, *Particulars of the Dreadful Tragedy in Richmond*, 17, 18.

37. Campbell, *Slavery on Trial*, 82.

38. Hammersley, *Particulars of the Dreadful Tragedy in Richmond*, 18; *Richmond Dispatch*, July 20 and July 22, 1852; On "Cary Street woman," see Susanna Delfino and Michele Gillespie, eds., *Neither Lady Nor Slave: Working Women of the Old South* (Chapel Hill: University of North Carolina Press, 2002), 157.

39. Hammersley, *Particulars of the Dreadful Tragedy in Richmond*, 10–11.

40. Takagi, *Rearing Wolves*, 104–05; Campbell, *Slavery on Trial*, 179; Schwarz, *Twice Condemned*, 21.

41. "Confession of Jane Williams" in Hammersley, *Particulars of the Dreadful Tragedy in Richmond*, 19; *Richmond Dispatch*, July 26, 1852; *Daily Telegraph*, July 28, 1852.

42. *Richmond Enquirer*, July 30, 1852; *Richmond Dispatch*, quoted in *Tri-Weekly Commercial*, July 27, 1852, *Weekly Commercial*, July 30, 1852, and *The Times-Picayune*, July 31, 1852.

43. "Confession of Jane Williams" in Hammersley, *Particulars of the Dreadful Tragedy in Richmond*, 19; *Richmond Dispatch*, July 26, 1852.

44. "Confession of Jane Williams" in Hammersley, *Particulars of the Dreadful Tragedy in Richmond*, 19; *Richmond Dispatch*, July 26, 1852; *Daily American Telegraph*, July 28, 1852,

45. Campbell, *Slavery on Trial*, 22–25 *passim*, 111; *Richmond Enquirer*, July 22 and July 23, 1852.

46. The name is a carryover from England.

47. Campbell, *Slavery on Trial*, 79; Marianne Buroff Sheldon, "Black-White Relations in Richmond, Virginia, 1782–1820," *The Journal of Southern History* vol. 45, no. 1 (February 1979): 30; *Acts of the*

General Assembly of Virginia Passed at the Session Commencing December 6, 1847, 162.

48. *Acts of the General Assembly of Virginia Passed at the Session Commencing December 6, 1847,* 162; Campbell, *Slavery on Trial,* 77, 111.

49. *Acts of the General Assembly of Virginia Passed at the Session Commencing December 6, 1847,* 162; Stroud, *A Sketch of the Laws,* 92; Campbell, *Slavery on Trial,* 91; Hammersley, *Particulars of the Dreadful Tragedy in Richmond,* 20; *Richmond Dispatch,* August 10 and August 13, 1852; Schwarz, *Twice Condemned,* 22, 24, 49.

50. Hammersley, *Particulars of the Dreadful Tragedy in Richmond,* 5–12, 17, 19.

51. Hammersley, *Particulars of the Dreadful Tragedy in Richmond,* 23; *The Abingdon Virginian,* September 18, 1852.

52. *Richmond Dispatch,* September 11 and September 14, 1852; *Richmond Enquirer,* September 14, 1852.

53. Campbell, *Slavery on Trial,* 82–83.

54. *Richmond Dispatch,* July 22, and September 16, 1852; *Richmond Enquirer,* September 17, 1852; *The Times-Picayune,* September 27, 1852; *The Daily Republic,* September 18, 1852; *Baltimore Sun,* September 16, 1852.

55. *Richmond Dispatch,* July 20, 1852.

56. *Richmond Dispatch,* October 25 and October 28, 1852.

57. Hammersley, *Particulars of the Dreadful Tragedy in Richmond,* 25; *Richmond Dispatch,* August 13, 1852; *Richmond Enquirer,* September 17, 1852.

58. Hammersley, *Particulars of the Dreadful Tragedy in Richmond,* 25–27; *Richmond Dispatch,* July 21 and October 25, 1852.

59. Hammersley, *Particulars of the Dreadful Tragedy in Richmond,* 27; *Richmond Enquirer,* September 17, 1852.

60. "Lord Cornbury to the Lords Commissioner of Trade and Plantations," February 19, 1708, John Romeyn Brodhead, *Documents Relative to the Colonial History of the State of New-York* (Albany, NY: Weed, Parsons, Printers, 1853), 39; James Riker, Jr., *The Annals of Newtown in Queens County, New-York Containing its History from its First Settlement, Together with Many Interesting Facts Concerning the Adjacent Towns* (New York: D. Fanshaw, 1852), 142–43; na, *History of Queens County New York with Illustrations, Portraits and Sketches of Prominent Families and Individuals* (New York: W. W. Munsell & Co., 1882), 269; Hall, "Not Killing Me Softly," 31.

61. *Phereby, A Slave v. The State (Alabama),* April 10, 1849, Alabama Supreme Court Case Files, Alabama Department of Archives and

History: https://digital.archives.alabama.gov/digital/collection/
supreme_court/id/12063/rec/2; *Commonwealth* v. *Agness*, January 17,
1850, Library of Executive Papers of Governor John Buchanan Floyd,
1849–1851, box 3, folders 7 and 8, box 4, folder 6, and box 5, folder 2.

62. The deceased family's name is alternately spelled Longgon in news-
papers. For details about the case, see *Weekly Conservative*, May 6,
1848; *The Weekly Mississippian*, April 28, 1848; *Vicksburg Weekly*,
April 26, 1848. The case went all the way up to the state supreme court.
See *Cicely* v. *State* (1849), High Court of Errors and Appeals of
Mississippi. Also see Mississippi Supreme Court, *Mississippi
Supreme Court Cases Argued and Decided in the Supreme Court of
Mississippi* vol. 21 (E. W. Stephens Publishing Company, 1850), 202–
23, and Joshua S. Morris, *Mississippi State Cases Being Criminal Cases
Decided in the High Court of Errors and Appeals and in the Supreme
Court of Mississippi* (Jackson: Joshua S. Morris, 1872). Cecily's con-
fession can be found in: *Weekly Advertiser*, June 12, 1850;
Washington Telegraph (Washington, AR), June 26, 1850; *Monroe
Democrat* (Aberdeen, MS), June 19, 1850; *Palmyra Weekly Whig*,
July 4, 1850.

63. *State of Texas* v. *Jane, A Slave*, May 16, 1853, Dallas Public
Library; Donna Gosbee, "Jane Elkins: A Female Slave, Becomes
the First Woman To Be Legally Executed in the State of Texas
When She Is Hung on Friday, May 27, 1853. Beside the Dallas
County Courthouse": www.humanrightsdallasmaps.com/items/
show/2. According to Daina Ramey Berry, after Elkins was buried,
members of a medical fraternity dug her body up and used her
cadaver for research. See Ramey Berry, *The Price for Their Pound
of Flesh*, 115.

64. *Salisbury Herald*, quoted in *Daily Dispatch*, January 26, 1857.

6 Nelly, Betsy, and Ellen

1. "Jesse Ewell to Phillip D. Lipscombe," December 26, 1856; *Alexandria
Gazette and Virginia Advertiser*, December 31, 1856.

2. Prince William County, Virginia, "Prince William County Infographic;
History of Prince William County": https://www.pwcva.gov/assets/
2021-07/aFY22-17-Appendix.pdf; Fairfax County History, "Timeline
of Fairfax County History from the 1700s to Today": https://research
.fairfaxcounty.gov/local-history/timeline; Loudon County, Virginia,
"History of Loudon County": www.loudoun.gov/174/History; Virginia
Places.org, "Prince William County": www.virginiaplaces.org/vacount/
prwillco.html.

3. Encyclopedia Virginia, "Tobacco in Colnial Virginia": https://encyclopediavirginia.org/entries/tobacco-in-colonial-virginia/; Damian Pargas, "Work and Slave Family Life in Antebellum Northern Virginia," *Journal of Family History* vol. 31, no. 4 (2006): 336.

4. Pargas, "Work and Slave Family Life," 337–39.

5. Richard, Edwards, *Statistical Gazetteer of the State of Virginia Embracing Important Topographical and Historical Information from Recent and Original Sources to 1854* (Richmond: Richard Edwards, Publisher, 1855), 350–51.

6. *Eighth Census of the United States, 1860: Slave Schedule: Prince William County, Virginia:* www.ancestry.com/imageviewer/collections/7668/images/vam653_1396-0167?backlabel=ReturnSearchResults&queryId=67dcb7af6de9d6c99efeb15f54541e52&pId=91267436.

7. The Weirs named their family mansion, Liberia, after the American colony in West Africa founded for the resettlement of African Americans.

8. *Eighth Census of the United States, 1860: Slave Schedule: Prince William County, Virginia.*

9. Virginia. *Death and Burials Index, 1853–1917. Fifth Census of The United States, 1830: Prince William, Virginia*, series M19, roll 196, page 68: www.ancestry.com/imageviewer/collections/8058/images/4411237_00139?treeid=&personid=&hintid=&queryId=17667a96c22cabe8d8c5e64e75c7ea27&usePUB=true&usePUBJs=true&_ga=2.1683 03201.1156299205.1607876067-113988525.1597812278&_gac=1.14 8604613.1607656315.CjwKCAiAq8f-BRBtEiwAGr3Dgdo84rsIaFvoBz 75QABEl5nBQvGtbMpbb2S2Ac1kVwqwjDoKaoyjChoC4IoQAvD_B-wE&pId=893981; *Seventh Census of The United States, 1850: Prince William, Virginia*, roll 970, page 97b: www.ancestry.com/imageviewer/collections/8054/images/4206392_00196?treeid=&personid=&rc=&usePUB=true&_phsrc=q5y-1822212&_phstart=successSource&pId=15450 161; Measuringworth.com: www.measuringworth.com/calculators/uscompare/relativevalue.php; *Seventh Census of The United States, 1850: Slave Schedule*, Record Group: *Records of the Bureau of the Census*, record group number 29: www.ancestry.com%2Fimageviewer%2Fcollections%2F8055%2Fimages%2FVAM432_992-0377%3Fbacklabel%3DReturnSearchResults%26queryId%3D8042 ce8dd617a11113612998e09346ea5%26pId%3D92961731.

10. *Commonwealth v. Nelly & Others*, January 26, 1857, Governor Henry A. Wise Executive Papers, 1856–1859. Accession 36710, box 6, folder 2, State Government Records Collection, Library of Virginia.

11. "J. B. Grayson to Governor Henry Wise," February 13, 1857, Governor Henry A. Wise Executive Papers, 1856–1859. Accession

36710, box 6, folder 3, State Government Records Collection, Library of Virginia.

12. The planting season began very early in the year. In February, they would have begun planting potatoes, peas, lettuce, and cabbage, which provided sustenance for them and Green. They also would have spent time ploughing and preparing the ground for corn and oats. In the early spring, the "winter wheat" that had been planted in the fall would be harvested. "Spring wheat," planted in the early spring, would be harvested in the fall. In order to plant wheat, enslaved people needed to rake and prepare the ground for planting. If the soil was not rich, compost would need to be spread. They would then need to spread and rake the seeds. The seeds then had to be covered by a thin layer of soil. Wheat crops required a great deal of maintenance. They had to be watered if not enough rain fell. The crops also needed to be weeded and protected from slugs and sawflies and other destructive pests. When wheat was ready to be harvested, it had to be raked, cut, bound, and stacked. After wheat was reaped it needed to be threshed, which is a process by which wheat kernels are knocked loose from the stacks by beating or flailing – a highly labor-intensive process. Oats were planted using a process similar to wheat. To harvest oats, farm workers had to cut the seed heads from the stalks. Once cut, the oats then had to be cured, or stored in a warm, dry area for several weeks. The harvesting, reaping, curing and threshing of the grains kept enslaved people working through most of the summer. Then, in early fall, the fall wheat had to be planted. Corn had to be planted in warm weather, in late spring to early summer, because it required a good deal of sun and moist soil. Corn was not a low-maintenance crop, by any means: it required regular deweeding and had to be protected from crows, birds, and worms.

13. Pargas, "Work and Slave Family Life," 342–43.

14. *Commonwealth* v. *Nelly & Others*, January 26, 1857.

15. *Commonwealth* v. *Nelly & Others*, January 26, 1857.

16. Austin Steward, *Twenty-Two Years a Slave, and Forty-Years a Freeman, Embracing a Correspondence of Several Years While President of Wilberforce Colony, London, Canada West* (Rochester: Richard Alling, 1857), 13–14; Pargas, "Work and Slave Family Life," 352.

17. *Commonwealth* v. *Nelly & Others*, January 26, 1857.

18. Eugene D. Genovese, *Roll, Jordan, Roll: The World the Slaves Made* (New York: Vintage Books, 1972), 569–74.

19. *Daily Dispatch*, December 29, 1856 and January 1, 1857; *Alexandria Gazette and Virginia Advertiser*, December 30 and December 31,

1856; *Wheeling Daily Intelligencer*, January 5, 1857; *Richmond Enquirer*, January 2, 1857; *Commonwealth* v. *Nelly & Others*, January 26, 1857.

20. *Commonwealth* v. *Nelly & Others*, January 26, 1857; *Alexandria Gazette and Virginia Advertiser*, December 27 and December 31, 1856; *Richmond Enquirer*, December 30, 1856 and January 2, 1867; *Daily Dispatch*, January 1, 1856; *Wheeling Daily Intelligencer*, January 5, 1857; *The Abingdon Virginian*, January 3, 1857; Prince William County, Virginia, "Coroner's Inquest: Statement of Eliza (Slave of G. A. Hutchinson), December 26, 1856," *Clerk's Loose Papers* vol. III.

21. Prince William County, Virginia, "Testimony of George B. Tyler, Coroner's Inquest: Killing of George E. Green, December 26, 1856," *Clerk's Loose Papers* vol. III. Library of Virginia; *Eighth Census of the United States, 1860: Non-Population Schedule: Prince William County, Virginia*: www.ancestry.com/imageviewer/collections/1276/images/t1132_14-00240?treeid=&personid=&rc=&usePUB=true&_phsrc=q5y-438791&_phstart=successSource&pId=2699889.

22. Prince William County, Virginia, "Testimony of Luther L. Lynn, Coroner's Inquest: Killing of George E. Green, December 26, 1856," by Jesse Ewell in *Clerk's Loose Papers* vol. III. Library of Virginia.

23. "Jesse Ewell to Phillip D. Lipscombe," December 26, 1856, *Clerk's Loose Papers* vol. III. Library of Virginia; *Eighth Census of the United States, 1860: Non-Population Schedule: Prince William County, Virginia*: www.ancestry.com/imageviewer/collections/1276/images/t1132_14-00240?treeid=&personid=&rc=&usePUB=true&_phsrc=q5y-438791&_phstart=successSource&pId=2699889; *Eighth Census of the United States, 1860: Slave Schedule: Prince William County, Virginia*: www.ancestry.com/imageviewer/collections/7668/images/vam653_1396-0167?backlabel=ReturnSearchResults&queryId=67dcb7af6de9d6c99efeb15f54541e52&pId=91267436.

24. Prince William County, Virginia, "Coroner's Inquest: Killing of George E. Green. December 26, 1856," *Clerk's Loose Papers* vol. III. Library of Virginia; Prince William County, Virginia, "Testimony of George B. Tyler, Coroner's Inquest: Killing of George E. Green, December 26, 1856," *Clerk's Loose Papers* vol. III. Library of Virginia; *Commonwealth* v. *Nelly & Others*, January 26, 1857.

25. Prince William County, Virginia, "Testimony of George B. Tyler," "Coroner's Inquest: Killing of George E. Green." December 26, 1856, *Clerk's Loose Papers* vol. III. Library of Virginia; *Commonwealth* v. *Nelly & Others*, January 26, 1857.

26. Genovese, *Roll, Jordan, Roll*, 569–74.

27. Prince William County, Virginia, "Coroner's Inquest: Killing of George E. Green, December 26, 1856," by Jesse Ewell in *Clerk's Loose Papers* vol. III. Library of Virginia.

28. Prince William County, Virginia, "Coroner's Inquest: Killing of George E. Green. December 26, 1856," by Jesse Ewell in *Clerk's Loose Papers* vol. III. Library of Virginia; *Alexandria Gazette and Virginia Advertiser*, December 31, 1856.

29. Prince William County, Virginia, "Coroner's Inquest: Killing of George E. Green, December 26, 1856," by Jesse Ewell in *Clerk's Loose Papers* vol. III. Library of Virginia.

30. Prince William County, Virginia, "Testimony of George B. Tyler, Coroner's Inquest: Killing of George E. Green, December 26, 1856," by Jesse Ewell in *Clerk's Loose Papers* vol. III. Library of Virginia.

31. Prince William County, Virginia, "Testimony of George B. Tyler, Coroner's Inquest: Killing of George E. Green, December 26, 1856," by Jesse Ewell in *Clerk's Loose Papers* vol. III. Library of Virginia.

32. Prince William County, Virginia, "Coroner's Inquest: Killing of George E. Green, December 26, 1856," by Jesse Ewell in *Clerk's Loose Papers* vol. III. Library of Virginia; *Commonwealth v. Nelly & Others*, January 26, 1857.

33. "Jesse Ewell to Phillip D. Lipscombe," December 26, 1856.

34. Higginbotham Jr. and Jacobs, "The Law Only as an Enemy," 986, 997, 998, 1003.

35. *Commonwealth v. Nelly & Others*, January 26, 1857; *Eighth Census of the United States, 1860: Slave Schedule: Prince William County, Virginia*: www.ancestry.com/imageviewer/collections/7668/images/vam653_1396–0167?backlabel=ReturnSearchResults&queryId=67dcb7af6de9d6 c99efeb15f54541e52&pId=91267436.

36. Before 1723, enslaved people could testify in court against whites. After 1723, they could not testify in a trial involving whites, but were permitted to do so in a trial involving all Black people. Schwarz, *Twice Condemned*, 14, 45–46, 70.

37. *Commonwealth v. Nelly & Others*, January 26, 1857.

38. *Commonwealth v. Nelly & Others*, January 26, 1857.

39. *Staunton Spectator*, January 21, 1857; *Alexandria Gazette and Virginia Advertiser*, January 8, 1857; *Commonwealth v. Nelly & Others*, January 26, 1857.

40. *Commonwealth v. Nelly & Others*, January 26, 1857.

41. Stroud, *A Sketch of the Laws*, 92; Schwarz, *Twice Condemned*, 24.

42. "Thomas B. Baless to Governor Henry Wise," January 24, 1857, Governor Henry A. Wise Executive Papers, 1856–1859. Accession 36710, box 6, folder 2, State Government Records Collection,

Library of Virginia; "Thomas K. Davis to Governor Henry Wise," February 9, 1857, Governor Henry A. Wise Executive Papers, 1856–1859. Accession 36710, box 6, folder 3, State Government Records Collection, Library of Virginia; "Philip D. Lipscomb to Governor Henry Wise," February 9, 1857, Governor Henry A. Wise Executive Papers, 1856–1859. Accession 36710, box 6, folder 23, State Government Records Collection, Library of Virginia; "Governor Henry Wise to the Senate and House of Delegates of the General Assembly of Virginia," May 1857, Governor Henry A. Wise Executive Papers, 1856–1859. Accession 36710, box 8, folder 1, State Government Records Collection, Library of Virginia; *Alexandria Gazette and Virginia Advertiser*, February 13, 1857.

43. *Alexandria Gazette and Virginia Advertiser*, February 18, 1857; *Shepherdstown Register*, February 28, 1857; *Daily Dispatch*, February 18, 1857.

44. *Alexandria Gazette and Virginia Advertiser*, February 18, 1856; *Shepherdstown Register*, February 28, 1857; *Daily Dispatch*, February 18, 1857.

45. Holden, *Surviving Southampton*, 68–69.

46. "J. B. Grayson to Governor Henry Wise," February 13, 1857, Governor Henry A. Wise Executive Papers, 1856–1859. Accession 36710, box 6, folder 3, State Government Records Collection, Library of Virginia.

47. "Invoice from Richard Beach to Prince William County for Transportation for Elias and Ellen," April 30, 1857, *Condemned Slaves and Free Blacks, Executed or Transported Records, 1779–1865*. Accession APA 756, box 9, folder 4, State Government Records Collection, Library of Virginia; "Bond for the Purchase and Removal of William and the Others," May 7, 1857, *Condemned Slaves and Free Blacks, Executed or Transported Records, 1779–1865*. Accession APA 756, box 10, folder 14, State Government Records Collection, Library of Virginia.

7 Lucy

1. A hurricane destroyed the Galveston courthouse in 1900, so there are no extant court records from 1858. All the details from Lucy's case come from local newspapers. *Civilian and Gazette*, January 5, 1858; *Galveston Weekly News*, January 5, 1858; *Civilian and Gazette*, August 19, 1858; *Marshall County Democrat*, May 27, 1858; *The Galveston Daily News*, August 8, 1873 and September 9, 1888; *Port*

Neches Midcounty Chronicle, November 24, 2004; W. & D. Richardson, *Galveston City Directory, 1859–1860* (Galveston, Texas, Richardson, 1859), University of North Texas Libraries, The Portal to Texas History: https://texashistory.unt.edu/ark:/67531/metapth636854/.

2. Robert S. Shelton, "On Empire's Shore: Free and Unfree Workers in Galveston, Texas, 1840–1860," *Journal of Social History* vol. 40 (2007): 718, 719.

3. Shelton, "On Empire's Shore," 724; Richard Lowe and Randolph Campbell, "Slave Property and the Distribution of Wealth in Texas, 1860," *The Journal of American History* vol. 63 (1976): 320.

4. Shelton, "On Empire's Shore," 725; Morrison & Fourmy, *Morrison & Fourmy's General Directory of the City of Galveston: 1859* (Houston, Texas: M. Strickland & Sons, 1859), 37: https://texashistory.unt.edu/ark:/67531/metapth908994/; University of North Texas Libraries, The Portal to Texas History: https://texashistory.unt.edu.

5. W. Richardson, *Galveston Directory 1866–67 Containing the Early History of Galveston, the Officers of the Existing City Government* (Galveston: "News" Book and Job Office, 1866), 9: https://texashistory.unt.edu/ark:/67531/metapth636852/?q=1866%20city%20directory%20galveston.

6. "Texas, County Tax Rolls, 1837–1910," *FamilySearch*, Galveston county > 1853 > image 34 of 77, State Archives, Austin; "Texas, County Tax Rolls, 1837–1910," *FamilySearch*, Galveston county > 1855 > image 9 of 100, State Archives, Austin; "Texas, County Tax Rolls, 1837–1910," *FamilySearch*, Galveston county > 1857 > image 17 of 118, State Archives, Austin; "Texas, County Tax Rolls, 1837–1910," *FamilySearch*, Galveston county > 1859 > image 18 of 141, State Archives, Austin; W. Richardson, *Galveston Directory 1866–67*, 69.

7. The names McDonnell and McDonald are both used in historical records. Both versions are Irish. I will be using McDonnell for consistency. Year 1850, Census Place: *Galveston, Galveston, Texas*, roll 910, page 244; The name of the Doughertys' son was found in "Will of Joseph Dougherty," November 30, 1861, Galveston County, *Probate Records 1838–1906* (Galveston County), 292.

8. W. & D. Richardson, *Galveston City Directory, 1859–1860*, 18, 21, and 216; *Texas Planter*, July 28, 1852; *Columbia Democrat*, January 31, 1854; *Galveston Weekly News*, June 10, 1856; *Civilian*

and *Galveston Gazette*, January 5, 1858; *Columbia Democrat*, January 31, 1854. In 1856, Banton announced in *The Democrat and Planter* that the hotel was opening under his management.

9. *Galveston Weekly News*, January 5, 1858; *The Eastern Texian*, January 16, 1858.

10. *The Weekly Telegraph* (Galveston), January 7, 1857; John R. Lundberg, "'Texas Must Be a Slave Country': Slaves and Masters in the Texas Low Country 1840–1860," *East Texas Historical Journal* vol. 53, no. 2 (2015): 36.

11. "Dougherty, Joseph A. Bill of Sale for Slavewoman," October 10, 1857, Texas State Library and Archives Commission: www.ancestry.com; *Texas, Memorials and Petitions, 1834–1929*: www.ancestry.com; *Civilian and Galveston Gazette*, January 5 and March 9, 1858; The details of Lucy's purchase can also be found in *Race & Slavery Petitions Project*, PAR number 11585901, Galveston, Texas, 1859: https://library .uncg.edu/slavery/petitions/details.aspx?pid=2176.

12. Steven Deyle, "The Domestic Slave Trade in America: The Lifeblood of the Southern Slave System," *The Chattel Principle: Internal Slave Trades in the Americas*, Walter Johnson, ed. (New Haven: Yale University Press, 2005), 93.

13. Jason A. Gillmer, *Slavery and Freedom: Stories from the Courtroom, 1821–1871* (Athens, GA: University of Georgia Press, 2017), 138–39.

14. Ramey Berry, *The Price for Their Pound of Flesh*, 130, 131, and 136.

15. "Louisiana, New Orleans, Slave Manifests of Coastwise Vessels, 1807–1860," Film # 103435696, database, *FamilySearch*: https://family search.org/ark:/61903/3:1:3Q9M-CSVF-V5HL?cc=2822773; NARA microfilm publication M1895, RG36. National Archives at Fort Worth, Texas, National Archives and Records Administration, 1986.

16. Ramey Berry, *The Price for Their Pound of Flesh*, 131, 132, 133, 134.

17. Lydia Plath, "'My Master and Miss ... Warn't Nothing but Poor White Trash': Poor White Slaveowners and Their Slaves in the Antebellum South," *Slavery & Abolition* vol. 38 (2017): 479, 480, 481.

18. Gillmer, *Slavery and Freedom*, 84, 202, fn 88. In 1858, Texas legislators were motivated to pass such protective legislation to deter third parties from harming their enslaved people; it was not motivated by belief in Black people's humanity or a desire to extend equal protection to them.

19. *Galveston Weekly News*, January 5, 1858; *Civilian and Gazette*, January 5, 1858; *The San Antonio Ledger*, January 16, 1858; *The*

Eastern Texian, January 16, 1858; *The Galveston Daily News,* September 9, 1888.

20. Steven W. Hackel, *Children of Coyote, Missionaries of Saint Francis: Indian–Spanish Relations in Colonial California, 1769–1850* (Chapel Hill: University of North Carolina Press, 2005), 325.

21. Glymph, *Out of the House of Bondage,* 25, 26, 33, and 46. Also see Jones-Rogers, *They Were Here Property,* 60, 61.

22. *Galveston Weekly News,* January 5, 1858; *Civilian and Gazette,* January 5, 1858; *The San Antonio Ledger,* January 16, 1858; *The Eastern Texian,* January 16, 1858.

23. *Galveston Weekly News,* January 5, 1858; *Civilian and Gazette,* January 5, 1858; *The Galveston Daily News,* September 9, 1888.

24. Holden, *Surviving Southampton,* 36.

25. *Galveston Weekly News,* January 5, 1858; *Civilian and Gazette,* January 5, 1858; *The Eastern Texian,* January 16, 1858.

26. *Galveston Weekly News,* January 5, 1858; *Civilian and Gazette,* January 5, 1858; *The San Antonio Ledger,* January 16, 1858; *The Eastern Texian,* January 16, 1858; *Colorado Citizen,* January 16, 1858.

27. *Texas Constitution* (1845), art. VIII, sec. 2.

28. Meaning "et cetera." This means that Lucy said additional things about her bad treatment, but the writer chose to abbreviate it with "&c."

29. *Civilian and Gazette,* January 5 and January 19, 1858; *Civilian and Gazette,* January 19, 1858; *Galveston Tri Weekly Civilian,* November 25, 1872; *The Weekly Telegraph,* January 20, 1858; *The Colorado Citizen,* January 30, 1858.

30. *Civilian and Gazette,* March 9, 1858.

31. *Civilian and Gazette,* March 9, 1858; *Galveston, Tri Weekly Civilian,* November 25, 1872; *Galveston Daily News,* September 9, 1888.

32. *The Colorado Citizen,* January 30, 1858.

33. The first place these exact words were reported is in the *Galveston Tri Weekly Civilian,* November 25, 1872 – some fifteen years later. The passage of time coupled with the fact that no contemporary source reported these words, leads to serious doubts whether these were Lucy's words or the words of the journalist.

34. *The Galveston Daily News,* September 9, 1888.

35. *State of Texas* v. *Jane, A Slave,* May 16, 1853, Dallas Public Library; Donna Gosbee, "Jane Elkins: A Female Slave, Becomes the First Woman To Be Legally Executed in the State of Texas When She Is Hung on Friday, May 27, 1853 Beside the Dallas County Courthouse": www .humanrightsdallasmaps.com/items/show/2. According to Daina Ramey Berry, after Elkins was buried, members of a medical fraternity dug her

body up and used her cadaver for research. See Ramey Berry, *The Price for Their Pound of Flesh*, 115.

Conclusion

1. Bertram Wyatt Brown, *Southern Honor: Ethics & Behavior in the Old South* (Oxford: Oxford University Press, 2007), 352–54, 368; Ira Berlin, "American Slavery in History and Memory and the Search for Social Justice," *Journal of American History* vol. 90, no. 4 (March 2004): 1264.

2. Kellie Carter Jackson, *Force and Freedom: Black Abolitionists and the Politics of Violence* (Philadelphia: University of Pennsylvania Press, 2019), 55–57.

3. On women's roles, see William Parker, "The Freedman's Story, In Two Parts," *The Atlantic Monthly: A Magazine of Literature, Science, Art and Politics* vol. XVII (Boston: Ticknor and Fields, 1866), 286, 288: https://docsouth.unc.edu/neh/parker1/parker.html; *Pennsylvania Freeman*, September 18, 1851; Erica Rhodes Hayden, "'Plunged into a Vortex of Iniquity": Female Criminality and Punishment in Pennsylvania, 1820–1860" (PhD diss., Vanderbilt University, 2013), 158; Thomas P. Slaughter, *Bloody Dawn: The Christiana Riot and Racial Violence in the Antebellum North* (New York: Oxford University Press, 1991), 43. On the mutilation of Gorsuch's body, see *The Lancaster Examiner* (Lancaster, PA), September 17 and October 1, 1851.

4. Lashawn Harris, "The 'Commonwealth of Virginia vs. Virginia Christian': Southern Black Women, Crime & Punishment in Progressive Era Virginia," *Journal of Social History* vol. 47, no. 4 (2014): 922–42 *passim*: https://sites.lib.jmu.edu/valynchings/virginias-rocket-docket/; *Alexandria Gazette*, April 10, 1912.

5. *The Washington Post*, June 22, 2020.

6. Brenna Ehrlich, "Should You Go to Prison for Killing Your Trafficker? Cyntoia Brown Long Weighs In," *Rolling Stone*, September 27, 2021.

7. *Ibid.*

ACKNOWLEDGMENTS

I first want to thank all the women in this book for fighting back with their hands against one of the greatest transgressions against humanity: chattel slavery.

I also would like to thank all of the archivists, librarians, and volunteers at the Library of Virginia, New York State Archives, New York Public Library, New York Historical Society, Massachusetts Historical Society, State Archives of North Carolina, Texas State Library and Archives Commission, Delaware Historical Society, Family History Library, Missouri State Archives, Cumberland County Historical Society, Clark County (Winchester, Kentucky) Public Library, American Revolution Institute, Pennsylvania Historical and Museum Commission, and the Library of Congress. They were generous with their time, information, advice, and always eager to assist. I especially appreciated the availability of so many of their materials online, especially during the pandemic when the archives were closed.

I am indebted to Cecelia Cancellaro who took a chance with this book and believed in the idea from the beginning. She moved mountains to get it reviewed at warp speed. My spirits were deflated when I went to her because of another experience and Cecelia sowed seeds of encouragement, support, and positivity from the first email. That is very rare in the brutal world of academic publishing. I am humbled, honored, and deeply grateful to her and Cambridge University Press. I also wish to thank the anonymous reviewers who sent glowing reviews, but who also took a great deal of time and attention in providing me with helpful advice.

I am grateful to have such generous colleagues at Howard University who encouraged and supported me in this endeavor, including Daryl Scott, Jeff Kerr-Ritchie, Carolette Norwood, and Hazel Edwards. One, though, stands above all: Ana Araujo. Dr. Araujo is a dream colleague, and an even better friend. She has encouraged and supported me through all manner of personal and professional ups and downs. She played a role in the birth of the idea for this book when she invited me to present an early iteration of it at her monthly seminar, "Slavery, Memory, and African Diasporas." Although the final book bears no similarity to that early paper, I still reflect on the insightful critiques from the audience that led me down the path that became this work. Dr. Araujo also read and critiqued drafts and encouraged me to reach out to Cambridge. In other words, she assisted me at every stage of this project and I appreciate all of it.

Only with an exceedingly supportive community can a department chair get her own work done. I wish to thank the entire Department of History faculty and students who were understanding when I frequently went missing from the office to go to an archive or revise certain chapters. My department offered two of our top graduate assistants to help me on the final lap of preparing this manuscript. Kendra and Sydney, your feedback, editing, and help transcribing primary sources has been invaluable. Sydney's editing, in particular, was professional level and drastically improved the manuscript. I am truly grateful.

Debbie Gershenowitz suggested that I organize the book using case studies as chapters. That innovation changed the game. I remain blown away by the advice Kellie Carter Jackson provided. Wrapped in love, support, and sisterhood, her advice and recommendations gave me the courage to be bolder in my analyses. I also thank Karen Cook-Bell, my friends Eric Jackson, Adah Ward Randolph and others who read drafts or allowed me to bounce new theories off them. Countless other friends, colleagues, students, and family members were indispensable on this journey.

To my immediate family: I am eternally grateful for, and indebted to, my partner in love, laughter, life, and all the things in between, Vincent. I used to dream about having this level of support from a partner. As a non-academic, he thinks it is a pretty big deal that I am writing a book: maybe it is. He never hesitated to mute his Dallas Cowboy games to patiently listen to me read countless versions of each chapter, ad nauseam. He gave me solid advice on chapter introductions, word choice, sentence construction, helped me get back on point when the text strayed, and filled my ego with so much praise that in my mind, this book is already a best seller. Everyone dreams of a partner as supportive and encouraging – not just in my career, but also in all the travails we have endured these last six years. He shows me unconditional love daily. What a wonderful gift.

I am fortunate to have a mother who taught me how to fight power using all the weapons I have at my disposal – the most powerful of which is the gift of writing.

Finally, to my forever muse and legacy, Kaia. She made a profoundly generous sacrifice of so much of her own time in medical school to assist and support me with this book. Between studying for licensing exams and hospital rotations, she would patiently listen to me summarize chapters and work through the theory. She gave very solid feedback and help. I was touched every time she expressed genuine interest in my latest archival discoveries and voiced excitement when I finished a chapter. We bonded over our full belly laughs about Rose Butler's antics. I would not be even half the historian I am without Kaia's imprint of love and support on every page of every book I have ever written.

SELECTED BIBLIOGRAPHY

Primary Sources
Newspapers

Alexandria Gazette
Baltimore Sun
Boston Evening Post
Boston Gazette
Carlisle Gazette
Civilian and Gazette
Columbia Minerva
Columbian
Connecticut Gazette
Daily American Telegraph
Daily Republic
Eastern Texian
Federal Gazette
Galveston Daily News
Galveston Weekly News
Independent Gazette
Mercantile Advertiser
New Hampshire Gazette
New-Hampshire Gazette and Historical Chronicle
New York Journal
Oracle of Dauphin
Philadelphia Gazette
Political Repository
Richmond Dispatch
Richmond Enquirer
Rinds Virginia Gazette

Scioto Gazette
Staunton Spectator
The New York Evening Post
The Times; and District of Columbia Daily Advertiser
Tri-Weekly Commercial
Washington Telegraph
Wheeling Daily Intelligencer

Trial and Court Records

Acts of North Carolina General Assembly
Certificate of Special Court for the Trial of Annis, A Negro Wench
Certificate of Special Court for the Trial of Cuffy
Clark County Probate Court Records
Commonwealth of Massachusetts. Probate Records (Middlesex County)
Commonwealth v. *Agness*
Commonwealth v. *Charlotte*
Commonwealth v. *Gus Depp's Jane*
Commonwealth v. *Nelly & Others*
Mary, A Slave v. *State of Missouri*
North Carolina Magistrates and Freeholders Courts 1770–1779
North Carolina Secretary of State Papers
Phereby, A Slave v. *The State (Alabama)*
Prince William County Clerk's Loose Papers
Prince William County Minute Book
Respublica v. *Negroe Cloe*
State of Missouri v. *Mary, A Slave*
State of Texas v. *Jane, A Slave*
Supreme Court of Missouri Historical Records
The People v. *Rose Butler*
Virginia. Condemned Slaves and Free Blacks, Executed or Transported Records

Other Primary Sources

A Few Lines on Occasion of the Untimely End of Mark and Phillis, Who Were Executed at Cambridge, September 18th for Poysoning Their Master, Capt. John Codman of Charlestown. Boston: 1755: www .loc.gov/resource/rbpe.0350150a.

Butler, Rose. *Statements of Confession*. New York Historical Society Museum & Library, 1819.

Federal Writers' Project, and Library of Congress. 2001. *Born in Slavery: Slave Narratives from the Federal Writers' Project, 1936–1938*. Washington, D.C.: Library of Congress: http://hdl.loc.gov/loc.mss/collmss.ms000008.

Goodell, Abner Cheney. *The Trial and Execution for Petit Treason, of Mark and Phillis, slaves of Capt. John Codman: Who Murdered Their Master at Charlestown, Mass., in 1755; For Which the Man was Hanged and Gibbeted, and the Woman Was Burned to Death*. Cambridge: John Wilson and Son, 1833. Pdf: www.loc.gov/resource/llst.023.

Governor Henry A. Wise Executive Papers, 1856–1859.

Hammersley, John D. *Particulars of the Dreadful Tragedy in Richmond, on the Morning of the 19th July 1852, Being a Full Account of the Awful Murder of the Winston Family: Embracing All the Particulars of the Discovery of the Bloody Victims, The Testimony Before the Coroner's Jury, and the Evidence on the Final Trials of the Murderess and Murderer, Jane and John Williams: Their Sentence, Confessions, and the Execution Upon the Gallows: Together With the Funeral Sermon of the Rev Mr. Moore, on the Death of Mrs. Winston and Daughter, and the Sermon of the Rev Robert Ryland on the Subject of the Murders*. Richmond: John D. Hammersley, 1852.

Index of Obituaries in Boston Newspapers, 1704–1795: Boston Athenaeum. Boston: G. K. Hall & Co., 1968: www.ancestry.com. *U.S., Newspaper Extractions from the Northeast, 1704–1930* [database online]. Provo: Ancestry.com Operations, Inc., 2014.

Journals of the House of Burgesses & Virginia.

Mark. *The Last & Dying Words of Mark, Aged about 30 years, A Negro Man Who Belonged to the Late Captain John Codman, of Charlestown; Who Was Executed the 18th of September, 1855 for Poysoning his Above said Master* (Boston: np, 1755). Held at the Massachusetts Historical Society.

Maryland. *Proceedings of the Council of Maryland, 1732–1753*. Virginia: Samuel Ogle, Governor, nd.

Maryland. *Proceedings of the Council of Maryland, 1753–1761*. Virginia: Horatio Sharpe, Governor, nd.

Nat Turner Project: www.natturnerproject.org.

New York City Directory 1818–19. Irma and Paul Milstein Division of United States History, Local History and Genealogy, The New York Public Library. New York Public Library Digital Collections: https://digitalcollections.nypl.org/items/8e1ed570-12ac-0137-9f2b-055502cc8899.

North Carolina. Stephen Beauregard Weeks, W. Laurence Saunders, Trustees of the Public Libraries. *The Colonial Records of North Carolina.* Raleigh: P. M. Hale [etc.] state printer, 1886–1890.

Parker, William. "The Freedman's Story, In Two Parts," *The Atlantic Monthly: A Magazine of Literature, Science, Art and Politics* vol. XVII. Boston: Ticknor and Fields, 1866: https://docsouth.unc.edu/neh/parker1/parker.html.

Ripley, Dorothy. *An Account of Rose Butler: Aged Nineteen Years, Whose Execution I Attended in the Potter's Field on the 9th of 7th Mo. For Setting Fire to Her Mistress' Dwelling House.* New York: John C. Totten, 1819.

Stanford, John. *An Authentic Statement of the Case and Conduct of Rose Butler, Who was Tried, Convicted, and Executed for the Crime of Arson.* New York: Broderick and Ritter, 1819.

Steward, Austin. *Twenty-Two Years a Slave, and Forty-Years a Freeman, Embracing a Correspondence of Several Years While President of Wilberforce Colony, London, Canada West.* Rochester: Richard Alling, 1857.

Stroud, George M. *A Sketch of the Laws Related to Slavery in the Several States of the United States of America.* Philadelphia: H. Longstreth, 1856.

Van Ness, William Peter and John Woodworth, eds. *Laws of the State of New-York Revised and Passed at the Thirty-Sixth Session of the Legislature, with Marginal Notes and References, Furnished by the Revisors.* Albany: H. C. Southwick & Co., 1813.

Watson, Alan D., ed. *Society in Early North Carolina: A Documentary History.* Raleigh: North Carolina Department of Cultural Resources, 2000.

Weld, Theodore Dwight. *American Slavery As it Is: Testimony of A Thousand Witnesses.* New York: American Anti-Slavery Society, 1839: https://docsouth.unc.edu/neh/weld/weld.html.

Whitman, Zechariah G. *The History of the Ancient and Honorable Artillery Company, From its Formation in 1637 and Charter in 1638, to the Present Time; Comprising the Biographies of the*

Distinguished Civil, Literary, Religious, and Military Men of the Colony, Province, and Commonwealth. Boston: John H. Eastburn Printer, 1842.

Williams, James. *Narrative of James Williams, an American Slave, Who Was for Several Years a Driver on a Cotton Plantation in Alabama.* New York: American Anti-Slavery Society, 1838: https://docsouth .unc.edu/fpn/williams/williams.html.

Secondary Sources

Aguirre, Adalberto and David V. Baker. "Slave Executions in the United States: A Descriptive Analysis of Social and Historical Factors." *Social Science Journal* vol. 36, no. 1 (January 1999): 1–30.

Aptheker, Herbert. *American Negro Slave Revolts.* New York: International Publishers. 1943.

Araujo, Ana Lucia. *Politics of Memory: Making Slavery Visible in the Public Space.* Ana Lucia Araujo, ed. New York: Routledge, 2012.

Baker, David V. "Black Female Executions in Historical Context." *Criminal Justice Review* vol. 33, no. 1 (March 2008): 64–88.
   Women and Capital Punishment in the United States: An Analytical History. Jefferson: McFarland & Company, 2016.

Berry, "Coroners and the Enslaved: CSI:Dixie," {Database] University of Georgia: https://csidixie.org/exodus/coroners-enslaved/

Banner, Stuart. *The Death Penalty: An American History.* Cambridge: Harvard University Press, 2002.

Bickford, Annette Louise. *Southern Mercy: Empire and American Civilization in Juvenile Reform 1890–1944.* University of Toronto Press, 2016.

Breen, Patrick H. *The Land Shall Be Deluged in Blood: A New History of the Nat Turner Revolt.* New York: Oxford University Press, 2015.

Bond, Richard E. "Shaping a Conspiracy: Black Testimony in the 1741 New York Plot." *Early American Studies* vol. 5, no. 1 (2007): 63–94.

Brown, Kathleen M. *Good Wives, Nasty Wenches, and Anxious Patriarchs: Gender, Race, and Power in Colonial Virginia.* Chapel Hill: University of North Carolina Press, 1996.

Camp, Stephanie M.H. *Closer to Freedom: Enslaved Women & Everyday Resistance in the Plantation South.* Chapel Hill: University of North Carolina Press, 2004.

Campbell, James M. *Slavery on Trial: Race, Class, and Criminal Justice in Antebellum Richmond, Virginia.* Gainesville: University Press of Florida, 2007.

Campbell, Randolph B. *Empire of Slavery: The Peculiar Institution in Texas, 1821–1865.* Baton Rouge: Louisiana State University Press, 1989.

Carroll, Joseph Cephas. *Slave Insurrections in the United States 1800–1865.* Boston: Dover, 2004.

Carter Jackson, Kellie. *Force and Freedom: Black Abolitionists and the Politics of Violence.* Philadelphia: University of Pennsylvania Press, 2019.

Catterral, Helen Tunnicliff and James J. Hayden. *Judicial Cases Concerning American Slavery and the Negro* vol. 5. Washington, D.C.: Carnegie Institution of Washington, 1937.

Cooper, Afua. *The Hanging of Angelique: The Untold Story of Canadian Slavery and the Burning of Montreal.* Athens: The University of Georgia Press, 2007.

Cooper, Francis Hodges, *Some Colonial History of Beaufort County, NC.* Raleigh: Edwards and Broughton Printing Company State Printers, 1916.

Crawford, Paul. "A Footnote on Courts for Trial of Negroes in Colonial Pennsylvania." *Journal of Black Studies* vol. 5, no. 2 (1974): 167–74.

Davis, T. J. *A Rumor of Revolt: The "Great Negro Plot" in Colonial New York.* Amherst: University of Massachusetts Press, 1985.

Delfino, Susanna and Michele Gillespie, eds. *Neither Lady Nor Slave: Working Women of the Old South.* Chapel Hill: University of North Carolina Press, 2002.

Deyle, Steven. "The Domestic Slave Trade in America: The Lifeblood of the Southern Slave System." In *The Chattel Principle: Internal Slave Trades in the Americas,* Walter Johnson, ed., The David Brion Davis Series, 91–116. New Haven: Yale University Press, 2004.

Duane, Anna Mae, ed. *Child Slavery Before and After Emancipation: An Argument for Child-Centered Slavery Studies.* New York: Cambridge University Press, 2017.

Egerton, Douglas R. *Gabriel's Rebellion: The Virginia Conspiracies of 1800 and 1802.* Chapel Hill: The University of North Carolina Press, 1993.

Espy, M. Watt and John Ortiz Smykla. "Executions in the United States, 1608–2002: The ESPY File." Inter-university Consortium for

Political and Social Research [distributor], 2016: https://doi.org/
10.3886/ICPSR08451.v5.

"The Database of Executions in the United States of America": https://
files.deathpenaltyinfo.org/legacy/documents/ESPYyear.pdf.

Fett, Sharla M. *Working Cures: Healing, Health, and Power on Southern
Slave Plantations*. Chapel Hill: University of North Carolina Press,
2002.

Flanigan, Daniel J. "Criminal Procedure in Slave Trials in the Antebellum
South." *The Journal of Southern History* vol. 40, no. 4 (1974): 537–64.

Forman, James, Jr. "Juries and Race in the Nineteenth Century." *Yale Law
Journal* vol. 113, no. 4 (January 2004): 895–938.

Frazier, Harriet C. *Slavery and Crime in Missouri*. Jefferson: McFarland &
Co., 2001.

French, Scot. *The Rebellious Slave: Nat Turner in American Memory*.
Boston: Houghton Mifflin, 2004.

Gellman, David N. "Race, the Public Sphere, and Abolition in Late
Eighteenth-Century New York." *Journal of the Early Republic*
vol. 20, no. 4 (2000): 607–36.

Genovese, Eugene D. *From Rebellion to Revolution: Afro-American Slave
Revolts in the Making of the Modern World*. Baton Rouge:
Louisiana State University Press. 1979.

Gerlach, Don R. "Black Arson in Albany, New York: November 1793."
Journal of Black Studies vol. 7, no. 3 (March 1977): 301–12.

Gillmer, Jason A. *Slavery and Freedom: Stories from the Courtroom,
1821–1871*. Athens: University of Georgia Press, 2017.

Glymph, Thavolia. *Out of the House of Bondage: The Transformation of
the Plantation Household*. New York: Cambridge University Press,
2008.

Greene, Lorenzo. *The Negro in Colonial New England*. New York:
Columbia University Press, 1942.

Hall, Rebecca. "Not Killing Me Softly: African American Women, Slave
Revolts, and Historical Constructions of Racialized Gender"
(2010): 1–47. *Freedom Center Journal* vol. 2: https://ssrn.com/
abstract=1874927.

Hardesty, Jared Ross. "'The Negro at the Gate': Enslaved Labor in
Eighteen-Century Boston." *The New England Quarterly* vol. 87
(March 2014): 72–98.

Unfreedom: Slavery and Dependence in Eighteenth-Century Boston.
New York University Press, 2016.

Harris, Jennifer. "Offering Nothing: Phillis Hammond and the "Bitter Effects of Sin." *Early American Literature* vol. 55 (November 2020): 395–418.

Hazen, Margaret Hindle, and Hazen, Robert M. *Keepers of the Flame: The Role of Fire in American Culture.* Princeton University Press, 1992.

Helg, Aline. *Slave No More: Self-Liberation Before Abolitionism in the Americas.* Chapel Hill: University of North Carolina Press, 2016.

Higginbotham, Jr., A. Leon and Anne F. Jacobs. "The Law Only as an Enemy: The Legitimization of Racial Powerlessness through the Colonial and Antebellum Criminal Laws of Virginia." *North Carolina Law Review* vol. 70, no. 4 (1992): 960–1070.

Higginbotham, Jennifer. *The Girlhood of Shakespeare's Sisters: Gender, Transgression, Adolescence.* Edinburgh University Press, 2013.

Hine, Darlene Clark. *Hine Sight: Black Women and the Re-Construction of American History.* New York: Carlson, 1994.

Hodges, Graham Russell. *Root & Branch: African Americans in New York and East Jersey 1613–1863.* Chapel Hill: The University of North Carolina Press, 1999.

Holden, Vanessa M. *Surviving Southampton: African American Women and Resistance in Nat Turner's Community.* Urbana: University of Illinois Press, 2021.

Holloway, Joseph. "Slave Insurrections in the United States: An Overview": http://slaverebellion.info/index.php?page=united-states-insurrections.

Horton, James Oliver and Lois E. Horton, *In Hope of Liberty: Culture, Community, and Protest Among Northern Free Blacks, 1700–1860.* New York: Oxford University Press, 1997.

Johnson, William. *Reports of Cases Argued and Determined in the Supreme Court of Judicature, and in the Court for the Trial of Impeachment and the Correction of Errors, in the State of New York* vol. XV. New York: Banks & Brothers Law Publishers, 1883.

Jones-Rogers, Stephanie E. *They Were Here Property: White Women as Slave Owners in the American South.* New Haven: Yale University Press, 2019.

Jordan, Winthrop D. *Tumult and Silence at Second Creek: An Inquiry into a Civil War Conspiracy.* Baton Rouge: Louisiana State University Press, 1993.

Kars, Marjoleine. *Blood on the River: A Chronicle of Mutiny and Freedom on the Wild Coast*. New York: The New Press, 2020.

Kay, Marvin L. Michael, and Lorin Lee Cary. *Slavery in North Carolina 1748–1775*. Chapel Hill: University of North Carolina Press, 1995. "'The Planters Suffer Little or Nothing': North Carolina Compensations for Executed Slaves, 1748–1772." *Science & Society* vol. 40, no. 3 (1976): 288–306.

King, Wilma. "'Mad' Enough to Kill: Enslaved Women, Murder, and Southern Courts." *Journal of African American History* vol. 92, no. 1 (Winter 2007): 37–56.

Kozel, Sue. "Why Wench Betty's Story Matters – The Murder of a NJ Slave in 1784." *New Jersey Studies: An Interdisciplinary Journal* vol. 6 (2020): 1–22.

Lee, Deborah A. and Warren R. Hofstra. "Race, Memory, and the Death of Robert Berkeley: A Murder … of … Horrible and Savage Barbarity." *The Journal of Southern History* vol. 65, no. 1 (February 1999): 41–76.

Lundberg, John R. "'Texas Must Be a Slave Country': Slaves and Masters in the Texas Low Country 1840–1860." *East Texas Historical Journal* vol. 53, no. 2 (2015): 29–47.

Maryland. "Hanged Slaves By Date": https://msa.maryland.gov/megafile/msa/speccol/sc2900/sc2908/000001/000819/pdf/chart28.pdf.

McConville, Mike, and Chester L. Mirsky et al. *Jury Trials and Plea Bargaining: A True History*. Oxford: Hart Publishing, 2005.

McCoy, Michael B. "Forgetting Freedom: White Anxiety, Black Presence, and Gradual Abolition in Cumberland County, Pennsylvania, 1780–1838." *The Pennsylvania Magazine of History and Biography* vol. 136 (April 2012): 141–70.

McCurdy, John Gilbert. *Citizen Bachelors: Manhood and the Creation of the United States*. Ithaca: Cornell University Press, 2009.

McLaurin, Milton. *Celia, A Slave: A True Story*. New York: Avon Books, 1991.

McNair, Glenn. *Criminal Injustice: Slaves and Free Blacks in Georgia's Criminal Justice System*. Charlottesville: University of Virginia Press, 2009.

Morris, Thomas D. "Slaves and the Rules of Evidence in Criminal Trials – Symposium on the law of Slavery: Criminal and Civil Law of Slavery." *Chicago-Kent Law Review* vol. 68 (June 1993): 1208–40.

Nash, Gary B. and Jean R. Soderlund. *Freedom by Degrees: Emancipation in Pennsylvania and Its Aftermath*. New York: Oxford University Press, 1991.

O'Shea Kathleen A. *Women and the Death Penalty in the U.S. 1900–1998*. Westport: Praeger, 1999.

Pargas, Damian. "Work and Slave Family Life in Antebellum Northern Virginia." *Journal of Family History* vol 31, no. 4 (2006): 335–57.

Pearson, Edward A., ed. *Designs Against Charleston: The Trial Record of the Denmark Vesey Slave Conspiracy of 1822*. Chapel Hill: The University of North Carolina Press, 1999.

Peterson, Mark. *The City-State of Boston: The Rise and Fall of an Atlantic Power, 1630–1865*. Princeton University Press, 2019.

Plath, Lydia. "'My Master and Miss ... Warn't Nothing but Poor White Trash': Poor White Slaveowners and Their Slaves in the Antebellum South." *Slavery & Abolition* vol. 38 (2017): 475–88.

Ramey Berry, Daina. *The Price for Their Pound of Flesh: The Value of the Enslaved from Womb to Grave in the Building of a Nation*. Boston: Beacon Press, 2017.

Rogers, Alan. *Murder and the Death Penalty in Massachusetts*. Amherst: University of Massachusetts, 2008.

Ryan, Kelly A. *Everyday Crimes: Social Violence and Civil Rights in Early America*. New York University Press, 2019.

Schwartz, Marie Jenkins. *Born in Bondage: Growing Up Enslaved in the Antebellum South*. Cambridge: Harvard University Press, 2000.

Schwarz, Philip J. *Twice Condemned: Slaves and the Criminal Laws of Virginia, 1705–1865*. Union: The Lawbook Exchange, Ltd., 1998.

Sesay, Chernoh M. "The Revolutionary Black Roots of Slavery's Abolition in Massachusetts." *The New England Quarterly* vol. 87, no. 1 (2014): 99–131.

Shapiro, Herbert. "The Impact of the Aptheker Thesis: A Retrospective View of American Negro Slave Revolts." *Science & Society* vol. 48, no. 1 (1984): 52–73.

Shelton, Robert S. "On Empire's Shore: Free and Unfree Workers in Galveston, Texas, 1840–1860." *Journal of Social History* vol. 40 (2007): 717–30.

Sidbury, James. *Ploughshares Into Swords: Race, Rebellion, and Identity in Gabriel's Virginia, 1730–1810*. New York: Cambridge University Press, 1997.

Soderlund, Jean R. "Black Women in Colonial Pennsylvania." *The Pennsylvania Magazine of History and Biography* vol. 107, no. 1 (1983): 49–68.

Takagi, Midori *Rearing Wolves to Our Own Destruction: Slavery in Richmond Virginia, 1782–1865.* Charlottesville: University of Virginia Press, 1999.

Tarlow, Sarah and Zoey Syndor. "The Landscape of the Gibbet." *Landscape History* vol. 36 (2015): 71–88.

Taylor, Nikki M. *Driven Towards Madness: Fugitive Slave Margaret Garner and Tragedy on the Ohio.* Athens: Ohio University Press, 2016.

Tushnet, Mark. "Essays in Honor of J. Willard Hurst: Part One." *Law & Society Review* vol. 10, no. 1 (Autumn, 1975): 119–84.

Warren, Wendy. *New England Bound: Slavery and Colonization in Early America.* New York: Liveright Publishing Corporation, 2016.

Watson, Alan D. "Impulse Toward Independence: Resistance and Rebellion Among North Carolina Slaves, 1750–1775." *Journal of Negro History* vol. 63, no. 4 (October 1978): 317–28.

"North Carolina Slave Courts." *The North Carolina Historical Review* vol 60, no. 1 (January 1983): 24–36.

Wayne County Historical Association and the Old Dobbs County Genealogical Society. *The Heritage of Wayne County, North Carolina, 1982.* Winston-Salem, Wayne County Historical Association, 1982.

White, Shane "Slavery in the North." *OAH Magazine of History* vol. 17, no. 3 (2003): 17–21: www.jstor.org/stable/25163595.

Wyatt Brown, Bertram. *Southern Honor: Ethics & Behavior in the Old South.* Oxford University Press, 2007.

Zaborney, John J. *Slaves for Hire: Renting Enslaved Laborers in Antebellum Virginia.* Baton Rouge: Louisiana State University Press, 2012.

Dissertations

Berry, Chelsea. "Poisoned Relations: Medicine, Sorcery, and Poison Trials in the Contested Atlantic, 1680–1850." PhD diss., Georgetown University, 2019.

Bouton, Christopher, "Against the Peace and Dignity of the Commonwealth: Physical Confrontations Between Slaves and

Whites in Antebellum Virginia, 1801–1860." PhD diss., University of Delaware, 2016.

Cashwell, Meggan Farish. "'To Restore Peace and Tranquility to the Neighborhood': Violence, Legal Culture, and Community in New York City, 1799–1827." PhD diss., Duke University, 2019.

Hayden. Erica Rhodes. "'Plunged into a Vortex of Iniquity': Female Criminality and Punishment in Pennsylvania, 1820–1860." PhD diss., Vanderbilt University, 2013.

INDEX

Printed in the United States
by Baker & Taylor Publisher Services